The IndieAuthor Guide

By

April L. Hamilton

*Dedicated to my
children, who remind
me daily that the correct
answer to the question,
"Why?" is, "Why not?"
- Mom*

Table of Contents

1 INDIE AUTHORSHIP: AN INTRODUCTION

1.1 A HISTORY LESSON

It's never been easy to get an original novel published in the U.S., and in fact there wasn't even an outlet for most of them prior to the 1940's. In the early 1900's there were three main types of book publishers in America: university presses, small commercial presses, and large commercial presses.

University presses published books for use in educational, academic and religious settings. Their domain was the land of textbooks, Bibles, academic tomes, encyclopedias, reprints of classic literature from the past, reference books and the like.

Small commercial presses churned out "dime" novels, the forebears of today's commercial fiction. These presses were entirely profit-driven, and run very much like the production office of a hit television show today. Every publisher had its various novel series, which were the literary equivalent of today's television series: highly entertaining stories centering on popular characters in interesting or amusing settings. Writers were hired to write new volumes in these series, but small commercial publishers weren't interested in publishing any completely original works from those writers. Given that the writers were expected to produce new installments at the rate of roughly one 30,000-word novel per week, they wouldn't have had time to create original works anyway.

Large commercial presses released literary fiction, poetry collections, essay collections, biographies, and other nonfiction: in a word, "important" books. These presses were owned by wealthy philanthropists who typically approached publishing as a family business. Such publishers were true patrons of the arts who were thrilled to discover a literary diamond in the rough, and were willing to invest many years and thousands of dollars to nurture a new talent. Their prime motivation was to enlarge and improve the canon of American literature—profit was a secondary consideration, and a distant one at that. It was typical for authors to have personal relationships with these publishers, and the relationships were not dependent on profit from book sales.

As you may have noticed, none of the publishers discussed so far had any interest in non-literary, original novels. University presses didn't publish new novels at all and small presses weren't interested in changing their highly-profitable business model. The owners of large presses sought art, and wouldn't risk their reputations as arbiters of literary excellence by stooping to publish mere entertainment, nor anything offensive to their high-society sensibilities.

The commercial novel wasn't born until Robert DeGraff founded Pocketbooks, the first press to release books in paperback format exclusively, in 1939 with funding from Simon and Schuster. Pocketbooks titles were sold at lunch counters, newsstands, train stations, grocery and drug stores for just 25¢ each, but ironically, bookstores snobbishly refused to carry these mere, popular entertainments until the 1950's. But thanks to its accessibility, affordability, and portability, the "mass market" paperback novel was a huge success. Pocket sold over 12 million books in 1941, and due largely to the new format's popularity among WWII soldiers, hit the 40 million book sales mark in 1945.

Big publishers couldn't ignore the sweeping reach of the popular paperback novel, but decided to publish their own paperbacks through differently-named subsidiaries or even entirely separate imprints so as not to sully the reputations of their flagship, literary presses. The postwar paperback market grew even larger with the passage of the GI Bill and subsequent expansion of American universities and colleges. Increasingly profit-minded big publishers introduced the trade paperback at about this time, releasing books they judged to be a cut above the typical mass-market paperback in a larger format and with a higher-quality binding. Since a hardcover binding was viewed as a mark of artistic legitimacy in the publishing field in those days, commercial novels were entirely excluded from hardcover release for decades.

Through the 1950's and 60's book publishing was a booming industry in the U.S., though its profit margins remained low: 4 – 6%, on average. Gone were the days of the patron publisher, as one by one, big publishers went public and became answerable to shareholders rather than their founders' sensibilities. The 1970's brought merger-mania to the publishing industry, with CEOs anxious to try out the successful business strategies of their peers in other industries. Mergers and acquisitions may have slashed costs and boosted the bottom line in manufacturing, finance and the service sectors, but publishing industry margins remained stubbornly narrow. The 1980's saw the birth of the media megaconglomerate: single, huge corporations with national or even global holdings in multiple media markets. Not content to dominate film, music, broadcast media, newspapers and periodicals, the media megas started buying up book publishers.

Thanks to over three decades of mergers, buyouts and consolidations, all of which were carried out with the motive of drastically improving profits, the U.S. publishing industry is now dominated by just six media megaconglomerates, Viacom, Time Warner and News Corp. among them. If these names sound familiar, it's because they also own and operate virtually every television, cable and radio broadcast network, as well as nearly all major magazines, newspapers, TV shows, movie studios, music labels, videogame franchises, cable channels and internet service providers in the United States. Media megas are bottom-line focused with a vengeance, and the blockbuster-centric mentality they've used to bring the mainstream film, music and TV industries to heel is now being forcibly applied to book publishing. Priorities have not just shifted, they've completely reversed. Sales forecasts are the primary driver when manuscripts are selected for publication; quality of the work is now the secondary, far distant consideration.

1.2   THE CURRENT STATE OF AFFAIRS

The six major publishing houses are now run like movie studios, which means they're increasingly risk-averse, sink most of their attention and resources into a few intended blockbusters, and view profit as the only worthwhile measure of their products' value. One of the first casualties of this new business model was the midlist, the publisher's catalog of books expected to sell no more than between 5,000 and 40,000 copies. Big publishers are no more interested in these "small" books than their movie studio subsidiaries are interested in "small" films. Many former midlist authors whose books sold reliably for years have been dropped by their publishers on the grounds that while their books may be successful, they're not quite successful enough.

The movie marketing machine is being brought to bear as well. Media megas typically hedge their movie bets by opening new films on as many screens as possible, to sell as many tickets as quickly as they can and keep a step ahead of any potentially bad word of mouth for at least a few days, and they've found a way to apply a similar scheme to books. By offering large discounts to booksellers on certain titles in exchange for maximum display space, reduced retail pricing and 2-for-1 deals, they "buy" the prime real estate at the front of bookstores, ensuring their favored titles will monopolize the display racks at the entrance to the store.

To make matters worse, display space in the rest of the store is getting smaller all the time. Anyone who's been to a chain bookstore lately knows that books seem like the least of their offerings anymore; next to the incredible shrinking book department, I find DVDs, CDs, stationery, candy, iPod accessories, games and even cosmetics in my local store. Struggling Borders is experimenting with a few different strategies in its Ann Arbor, MI store, chief among them a 5 - 10% reduction in book stock. The store no longer carries books that move only 1 or 2 copies a month, and the liberated shelf space is being used to display more books "face out": with the front covers, rather than the spines, facing into the aisle. The bad news for all of us is that the store is reporting a spike in book sales since the change, which means the same strategy will no doubt be coming to a bookseller near you in the coming months.

Unless you're a prestige, celebrity or bestselling author, it's not necessarily good news when you learn a major publisher has decided to buy your manuscript. Advances are shrinking and promotion has turned into a vicious circle for such authors: they can't get their media mega publisher to spend money on promotion until they've proven their books will sell, but their books won't sell without promotion. Yet if an author's book doesn't earn enough he'll be dropped by his current publisher (along with all their many imprints), and viewed as damaged goods by the few other publishers in town. Meanwhile, publishers lavish money, publicity, book tours and huge promotion budgets on a few, favored authors. It was once safe to assume that if you were published by a major house you'd at least get to see your book on the shelf in brick-and-mortar stores, but even this small bit of writer wish fulfillment is no longer a given.

Non-bestselling authors often find they have little choice but to take their meager, long-awaited advances and immediately spend the funds on their own marketing campaigns. Accurate statistics in this area are hard to come by, but a figure frequently quoted at writers' seminars is this: fewer than 200 American novelists earn enough to support themselves through book sales alone.

When this type of slow, inexorable crawl toward mediocrity and scorn for artists came about in film and music, hopefuls jumped at the chance to take their careers into their own hands by going independent. You may wonder, as I have, why writers aren't following suit now that we have quality, affordable tools at our disposal to publish, distribute and market our books without any help or involvement from mainstream publishers. In a word, stigma.

1.3   INDIE VS. VANITY

Before consolidations began, there was a lot of truth in the assumption that the only author who resorts to self-publication is an author whose work isn't good enough to attract a "real" publisher. Anyone could pay a press to publish a minimum print run of his book, but it was very expensive and bookstores generally refused to carry the finished product. Because the author was assumed to be more or less bribing his way into print the entire process was viewed as an exercise in vanity, hence the term, "vanity publishing". The "vanity press" of yesteryear is a far cry from today's eBooks and print-on-demand self-publishing, but the "vanity publishing" label continues to be broadly, incorrectly affixed to any self-publication endeavor.

Today's self-published authors are on much the same path as their peers in independent film and music, choosing to release quality work that may not appeal to a massive enough audience to interest a media mega publisher, but may be greatly appreciated by a smaller audience. Those former midlist authors who've been dropped by their publishers often find self-publication is the only means at their disposal to keep serving their readership, and authors of niche nonfiction, poetry collections, short story collections, or any material deemed to have limited commercial appeal are in the same boat. The fact that these books aren't likely to become bestsellers is no indication of their quality. Such manuscripts are the literary equivalent of the independent film, which is generally regarded as the last stronghold of meaning and originality in American filmmaking. Such authors are not "vanity" authors, desperate to see their names in print for bragging rights alone, but "indie" authors.

1.4   BIAS AGAINST SELF-PUBLICATION

Unfortunately, the characterization of self-published authors as talentless hacks persists, and big publishers definitely use it to their advantage. As any book doctor, editor or literary agent can tell you, no major publisher will want to have anything to do with you if you've self-published. Why? Because in the highly unlikely event you ever manage to sell a manuscript to one of them and go on to make the bestseller list, your publisher will want to immediately cash in on any other, unpublished manuscripts you may have lying around—even manuscripts they themselves have previously rejected!

The media megas know the old bias against self-published authors doesn't hold much water anymore, but they pretend otherwise to keep their future purchasing options open. Far more appalling is the fact that the same prejudice exists among writers as well. Many, if not most, mainstream-published authors view all forms of self-publishing as "vanity" publishing, and believe it or not, the same opinion is commonplace among unpublished writers too. These anti-indies believe self-published books should be excluded from editorial reviews by mainstream media outlets, as well as from major awards and recognition for writing excellence among published books, and that self-published books should be labeled in a specific way in online bookstores as a warning to potential buyers. It's as if there's some sort of bizarre Stockholm effect at work, in which writers not only accept the conditions of career captivity at the hands of the media megas, but have come to believe there's some value inherent in those conditions. Can you imagine anyone seriously remarking to a friend, "Well, I'm just glad we've got the megaconglomerates deciding what movies and music get made. If it weren't for the work of those fine people, we might be exposed to just any old thing!" More ludicrous still, can you imagine a filmmaker or musician saying it?

Attitudes are changing and minds are opening, but slowly. As the history I've provided in this chapter demonstrates, the American publishing industry has always been elitist and resistant to change. Just as the publishing establishment once looked down its collective nose at the paperback novel, it now looks down on the self-published book. When paperback novels gained public acceptance on a scale publishers could no longer afford to ignore, the format became an accepted and respected part of American publishing. Now, as then, public acceptance is the key. Fortunately, readers don't share big publishers' tastes, views or biases. Readers buy books that appeal to them regardless of where the books came from. All that indie authors need to cross over, as the paperback did, is enough quality work being independently released to prove indies' work is every bit as good as that of their mainstream peers—and in some cases, better.

1.5   COMMON MISPERCEPTIONS ABOUT INDIE AUTHORSHIP

There's a lot of misinformation out there about what it means, and what it's like, to be an indie author. Let's tackle these old wives' tales one by one, shall we?

I'd never go indie because I'm a writer, not a salesperson.

Guess what? Big, mainstream publishing houses only offer promotional services and budgets to their celebrity, prestige and bestselling clients. With the exception of authors lucky enough to sign with a small press that treats all its authors equitably, *everyone* else is on the hook to promote his own work. While it's true that only mainstream-published authors have access to mainstream editorial reviews, the mere fact that you were published by a Penguin or Harper doesn't guarantee you'll get any mainstream editorial reviews. Hundreds of books come out every year, and of course major magazines are much quicker to review the latest book by a 'name' author than a debut from an unknown. Anyway, a recent Publisher's Weekly survey demonstrated that word of mouth is a far more effective sales tool for books than reviews by professional critics.

Since brick-and-mortar stores won't stock self-published books, indie authors can't ever earn as much as mainstream-published authors.

As explained previously, brick-and-mortar bookstores are struggling as more and more readers turn to the web, discount stores and 'big box' stores like CostCo to buy their books. Discount stores and big box stores only carry bestsellers, gift books and bargain books, so non-bestselling mainstream authors won't find their books in those outlets. Increasingly, brick-and-mortar bookstores heavily promote each big publisher's favored authors while relegating everything else to the back of the store. Getting your book on the shelves of your local Borders doesn't provide much of a sales boost if the only people who know about it are you, your friends and family. After all, *those* people would've bought your book even if you had to sell it out of the trunk of your car.

Online booksellers level the playing field, enabling indie authors to compete as effectively as their mainstream-published peers. In fact, indies actually have an advantage over the mainstreamers on the web because mainstreamers, for the most part, have yet to accept the fact that they're responsible for promoting their own books and have therefore been slow to acquire the necessary skills.

Moreover, recall that very, very few authors earn enough to support themselves through sales of their books alone, regardless of who published them. Signing with a big publishing house does not guarantee strong earnings.

My chances of becoming a bestseller are much better with a big publisher.

If you happen to be a favored client of your big publisher, one behind whom they intend to put considerable promotional effort and money, then you're absolutely right. Otherwise, not so much. Only about 1-2% of all books published go on to become bestsellers, so your book isn't really *likely* to become a bestseller no matter how good it is or who publishes it. The question shouldn't be one of who's more likely to become a bestseller, but who's more likely to become a favored client. Here again, indies have the advantage because an indie's book is a proven quantity by the time it comes to the attention of a big publisher. This gives the indie author more leverage to negotiate favorable promotion terms with a big publisher, and gives the big publisher more and better reasons to give the acquired indie book a promotional push.

Indie is fine for publishing one book, but I intend to have a <u>career</u>.

Where a mainstream author has a chance, a very small chance, at career longevity, an indie author chooses for herself how long her career in authorship will last. Recall that a first-time author's book must perform very well in order to "break out", and if it fails to do so the author will be dropped by her publisher and seen as damaged goods by the few other major publishers in existence. With no promotional backing from the publisher, the chances that the author's book will break out are very slim indeed. Even if it does, the literary landscape is strewn with the career wreckage of authors who had one or more bestsellers, only to drop gradually into obscurity thereafter. It is extraordinarily rare for any author to have the kind of career longevity enjoyed by the serially-bestselling likes of a Michael Crichton or Tom Clancy, and thanks to the death of the midlist, it's only becoming rarer.

While it's virtually unheard of for an indie author to scale those same career heights in terms of consistently high sales, they don't face the performance pressure foisted on mainstream authors. If an indie's book only sells modestly, there's no one stopping him from publishing another. Furthermore, because indies earn much higher royalties than mainstreamers, don't have an agent taking a cut and don't have an advance to pay back, it's entirely possible for an indie author to earn a steady, if modest, income off his writing. There's no analog in the mainstream publishing world, since an author who's earning only modestly for his publisher won't be with that publisher for long. There are numerous examples of non-fiction indies who earn their entire living off their writing, mostly by serving niche audiences and relentlessly promoting.

1.6   PORTRAIT OF THE INDIE AUTHOR

The active term in "indie authorship" is indie, or independent. An independent filmmaker produces his own films. An independent musician produces his own recordings. Likewise, an independent author produces his own books.

An indie author controls the entire process of creating, publishing and promoting his book from beginning to end. This doesn't necessarily mean he performs every task along the way himself, he may pay others for specific services like editing, cover art design or website design, but he's the one calling the shots, he retains all rights to his work, and he keeps all the profit.

Indie authorship demands a certain amount of entrepreneurial spirit, sometimes referred to as a "can-do attitude". Working outside the publishing mainstream affords authors complete freedom over their work, but it also places sole responsibility for their careers squarely on their own shoulders.

The ideal candidate for indie authorship is the writer who's spent years honing her craft and has acquired a basic understanding of how the publishing and bookselling industries work, but can't garner the interest of an agent or mainstream publisher because her manuscripts don't fit the extremely limited parameters of today's highly-consolidated publishing industry. Her work is well-reviewed and might even have won or placed in contests, yet she can't get a nibble from the big boys. She's got some computer tools and skills, she's willing to learn, she wants to redirect her energies toward something productive, and she's ready to boldly go where few authors have gone before.

One more thing: the indie author must believe very fervently in the indie movement, because she will face repeated episodes of prejudice, ignorance and possibly even mockery from those in the mainstream who continue to cling to the publishing model of yesteryear. Remember, prior to Pocketbooks' founding, the Stephen Kings, James Pattersons and Sue Graftons of the world were mocked and dismissed by the establishment, too. And in any event, an indie author doesn't need the establishment's approval anyway; she will be marketing her books directly to the reading public, and history has shown they're a reliably pragmatic and open-minded lot.

1.6.1   TOOLS OF THE INDIE AUTHOR TRADE

The tools and skills needed to create and promote a book independently vary according to each author's needs and preferences. For example, an author who intends to hire a publicist doesn't need all the computer and graphics skills required of an author who intends to do all his own promotion.

The tools in the table on the following page will enable you to do everything covered by this book yourself, from manuscript formatting to issuing online press releases. The greater your skills and better your tools the easier it will be to accomplish each task along the way, but even someone with basic skills and a willingness to learn can be successful with the step-by-step instructions in this book. After all, if you were already an expert with everything on the list you wouldn't need this book.

Item	Required For
Computer	Almost everything in this book
Word processing program (i.e., MS Word, Open Office Writer)	Manuscript preparation, promotional activities
Graphics editor program (i.e., Microsoft Digital Image Pro, Corel Draw)	Cover art design, promotional activities, author photo
Clipart (comes with graphics editor program, additional collections can be purchased separately)	Cover art design, promotional activities
File archiving program (i.e., WinZip, WinRar, etc.)	Compression of manuscript and cover art files for upload to publisher
Internet access & skills (i.e., email with attachments, ability to post to online discussion groups)	Upload of manuscript and cover art files to publisher, promotional activities, correspondence
Basic HTML knowledge	Online promotional activities—don't worry, there's an HTML primer in this book
Digital camera	Author photo

1.6.2   GOALS IN INDIE AUTHORSHIP

Some authors' definition of career success has more to do with how much readers enjoy their books than it does with how many readers buy their books. Others take the totally opposite view, using sales as the primary yardstick for measuring their career success.

Independence is a viable option for any author, but the former type will be content to remain indie for his entire career in authorship while the latter type will generally view indie authorship as a stepping stone to mainstream publication. Either way, the initial goals are the same: to produce quality work and get people to read it.

Given that the mainstream publishing industry looks down on indie authorship, it may seem counterintuitive to use indie authorship as an entrée to that world. However, as with the paperback novel, in the end it all comes down to money. The publishing establishment only remains snobby toward indie books so long as it can afford to do so. As crossover successes like *The Celestine Prophecy*, *Diary Of A Wimpy Kid*, and *Eragon* have repeatedly shown, publishers will welcome commercially successful self-published authors with open arms.

2 PUBLISHING OPTIONS

The terms "self-publishing", "subsidy publishing", "vanity publishing" and "print-on-demand" are often used interchangeably when people speak of self-publishing, but these terms aren't synonymous. Rather, they describe different self-publishing options or processes.

2.1 SELF-PUBLISHING

In common usage, "self-publishing" has become a catch-all term. People using it may be talking about subsidy publishing, vanity publishing or print-on-demand (POD), but ironically, they're rarely talking about true self-publishing.

In the strictest sense, self-publishing is exactly what it sounds like: doing your own publishing. This is also known as "desktop publishing," since it's generally done with an ordinary computer, or 'desktop' computer.

Typical self-publishing projects include club or family newsletters, brochures, booklets and research papers, any of which can be created using a standard word processor. There are also dedicated desktop publishing computer programs that enable the user to create more sophisticated and lengthier publications. Either way, desktop publishing isn't a workable solution for book manuscripts because binding options are severely limited.

Office supply stores and print shops offer several types of binding, and can generally bind up to 300 pages. However, all their binding options are more fitting for reports or business documents than books. The pages may be hole-punched and placed between two report covers, or drilled for comb- or spiral-binding. The finished product will have a binding, but even if you customize the report covers with artwork and a book title, it won't look like a book. You won't be able to duplicate the look of a "real" book, which has pages glued or sewn into a wrap-around cover at the spine. Furthermore, having manuscripts bound individually is very expensive.

2.2 VANITY PUBLISHING

As described previously, vanity publishing is the process whereby an author pays a publishing service to format and publish a minimum number of copies of his book. The publisher usually offers related services on a fee basis, from editing to cover art design and even promotion. The author is essentially paying to have his book printed, and so long as he's willing to pay the required fee, the publisher will not turn him away. It is because of this fact that as a group, books from vanity publishers are presumed to be of poor quality.

This bias is the primary downside to vanity publishing, but expense comes in at a close second. An author who chooses to go with a vanity publisher must pay all production costs for a minimum 'print run' of his book, generally at least 200 copies. Cost per book goes down as quantity goes up, but in most cases the author can expect to pay anywhere from US$5 - $10 per copy for a trade paperback edition and between US$8 - $16 for a hardcover. Multiply those figures by 200, then add hundreds more dollars in flat fees for project setup, optional ISBN assignment, proof corrections, project management and delivery. Add another thousand or two if the author pays for related services.

The third downside to vanity publishing is distribution, or lack thereof. When the print run is finished, all the books are delivered to the author and it's up to him to store them, sell them, give them away, or otherwise dispose of them. With few exceptions, brick-and-mortar bookstores won't stock *any* type of self-published book. They're particularly leery of books from vanity publishers, all of whose names are widely known in the publishing and bookselling industries.

More recently, vanity publishers have begun addressing the distribution problem by setting up online bookstores to stock their clients' work, but the sites don't get much traffic because they only stock the vanity publisher's books, and again, most people assume those books aren't very good. Enterprising authors can turn a profit selling their books themselves, on their own website, at community fairs, through direct mail and so on. Occasionally one will even do well enough to attract the attention of a mainstream publisher, but this is very rare.

Lastly, even though vanity publishers are only providing services for a fee, they act like conventional publishers when it comes to contracts and rights. As part of the publishing arrangement, the author will be required to sign a contract granting certain, exclusive rights to the publisher. The contract may stipulate that the author cannot publish the same work in the same format, or any other format, for a set period of years. In this way, the publisher ensures the author must go back to the same publisher to order additional print runs if the book is successful enough to sell out its first print run. The contract will also specify whether or not the author can buy his way out of the contract before the term is up, and if so, what it will cost. This stipulation lines the vanity publisher's pockets in the event a mainstream publisher wants to publish the book.

2.3   SUBSIDY PUBLISHING

Subsidy publishing is virtually identical to vanity publishing, except that subsidy publishers will not publish every manuscript submitted to them. Instead, they accept submissions (sometimes for a fee) and choose the manuscripts they wish to publish. Subsidy publishers sprang up as a legitimate self-publication alternative to vanity publishing. Subsidy publishers aren't all created equal, however. Some are hardly more discerning than vanity publishers, while others are so selective as to rival mainstream publishers.

The worst subsidy publishers are ripoff artists par excellence, assuring every prospective client her manuscript is a diamond in the rough that is practically guaranteed to become a bestseller if she will only pay for professional editing, artwork, promotion, and other services—all of which just happen to be offered by the publisher or a company referred from the publisher.

The best subsidy publishers truly strive to distinguish themselves by putting out quality books and dealing fairly with authors, but even in that case the author must contend with all the same downsides as she would face with a vanity publisher. She must pay for a minimum print run and related services, she must sign over at least some of her publication rights in a contract, and she faces all the same distribution challenges as a vanity-published author.

2.4 PRINT ON DEMAND

While vanity or subsidy publishing is fine for a book with a built-in customer base, such as a textbook published by a college professor for use in his class, Print On Demand (POD) is the best way to go for an author who intends to sell her book to the general public. As with vanity publishing, an author who chooses POD is essentially paying for printing services. There is no selection process on the part of the publisher. Also as with vanity and subsidy publishers, POD companies may offer related services for a fee, and the published books aren't likely to be carried by brick-and-mortar stores. That's where the similarities end, however.

There is no minimum print run to order and pay for with POD because the publisher stores POD books in digital format. Individual copies of the book are printed and bound by automated systems "on demand", meaning each time an order for the book is received. The author doesn't pay to have on-demand copies produced. Instead, the printer keeps a share of the book's price to cover its production costs and pays the remainder to the author as a royalty.

POD publishers may offer services related to publishing for a fee, but they are also prepared to accept print-ready files from authors. This is where the author can save thousands of dollars, by using the information in this book to do all those related tasks himself instead of paying for services. Most POD publishers don't charge a set-up fee, and at least one (CreateSpace) even throws in an ISBN and EAN for free. Often, the only expense shouldered by the author is the cost of proof copies, which must be printed in order for the author to review the book before approving it for publication.

With a POD publisher, the author retains all rights to his work. If there's any contract at all, its terms are limited to the details of fees, royalty payment, services provided and the responsibilities of each party. If your publisher requires you to order a minimum print run or sign over any of your publication rights, it's a subsidy publisher.

Most POD publishers have distribution relationships with major, online booksellers such as Amazon and Barnes and Noble, through which the bookseller agrees to sell the POD publisher's books on its website. Some POD publishers only offer this as an optional service, and only for a fee. Another service some POD publishers offer, always for a fee, is 'guaranteed returns', whereby brick-and-mortar stores are allowed to return any unsold copies of POD books to the publisher. This is supposed to encourage brick-and-mortar stores to carry POD books, since many cite 'un-returnability' as a reason not to carry them, but in reality the centralized purchasing departments and computerized inventory systems of chain bookstores present obstacles at least equal to concerns about money lost on unsold copies.

All POD publishers can print paperback books in various, standard sizes, both in black and white and full color, but only some of them can print books in hardcover editions. When the hardcover option is available, the production cost for it is much higher than that charged for paperbacks.

Since an author who goes the POD route can still opt to pay for certain related services as desired, vanity and subsidy publishers have no advantages to offer the typical indie author. Why pay stiff fees upfront, warehouse your books, and sign away your publication rights if you don't have to?

2.5   RIGHTS, ROYALTIES AND ADVANCES

In a traditional publishing scenario, an author grants a publisher the right to package, publish, promote and distribute his content for commercial sale for a set time period, in exchange for a percentage of the profit from those sales. The details of the exchange are laid out in a contract, which is negotiable and therefore unique for each manuscript sold.

2.5.1   MAINSTREAM RIGHTS

Publication rights are many and varied, covering all the different ways the manuscript's content can be published for distribution to the public. Rights to publication of the entire manuscript in different formats include hardcover, softcover, trade paperback, mass market paperback, audiobook on CD or tape, audiobook digital download, and eBooks in various formats. Rights to portions of the manuscript include excerpts to be distributed for promotional purposes at no cost to consumers, reprints of entire chapters to be sold as standalone articles or short stories, reprints of art or text from the manuscript for reproduction and sale in a different product format (i.e., calendars), and reprints of excerpts to be included in subsequently published anthologies.

Other content rights include screenplay rights, broadcast rights and licensing rights. Licensing rights govern the terms under which manuscript text, artwork or character likenesses can be printed on t-shirts, mugs, or other merchandise offered for sale. Broadcast rights pertain to the terms under which the manuscript (or portions thereof) may be broadcast over television, satellite or radio waves, and usually pertain to broadcast of audiobook editions or live readings. Screenplay rights cover situations where someone wants to make a film or television show based on content from the manuscript.

Mainstream publishing contracts grant the publisher any or all of the above rights for a certain number of years. Megaconglomerate publishers may negotiate for publication, broadcast, licensing and screenplay rights simultaneously, offering a flat-fee payment or profit-sharing terms for non-publication rights in addition to the royalties (see sections 2.5.3 and 2.5.4) offered on book sales.

Smaller publishers will typically sign on only for publication rights, leaving the author free to sell the remaining rights to other parties. In that case, the author's agent or manager may attempt to sell the remaining rights on the author's behalf.

2.5.2 INDIE RIGHTS

Indies who go the vanity or subsidy route are subject to rights contracts just like mainstream authors, but the contracts are usually limited to publication rights and the author doesn't get royalties or advances in return. In a basic vanity or subsidy publisher situation the author sets her own price and sells her own books, so her earnings are a function of how many books she sells and how she prices them. If she manages to get them into a bookstore, she'll be subject to the same 40% bookseller fee (see next section) as any other author.

Indies who go the POD route retain all rights to their work, leaving them free to negotiate for the sale of those rights with whomever they wish, under whatever terms they wish.

2.5.3 MAINSTREAM ROYALTIES

The "percentage of the profit from those sales" to be paid in exchange for rights is called the 'author royalty'. Among mainstream publishers, author royalties are somewhat standard according to the type of book and publication format, but are open to negotiation before the contract is signed. Bestselling and prestige authors can demand higher royalties than other authors, and usually get them.

For everyone else, royalties are usually figured either as a percentage of the book's list price, or as a percentage of the net profit from the book.

Consider a manuscript to be published as a trade paperback book with a list price of US$14. Typical royalties offered on ordinary trade paperbacks are 8-10% of the list price, or alternatively, 15-25% of 'net' from each sale.

The list price is the suggested retail price. 8% of $14 is $1.12 and 10% is $1.40, which makes the 'net' option look a whole lot more attractive at first blush.

Net is calculated as list price - production costs - bookseller fee. Production costs for a typical black and white trade paperback book of average length run anywhere from $2 to $4 per copy, depending on the quantity of books in the print run (as quantity goes up, cost per copy goes down), paper and binding quality. Let's say our book's production cost is at the low end, $2 per copy. The standard bookseller fee is 40% of the list price, meaning that every time you buy a book in a store, whether in person or online, the seller keeps 40% of the list price as his fee. On our $14 book the bookseller fee is $5.60. This leaves a net of $14 - $2 - $5.60, or $6.40. 15% of $6.40 = 96¢, and 25% of $6.40 = $1.60. Royalties calculated from net can vary widely based on the size of the print run, due to the variance in production costs.

Royalty percentages for hardcover, mass-market paperback, eBook and audiobook formats are calculated in a similar way, though standard percentages vary for each different format. Also, it's typical to reward the author with a higher royalty percentage on additional print runs after the first run sells out, but bestselling authors are usually the only ones in a position to collect that reward.

Any way you slice it, less than $2 per copy sold is not a lot of money. At $2 per copy you'd need to sell 15,000 copies to earn $30,000, and that's *before* taxes and fees for professional services (see Paying the Piper(s), next page).

Royalty Advances

The contract may require the publisher to pay the author an "advance", or up-front, lump-sum payment. The advance is not a free-and-clear payment, such as a professional athlete's signing bonus, however. It's actually a loan against future royalties. When an advance is paid, the publisher enters it into the author's royalty account as a negative amount, indicating the author owes the publisher that much money. The publisher keeps track of sales, calculates the author's royalty on each sale and deposits the funds into the author's royalty account. No royalties are paid to the author until the advance loan is paid off.

Since it takes time for earnings to cancel out the advance, it's not unusual for authors to wait many months after their book is published to see that first royalty check. In many, if not the majority of cases, the book doesn't ultimately sell enough copies to pay back the advance. The publisher won't make the author pay back the difference out of his own pocket, but the publisher will not want to publish the author again, either. The larger the advance, the bigger the author's risk of committing career suicide.

Paying the Piper(s)

If the author has contracted with a manager, agent or attorney for services, each of them will take a percentage of the author's advance, flat fees, profit-sharing proceeds and royalties. It's easy to see why so few authors actually make a living on their writing, regardless of who published their books.

2.5.4   INDIE "ROYALTIES"

Indie authors don't truly earn 'royalties', they earn net profit. However, self-publishing companies tend to refer to the author's net profit on each book sold as a "royalty" in order to mimic the terminology of the mainstream. Indie net profits are calculated according to list price, production costs and bookseller fees, just like mainstream author royalties.

The Production Cost Problem

Production costs for indie books are two to three times higher than mainstream books due to economies of scale. Recall that production costs go down as quantity of books printed goes up. Big publishers order print runs in the tens of thousands. Vanity and subsidy publishers order print runs in the hundreds, or occasionally, the low thousands. POD publishers order one book at a time.

This problem can be a major stumbling block for indie authors, since they may be forced to set their books' list prices higher than comparable mainstream books to earn as much per book as a mainstream author. This situation also feeds the bias against self-published books since customers are being asked to pay more for untested, self-published books than they would for a bestseller.

The Production Cost Solution

Self-publishing companies realize the production cost problem alone can be enough to deter authors, so some now offer reduced production costs in exchange for flat fees, annual dues, or a combination of both. One example is CreateSpace, the publisher I use for POD. Authors who opt for reduced production costs can set their books' pricing equal to comparable mainstream books and still earn royalties three to five times higher than most mainstreamers.

Such fees range widely from publisher to publisher, so authors should do some 'what if' calculations to figure out what their net profit will be at various list price points, both with and without the production cost discount, and how many books they must sell at each price point to cover the cost of the fee.

Another consideration is author copies; authors can buy copies of their self-published books for the cost of production alone, so reduced production cost means less money spent when ordering author copies. If the author intends to order 20 or more copies of his book to give to friends and family, he may find the savings on author copies alone are enough to cover the fees. Authors who buy larger quantities of their books to sell at signings, appearances and through bookstores (see Promotion chapter) will almost certainly find the savings in author copies makes it worth paying for reduced production costs.

2.6 WHAT'S THE DEAL WITH ISBNS?

Any commercially-sold, physical book must have a unique International Standard Book Number, or ISBN, assigned, and each different edition of a given book (i.e., hardcover, paperback, audiobook) must have its own ISBN. EBooks, which are essentially digital files, don't require ISBNs. The ISBN is a unique identifier assigned to all commercially-sold books being sold in any physical format, consisting of a 10- to 13-digit number and associated barcode. Bowker (http://www.bowker.com) is the only agency allowed to distribute ISBNs in the U.S. Bowker sells ISBNs to publishers and authors in blocks of ten at the minimum. It's not unusual for self-published authors to purchase their own ISBN blocks, though unless you're very prolific or issue your books in multiple editions, you may not ever use up a whole block of ten.

Some publishers require authors to obtain their own ISBNs at their own expense, some will provide ISBNs to authors for a separate fee, and still others include ISBN assignment as part of their standard publishing package. If you buy your own block of ISBNs, each ISBN in the block can only be used once, and only for a specific edition of your book.

For example, let's say you use the first ISBN in your block for a paperback edition of Novel A, the second for a hardcover edition of Novel A, and the third for an audiobook edition of Novel A. A couple of years later, when you're ready to publish Novel B, you must assign ISBNs to all its editions beginning with the fourth ISBN in your block. Once assigned, an ISBN can never be re-used, not even if the book to which it was assigned goes out of print.

In Europe, books are tracked with a European Article Number, or EAN. Some publishers can assign an EAN to your book, but check with your publisher to be sure that service is available if you intend to sell your book in Europe, or through online vendors that accept international orders.

2.7 WHAT ABOUT BOOKSTORES?

You may be wondering how you can sell significant quantities of your books when it's nearly impossible to get brick-and-mortar stores to stock them. The answer is, you don't *need* brick and mortar bookstores to stock them.

Until fairly recently, brick-and-mortar bookstores were the biggest sellers of books. Now that books are sold in discount stores, grocery stores, 'big box' retailers and online, this is no longer the case. As of this writing, Amazon is the #1 seller of books worldwide and #2 in North America. Barnes and Noble is the #1 bookseller in North America, with that rank including both its brick-and-mortar and online stores.

Recall from the introduction, even if you can get a chain bookstore to stock your book, since major publishers have bought up all the prime real estate in the store your book most likely *won't* be prominently featured. An exception to this is the bookstore with a 'local authors' display, but again, your book will only be highlighted in that one display, in that one store. Getting a brick-and-mortar chain store to stock your book does not guarantee any increase in sales.

Another consideration is the fact that you must provide copies of your books to brick-and-mortar stores willing to stock them. While author copies are sold at a much lower price than retail copies, you still have to pay for them to be produced and shipped to you. Then you have to deliver or ship them to the bookseller, who isn't likely to stock more than two or three copies at a time, and work out arrangements for collecting your net profit if your books sell.

The standard 'cut' for any bookseller, be it Amazon or a local mom n' pop store, is 40% of the book's list price. If the list price for your book is $14, the bookseller's cut for each sale is $5.60. Assuming the author copy price is $6, you will only earn $2.40 per book sold in the store. Granted, this is a much higher royalty percentage than that earned by mainstream authors on the same book, but even if all three copies of your book sell, it's an awful lot of up-front trouble and expense for a measly $7.20 profit. If you had to ship your books to the store, or pay for gas to deliver them yourself, your net profit is even less.

While it's true that Amazon or any other online bookseller will take the same 40% as a brick-and-mortar store, the advantage of working with an online seller is that you don't usually have to order, pay for, or deliver any books up front. Most online sellers can list your book on their sites, and when a customer orders your book, send an electronic order to the publisher. The book is printed and sent directly to the customer with no involvement from you whatsoever. The online seller gets its 40%, thereby reducing the amount of royalty paid to you, but you haven't incurred any expense or hassle in the process.

2.8   CHOOSING A PUBLISHER

Your choice of publisher depends on your goals as an indie author and the resources you're prepared to expend in the endeavor—not just money, but time and skills as well. As with so many things, the best way to find a good publisher is on the basis of a recommendation from a trusted third party. If you know any self-published authors, get their input.

If you don't know any self-published authors, or the ones you know recommend *against* the publishers they used, do an internet search on "self publish" or "POD" to find publishers and what people are saying about them. Narrow the field to just two or three candidates, then review each one's Terms of Service (sometimes called a Membership Agreement), submission guidelines and FAQ sections to determine which will be the easiest for you to work with, according to your specific needs and priorities.

For example, if you intend to minimize costs by doing as much as possible by yourself, it doesn't make sense to go with a publisher whose most basic package charges upfront fees for providing services you don't need. On the other hand, if you know you'll need to pay for certain professional services, such as editing or book cover design, it doesn't make sense to go with a publisher that doesn't offer those services.

If you're hoping to make a profit selling your books online, crunch the numbers for various publishers. Compare the setup costs, production costs and publisher fees for production of the same book. If a publisher's production costs will force you to price your book higher than a comparable mainstream book just to break even after taking the 40% bookseller fee into account, find out if they offer any programs or membership upgrades that will reduce production costs. If not, cross that publisher off your list of candidates. Working with a list price that's typical for a mainstream-published book of the same type, see what you will earn per book for sales through booksellers and and through each publisher's online store (if applicable).

Look at the tradeoffs. One publisher may have excellent tech support and customer service through the setup and publication process, but charge stiff setup fees or production costs. In contrast, a different publisher may offer tech support and customer service via email only, but charge much lower fees. Remember that the eventual buyers of your book won't care how easy or hard your publisher was to work with, they only care about the physical quality of the book, how good it is, and how much it costs. If going with the first publisher requires you to set the list price for your 6x9" trade paperback at $16 just to net $1 in profit (when mainstream books of the same type and dimensions are selling for $14 or less), in the final analysis it won't matter how great their service is: your book will be hard to sell.

Rights will be a primary concern if your goal is to attract a mainstream publisher. You won't be able to negotiate with any other publishers if you've already locked up publishing rights with a subsidy or vanity publisher. However, as discussed previously, subsidy and vanity publishing don't offer any advantages over POD publishing these days, so there's no reason for an indie author to sign away his publication rights in the first place.

Finally, consider how you intend to sell your books. The online bookstores publishers run to sell their clients' books typically charge a bookseller fee substantially lower than the standard 40%, but those stores also get less traffic than say, Amazon. You can link to your books in the publisher's store from your website or elsewhere, but you won't get as many sales from customers 'browsing' the virtual shelves since Amazon has far more customers than a publisher's bookstore. Personally, I feel that an Amazon store listing is critical if you hope to turn a profit on your self-published books, not only due to Amazon's huge market share but also due to the greater promotional opportunties available for products listed on Amazon's site (see Promotion chapter). Verify that the publishers you're considering can do this, and if they charge a fee to do so, that the cost isn't prohibitive.

If you've got all the tools recommended in the first chapter and are proficient with them, this book will provide all the help and information needed to do everything from formatting your manuscript to promoting the finished book by yourself, so don't make any hasty decisions when it comes to paying for related services until you've thoroughly perused the remaining chapters.

3 GETTING ORGANIZED

Keeping your digital work organized is a critical but often overlooked step in successful authorship. As you work on a manuscript, you need your research, notes and drafts at your fingertips. When you begin iterations of revision, you need to keep tabs on the feedback you receive and make sure that feedback is readily available when you need it. After the manuscript is completely polished, proofed, and "locked" against further changes, you need to maintain separate 'containers' to hold the files for each type of release you intend to make available (i.e., POD, eBook, Kindle edition, etc.). Finally, you will want to archive all the files related to former works in progress, as you never know when those notes and ideas will come in handy as you work on some future project.

3.1 HARD DRIVE HOUSEKEEPING AND ORGANIZATION

It's essential to set up an organized filing system for all of the writing-related files on your computer. This will save you a great deal of time and energy in the future, when any file related to any one of your manuscripts will be easy to locate with just a few mouse clicks. A well-organized, centrally-located filing system also simplifies and speeds the backup process---which of course, you're doing regularly, right?

The question of specifically how to organize your files is a matter of personal preference, and what makes sense to you. Most people will have a top-level folder called "Writing," "Manuscripts," or something similar. Beneath that, some will create a separate folder for each different manuscript, using the manuscript's title as the folder name, and then create sub-folders within each manuscript folder to hold each different type of file: rough drafts, notes and research, proofs, eBook versions, etc. Others will prefer to create folders for each different file type within the main, "Manuscripts" folder, and then place files for each different manuscript within the file type folders: all proof versions in the 'Proofs' folder, all eBook versions in the 'eBooks' folder, etc. etc. My own filing system is a combination of the two, as illustrated by the screenshots below.

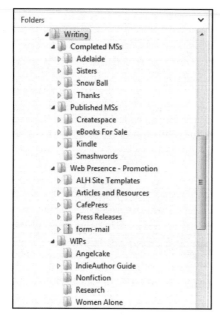

Within my Writing folder, I have a folder for Completed Manuscripts, Published Manuscripts, Web Presence – Promotion, and Works In Progress (WIPs). Within the Completed Manuscripts, Published Manuscripts and WIPs folders, there are subfolders for each manuscript. Within the Published MSs folder, there are subfolders for each different publisher. The Web Presence – Promotion folder contains subfolders to store all documents, notes and information related to my websites and promotional activities.

The screen shot at right shows how my work is organized within each manuscript folder in the Completed MSs and WIPs folders. There are subfolders for Correspondence, Current Version (for the most recent version of the manuscript, or in the case of published manuscripts, the final version), Drafts, Excerpts, Graphics

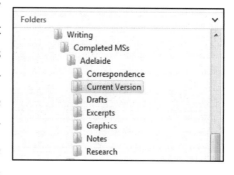

(for cover art or any images appearing in the manuscript), Notes (for workshopping feedback) and Research.

3.2 EMAIL HOUSEKEEPING AND ORGANIZATION

Just as on your hard drive, a logical, tidy email filing system will save you a lot of time and headaches when you're desperate to locate a specific note, name or contact information. Just as with your hard drive filing system, your email filing system should be organized in a way that makes sense to you, but there are some overall guidelines that will probably make sense for everyone.

Typically, you correspond with many of the same people about all your different works and it may initially seem like a good idea to set up a separate folder for each of those people, containing all emails you send to, and receive from, each individual. However, if you set`up your email files this way, when you need to find a specific email from Susan Editor about your My Super Fantastic Career manuscript, it may not be easy to locate among all the other emails from Susan Editor pertaining to all your other manuscripts. I suggest creating a separate folder for each manuscript and storing all relevant correspondence accordingly. Separate folders can also be created for correspondence not specifically related to any particular manuscript. And don't forget, you need to periodically archive and back up your email too!

4   CREATING YOUR BRAND

In the context of indie authorship, what is a "brand" and why do you need one? Your brand is the name that stands for the public image encompassing both you, the author, and the body of work affiliated with that name. For most writers the name will be the same as that listed on their books for "author", but it can also be an alias or company name.   Establishing a known, consistent and reliable brand is key to marketing success, regardless of what you're selling, and it's a big mistake to think marketing products like detergent and soda pop is all that different from marketing books and authors.

A brand becomes a placeholder in the consciousness of the customer, a bucket containing all the good or bad associations, opinions and factual observations the customer has come to connect with a given product line.   Consider Ben and Jerry's ice cream.   The Ben and Jerry's name typically calls to mind premium ingredients, wild flavor combinations, and socially-conscious executives. Ben and Jerry's products are also known to be more expensive than supermarket ice creams, but this is an acceptable trade-off for fans of the brand.

Now take the example of author Terry Pratchett. Common ideas about his work, and by extension about Mr. Pratchett himself, are fantasy, dark humor, imagination, whimsy and a touch of the philosophical. These associations are so strong that when a new Pratchett book comes out, many people will buy it without having any idea of the plot or characters, on the strength of the Pratchett reputation alone. Each new book that delivers on the promise of that reputation further solidifies the brand and serves as cross-promotion for every other book Pratchett has written in the past or will come to write in the future.

Conversely, readers who don't care for dark humor and whimsy in their fantasy books know to avoid Pratchett's work. It seems counterintuitive, but this helps the author as well. Readers whose tastes don't align well with Pratchett's brand will not enjoy his books, and if they buy one with unrealistic expectations they will go on to become dissatisfied customers. Dissatisfied customers tend to share their dissatisfaction with everyone they know, and bad word of mouth has a way of spreading.

4.1   SHOULD YOUR NAME BE YOUR BRAND?

The answer to this question is, "It depends." It depends on you, your work, your past history, your current life situation, and your future plans.

The "you" part of the equation comes down to your tolerance for fame, however small or large that fame may be. Remember that if you use your real name as your brand name, not only you, but your relatives, friends and even hometown may one day come to national media attention. For many writers this is entirely welcome, and in fact the ultimate goal. For others, it's far preferable to have one persona for public consumption and another for private life.

If you're writing a tell-all type of book, or a fictionalized memoir in which your thinly-veiled characters are based on real people who may be recognized by readers (regardless of their phony names and the way you altered their physical descriptions), using a pen name is your safest bet. Outside these narrow circumstances, the "your work" part of the equation comes into play primarily when there's something about it that could be controversial, as you'll see in the following examples.

For instance, suppose a former child star from a squeaky-clean family sitcom now writes gory crime thrillers. If he wants to leave his former, child-star persona intact, or if he worries people may not take him seriously as a writer because they've pigeonholed him as an actor, the author should publish under a different name. However, if he wants to capitalize on his fame and create buzz from the shock value of turning his former image on its ear, publishing under his celebrity name will accomplish his goals.

Also consider any existing body of work. Having a series of finance books in print under your real name may nudge you in the direction of taking a pen name for publication of fiction. Conversely, if you've got a few volumes of arty poetry in print and now want to turn your efforts toward writing books about tax law, establishing a separate brand for your new line may be a good idea because people don't generally look to poets for advice about tax law.

Look at your current circumstances as well. If you're a grammar school teacher, publishing a series of steamy, borderline erotica romances under your real name is a bad idea. Similarly, if you live in a very small community where everyone knows everyone else, you may not welcome the notoriety that comes with having published anything provocative or controversial. Consider the general character of your community, and whether your friends and neighbors might feel what you've written reflects negatively on them or the community in any way. If you have children, consider any possible impact your work may have on them.

Finally, think about your future. If you hope to someday occupy a spot in the public eye for anything other than your writing (i.e., public office, acting, singing, etc.), or hold a position of authority over children (i.e., Scout leader, cheerleading coach, middle school teacher), consider how your published work will be viewed in the future.

4.2   YOU VERSUS YOUR BRAND NAME

First, the usual caveat: I am not, nor have I ever been, a lawyer, and nothing in this book should be construed as professional legal advice. If you have any questions or concerns about publishing under a name other than your legal name, please consult an attorney.

However, one thing I can tell you is this: if you choose to publish under a brand name that is not the same as your legal name, which is also known as taking a "pen name," you are still required to conduct all financial and legal business under your real, legal name. In other words, when Sting files his taxes, signs contracts, applies for a passport, receives his earnings from the record label or reports his earnings to the government, he does so under his legal name, "Gordon Sumner". Likewise, the man known to readers as "Mark Twain" was known to the U.S. government as Samuel Clemens. If you attempt to conduct financial or legal business of any sort under a pen name, you will run afoul of the authorities.

4.3 WHAT'S IN A NAME?

There are many things to consider in choosing your brand name, even if you've elected to go with your real name or some variation of it. When marketing types come up with new brand names, they try to convey some sense of the product line, or some favorable associations, through that name. For example, Mr. Clean evokes the image of an efficient and polite cleaning expert who's very serious about his job. An author's brand name doesn't have to convey anything about the content of her books, but it shouldn't clash with them, either.

If your name naturally evokes certain feelings or ideas, think about how well those feelings or ideas mesh with the work you intend to publish. "Bambi Waverly" would be a good fit for romance, children's books or fantasy, and is probably fine for general fiction as well, but may not convey the necessary authority desirable in nonfiction reference, nor the sobriety the author may be aiming for in literary fiction. In such a case, if the author doesn't want to use a pen name she can go with a variation of her real name, such as "B. Waverly".

4.4 CONSISTENCY IS KEY

Consumers know the Big Mac and Quarter Pounder are both McDonald's products; likewise, you want to make it easy for readers to find all your various works and know they came from the same source. You don't want to publish one book under the brand "Joe Blow", a second under "Joseph B. Blow", a third under "J.B. Blow", and so on. In bookstore listings and library card catalogs, it won't be at all clear that the books were all written by the same person. If you already have books in print and want readers of your new books to know you are also the author of those prior works, you pretty much have to go with the name you used previously.

There is one exception to the consistency rule: authors who have more than one "product line". Gothic fiction author Anne Rice has written erotica under the pen name of "A.N. Roquelaure" for example, to keep the two bodies of work separate and distinct from one another. Some authors use one version of their name for nonfiction and another for fiction, so that their reputation as a writer of fiction doesn't dilute their authority in the world of non-fiction. The respected author of highly technical computer manuals risks being viewed as little more than a goofy fanboy if word gets out that he writes sci-fi novellas on the side.

Think very carefully about what you stand to gain and lose in choosing separate brands for separate "product lines", however. An author with ten books in print under the same brand has ten promotional tools at his disposal, all of which build up his reputation, with each book acting as a cross-promotional tool for every other book in the line. If that same author published five books under one brand and five under a second brand, he has two separate avenues of promotion but each is only half as powerful as if they were combined into a single line.

And don't forget, the latter author has easily twice as much work in keeping the marketing fires stoked for two separate product lines because he must cultivate and maintain two separate brands, and possibly even two separate identities if he intends to give interviews, blog or otherwise communicate with his readership.

4.5   TAKE THE LONG VIEW

Never forget, your brand will be a constant throughout your career and life, it should not be based on fads or specific reader age demographics.   As a twentysomething author of gossipy chick lit, you may find a name like "Snark E. Gurl" very clever and so will your intended audience.   But if you hope to have some career longevity as a writer, flash forward another twenty years and see if that name doesn't sound ridiculous hanging over the head of a fortysomething author of hen lit or literary fiction.   When the day you must switch to a more mature-sounding name inevitably comes, poof!   All the promotional and brand-loyalty equity you've built up will vanish.

Also remember, your brand name will be used as a single point of reference to stand for you and your body of work in every venue.   Your chosen name will not only appear on book covers, but also in interviews, on websites, press releases, merchandise related to your books, publicity materials and so forth.   If you absolutely hate your middle name, don't make it part of your brand name because you'll have to hear people calling you by that name for the rest of your career.

4.6   BEWARE THE COMMON NAME

Common names like "John Miller," "Susan Wilson," and the like can be easy for your readers to forget because more often than not, they will only remember that the name was "something common, like Smith or Jones."   If you want to stand in for the Everyman or Everywoman in your writing, "John Smith" or "Joan Smith" may be a good pen name.   Otherwise, you can either choose a pen name totally different from your real name or choose a variant of your real name. "John Miller" could be "J. Lee Miller," and "Susan Wilson" could be "Susan Nicole Wilson," for example.

4.7   THE SAME NAME GAME

When you've settled on your brand name, do some research to ensure no one else is publishing, or doing anything you find objectionable, under your chosen name. Ideally, you want to be the only one using your chosen brand name in a noticeable way.

First, do an internet search. In my own case, a search on "April Hamilton" turned up nearly 5,000 hits, with everyone from an interior designer to a professional soccer player among them. The same search on "April L. Hamilton" returned only references to me, so I chose that variant of my name.

You don't have to rule out your chosen name if your search turns up just a small number of references to people other than yourself, on two conditions: first, none of them are authors, and second, none of them are doing anything you find objectionable under that name. For example, if you find only one other person listed with your name but that person is on the FBI's most wanted list, you don't want to risk having people confuse you with that other person when they go looking for you online. Likewise, if one of the same-name people is prominently featured on an adults-only website or in embarrassing online videos, it's probably best to go with a variation or a completely different name.

Just to cover all the bases, also do a search on the name at Amazon.com. On the off chance someone else is publishing under your chosen brand name and it's escaped the attention of internet search engines, you'll find out about it at Amazon.

4.8   BECOME THE MASTER OF YOUR DOMAIN

Once you've got your name and you're confident you're the only one using it in much of a public way, check its availability as an internet domain. Go to the Network Solutions site (http://www.networksolutions.com) and do a domain search on the name you've chosen with a .com extension, as shown below. Just type the name you've chosen into the search box under "Find a Domain" and

leave the extension box to the right set to its default value of ".com". If the internet gods are smiling on you, your brand name will be available as a .com domain name, and if it is, immediately reserve that domain name before someone else grabs it.

Don't make the mistake of taking a .net domain when someone else has the same domain with a .com extension, because in the minds of the general public, everything online has a .com address. Many of those looking for you will end up at that other person's website. This will annoy the people who are looking for you, as well as the owner of that other domain when he starts getting confused emails from people who think he's you, demanding to know why there's nothing about your books on his site.

Even if you don't have the time, skills or funds to set up a website for the foreseeable future, you should still reserve the domain and keep it. Remember how carefully you chose your brand name, how you searched the 'net to make sure your good name wouldn't become wrongly affiliated with some other person? It's a safe bet there's an exotic dancer, drunk frat boy or crazy shut-in out there in the world with your chosen name, and there's nothing stopping them from reserving your .com and building a website that will unravel all your due diligence the day their site goes live.

As of this writing it costs less than US$40 to reserve a .com domain on a year-to-year basis through Network Solutions, with a downward sliding price scale when you reserve it for more than one year. Going through a hosting service can get you the domain name reservation for free, but you must sign up for fee-based monthly hosting services. You may want to check out some hosting providers and shop around for the best deal, even if you don't intend to build a full-fledged website. If you know anyone who has a website, ask which service he or she uses for hosting, how much it costs, and whether or not the service is satisfactory. If not, you can look for service provider reviews on sites such as CNET.com. As a last resort, you can just do an internet search for "web hosting" and do your own research.

If your chosen brand is not available as a .com, I strongly recommend you choose a different brand name. The existence of a .com website is taken as a sign of "realness" and professionalism in the eyes of the public. Think about it: if you hear about a hot new toy company called 'Whoozit', you'll tend to assume you can go online to the Whoozit.com website to learn more about their products or even order something from them. If there is no Whoozit.com website, or if the Whoozit company site address is something like Whoozit.funpages.net, suddenly Whoozit Corp. starts looking a little fly-by-night to you, doesn't it? Don't risk making the same bad impression.

5   DIY FORMATTING FOR POD

If you're using a vanity or subsidy publisher, you don't need these formatting instructions because your publisher will either do the formatting for you or provide its own, very specific formatting requirements. This chapter explains how to format your book by yourself for print through a POD or eBook publisher. You may be familiar with standard formatting conventions for manuscripts to be submitted to an agent or editor, but formatting for POD is entirely different.

The manuscript you submit for print must be formatted as print "galleys": pages that look *exactly* how they should look in the published book. Therefore, it's up to you to ensure everything from page dimensions to headers and footers are properly formatted before sending your manuscript off for print.

The keys to success with formatting a proof manuscript are minimalism and consistency. Use as few different formatting options as possible, and apply them consistently. Ideally, you should start with a pre-formatted document "shell" so that your pages will be properly formatted as you write, but you can also set up a shell, copy text from your existing manuscript and paste it into the shell as 'unformatted text' so that it will acquire the correct formatting from the shell.

In this chapter, I'll be demonstrating how to build and use a manuscript shell in Microsoft Word 2003. All the program features and options shown should be available in any word processing program from that year or later, and since MS Word has been the leading word processing program for decades most other word processors are designed to mimic Word's interface and layout. If your word processor is substantially different, you'll have to consult your program's menus and help files to locate the features shown and learn how to use them.

5.1 STYLES

Every modern word processing program has 'Style' functions built into it. Styles are a way of storing formatting options, such as font size, line spacing and so on, so you can easily apply all those same options to other sections of text with a single click. In Microsoft Word, Styles are accessed under the Format menu.

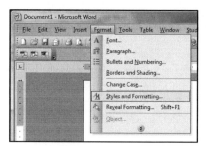

When you open a new, blank document in your word processor, certain default Styles are already assigned to the document. If you just start typing into your document, the default Styles specify what font face and font size will be used, among other things.

Clicking on the Styles and Formatting menu item in MS Word 2003 will display a list of all Styles currently available for use in the document. The default Styles for a new document in MS Word 2003 are shown below (on the right).

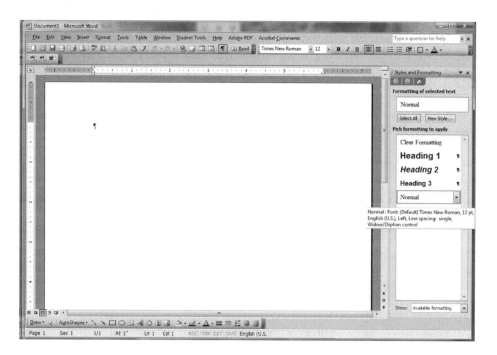

Mousing over a Style in the list pops up a little box displaying all the formatting options being used in that Style. As shown above, the Normal Style is defined as Times New Roman, 12 point text, using English language conventions (i.e., no umlauts or Chinese characters will be needed), with text left-aligned, lines single-spaced, and widow/orphan control (explained later in this chapter) turned on. Notice that Style names are displayed with their respective formatting options applied, to give you a preview of how your text will look when each Style is used. For example, the Heading Style names are all displayed in boldface because each of those Styles applies boldface to text.

Three Heading Styles are available in the default list; Headings are formatted differently from ordinary text, and are intended for use as chapter and section headings in a document's Table of Contents. In Word, when you insert a Table of Contents (demonstrated later in this chapter) the program locates every piece of text with a Heading Style applied to it and includes that text in the Table of Contents. The Clear Formatting command appears above the listed Styles.

Using Styles in Word is simple: just highlight the text you want formatted, then click the Style containing the formatting options you want. However, it's obvious that this only works if there's an applicable Style containing all your desired formatting options in the list.

People who don't know how to use Styles apply formatting changes to the text in their documents "on the fly," meaning as they go, by selecting the text they want to change and applying their desired formatting manually through use of the toolbar (shown below).

Each time the user does this, Word stores the chosen formatting options as a new Style and adds that Style to the list. The newly-created Style is named in the list like this:

[name of Style before changes] + [list of changes applied, in order applied]

For example, if you select text formatted as the default, Normal Style and apply boldface and italics to it using toolbar buttons, the new Style will be named:

Normal + bold + italics

If you applied the italics first, then the boldface, the new Style would be named:

Normal + italics + bold

As you can imagine, it's easy to quickly build up a huge number of differently-named Styles, many of which are duplicates in terms of the formatting changes they apply. The on-the-fly approach is fine for personal documents, letters, notes to yourself and the like, but not for a word processing file to be submitted to a POD publisher. This is because the publisher must convert word processing files into a format that's readable by their printing programs and equipment.

You probably know that some computer programs place a limit on how many characters you can use for a filename; similarly, POD publishers' conversion tools have internal limits on how many characters of a Style name they can read. If a given document has four different Styles that all begin with "Normal + bold + italics," each of which goes on to set different options for line spacing, indenting, font face or anything else, the publisher's file converter may not 'read' beyond "italics" in the Style names. It will assume that all four Styles are the same, ignore the latter three 'duplicates' and apply only the first instance of "Normal + bold + italics" to all the text that was originally formatted using four *different* Styles. It will still apply all the formatting options specified by that first Style, it won't stop at "italics," but any formatting changes applied by the latter three Styles will be lost and you'll get an unpleasant surprise in the proof copy.

It's far better to determine all the different formatting required in your manuscript ahead of time and create differently-named Styles for each. Note that if you only intend to publish in eBook formats *other* than pdf (i.e., prc, pdb, lrf, html, Kindle), you should keep the number of Styles you use to a minimum and keep them very simple, because when you're done formatting you will have to convert your finished document into the desired format(s) and all but the most basic formatting options will be lost. See the Publishing For The Kindle and Publishing To Other Ebook Formats chapters for more details.

What About PDF Files?

Some POD publishers accept pdf file submissions in addition to, or instead of, word processing files (i.e., .doc, .txt. .rtf, etc.). In that case, no file conversion is needed at the publisher's end. Their processing programs and equipment print the pdf file exactly as-is, so you can feel confident your published book will look exactly like the pdf file you submitted. This is one reason why I include a pdf maker program in the indie author's required tools of the trade.

However, turning a word processing file into a pdf is also a file conversion process. A pdf file is essentially a series of images; it's as if the pdf maker program takes a photograph of each page in the source document and assembles all those pictures into a single file. The pdf file looks just like the word processing source file, but you can't edit it with a word processor. The pdf file is also a lot smaller than the source file in terms of bytes, because it doesn't contain all the behind-the-scenes formatting details and instructions that were present in the source file.

There are many pdf maker programs, and some of them are available online as a free download. Do an internet search on "pdf maker" + free to find them. Open

Office (http://www.openoffice.org), a free, open-source alternative to Microsoft Office, includes pdf maker functionality right inside all its programs. The granddaddy of them all is Adobe Acrobat, the first pdf maker invented. Adobe distributes its Acrobat Reader software free of charge, but that program can only *read* pdf files. The full Acrobat program is needed to *create* pdf files.

Every pdf maker program creates pdf files, but they don't all use the same file conversion process. Some don't take source file Styles into account, but those that include a feature enabling the user to convert pdf files back into word processing files might. Adobe Acrobat's conversion engine generally disregards Styles, but it sometimes falters with heavily-formatted documents due to the large amount of data in the file. This isn't necessarily a problem with the Acrobat program itself, but with the demands it makes on your computer's processing power. Formatting your word processing document through the use of a small number of consistently-applied Styles keeps file size to a minimum.

5.1.1 CREATING CUSTOM STYLES

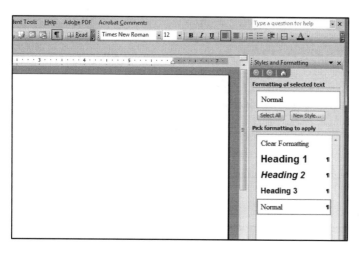

Open a new, blank document and open the Styles and Formatting feature. Click the New Style button above the Styles listbox, shown in the screen shot at left. The New Style dialog box (shown on next page) is displayed.

Begin by specifying a name for your Style. Custom Style names must be different than any of the Style names already included with your word processing program, so you can't name your Style "Normal," for instance. Recall that this name is what will be shown in the Styles listbox, so choose something that will be easily recognizable to you in the list.

The Style name I chose for normal body text is "IAG Normal Body Text". Consider beginning your custom Style names with a specific designation so they will all appear together in the alphabetical Styles list. For example, the names of all the custom Styles I created for use in this book begin with "IAG", which is a designation for IndieAuthor Guide.

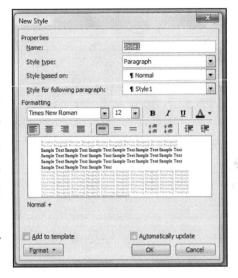

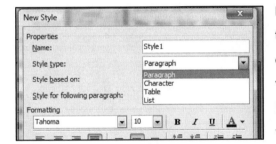

Next is 'Style type'. As shown in the screen shot at left, there are only four choices. The only ones you're likely to ever need are Paragraph and List. If your Style will be applied to blocks of text, choose Paragraph. If it will be applied to numbered or bulleted lists, choose List.

The 'Style based on' box (shown on next page) lists every Style that comes pre-installed in your word processing program. Select any Style from the list to see its formatting options. The goal is to find the pre-existing Style whose formatting options are closest to the custom Style you're creating. For example, for the main title on the title page of this book, I selected "Title" for 'Style based on," then merely changed the font face and font type. All the other pre-selected formatting options were fine as-is.

In the screen shot below, I've selected "Title". The Formatting section is updated to reflect all the options applicable to the chosen Style, and the display box shows an example of how text formatted with the Style will look.

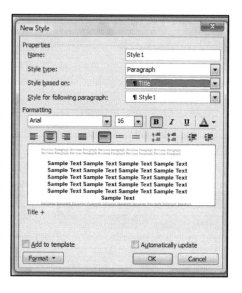

The most commonly-used formatting options are right there on the New Style dialog box, and all other options are accessible through the Format button, located in the lower left-hand corner of the dialog box. Click the button to access a pop-up menu of choices (shown below).

Each list item links to the same formatting dialog boxes that are accessible from the main toolbar under 'Format' (shown at right).

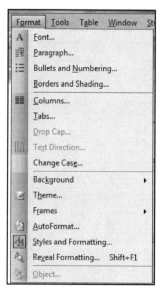

A whole chapter could be written on each option item in the pop-up menu, but this chapter assumes you are already versed in at least the basic use of each one. If not, refer to your word processing program's help files for further detail. If you write novels the options you will use most often are Font and Paragraph. In a nonfiction book (like this one), you may also need Styles that incorporate settings for Tabs, Border and Numbering.

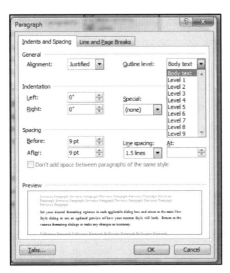

When creating a chapter heading Style be sure to check the options set for Paragraph, because that's where you specify an outline level for heading Styles to ensure they will show up as you want them to in your table of contents. As shown at left, use the drop-down list to select an outline level for each header you create.

Styles with an outline level of 'Body text' won't appear in the table of contents. Outline level 1 Styles will appear as left-aligned text in the table of contents. This is the level you'll select for your chapter headings. Outline level 2 Styles will appear in the table of contents as text indented five spaces in from the left-aligned Outline level 1 Styles. This is the level to choose for chapter sub-headings. Outline level 3 Styles will appear in the table of contents as text indented five spaces in from the indented level 2 Styles. This is the level to use for headings beneath sub-headings. The pattern continues from there, but for the sake of easy readability it's a good idea to limit your table of contents to just three outline levels. The table of contents for this book shows three levels.

Set your desired formatting options in each applicable dialog box and return to the main New Style dialog to see an updated preview of how your custom Style will look. Return to the various formatting dialogs to make any needed changes.

Make a selection in the Style For Following Paragraph drop-down box, specifying the default Style to apply to paragraphs beginning immediately after the Style you're creating. For example, when working with a Header Style, the Style For Following Paragraph is generally Normal Body Text (or your custom Style version of it). This setting can save you a lot of time and hassle as you work on your chapters, so make good use of it. When you're happy with your Style, click on the Add To Template checkbox above the Format button to select it, and click the OK button to save the Style. When the New Style dialog box closes, you'll see your custom Style has been added to the Style list.

5.1.2   WHAT STYLES ARE NEEDED?

To figure out how many custom Styles you need to create for a POD book, and how they should be formatted, look through the pages of a book that's the same type as your intended book (i.e., novel, user guide, software manual, textbook, reference book, nonfiction, etc.). You will notice that the book employs different Styles for different types of text. For example, main body text, footer text, header text, title page text and the table of contents will all probably employ different formatting options. Some text may be printed in a different font or indented to set it apart from blocks of normal body text. The following table lists the Styles most commonly used for different types of books.

Style Type	Needed For	Fiction, Poetry or Nonfiction Prose	General Nonfiction
copyright	copyright info page	✔	✔
title	title page, main title	✔	✔
subtitle	title page, subtitle	✔	✔
byline	title page, author name	✔	✔
dedication	dedication page	✔	✔
TOC heading	table of contents page, table of contents heading	✔	✔
body text, normal	within chapters	✔	✔
body text, italics	within chapters	✔	✔
body text, bold	within chapters	✔	✔
chapter heading	start of each chapter	✔	✔
chapter sub-headings	within chapters, one for each 'level' of subheading		✔
index	index		✔

The table is just a starting point. You may not need all the Styles in it for your book, or your book may require additional Styles for things like captions to describe illustrations, indented text blocks, or bulleted or numbered lists.

5.1.3 ABOUT INDUSTRY STANDARDS

You may have noticed that a lot of published books look alike in terms of layout and the Styles they employ, and this is due to 'industry standard' formatting. Each different "imprint", or subsidiary, of a big, mainstream publisher will have its standard font, layout and sometimes even cover design. Rules and guidelines dictate everything from line spacing to header and footer height. About the only place you see much variety in the look of published books anymore is children's books, in which more creative layouts and unusual fonts are still acceptable.

There are plenty of how-to books and articles out there admonishing indie authors to school themselves on industry standards, and strictly apply those standards to their self-published books in order to avoid an "amateurish" look. Not surprisingly, I do not share this viewpoint.

First of all, nobody but publishing professionals know the industry standards for book formatting. The general public may be aware that books from a given imprint all look sort of the same, but they don't know or care why. The general public judges the professionalism of a book by the quality of its binding and cover, and the readability of its content. The average reader will not discard a book in disgust, exclaiming, "Verdana isn't an industry standard font!"

Secondly, industry standards were established around mechanical typesetting, before the digital age began. In those days, each letter and character of text was carved into a tiny metal block, and the blocks were all laid out in a frame to create a massive stamp of each page of text to be printed. The entire frame could be inked and then stamped onto a page. Publishers and typesetters didn't think of fonts as design elements, or experiment with different fonts, because the process of creating a whole new set of those tiny metal blocks was very expensive and time-consuming. Similarly, in the old days line spacing was built into the frames used to hold the tiny character blocks. Access to a variety of line-spacing options required a variety of different frames, and this was another expense to be avoided. When digital design came along a whole plethora of fonts and page layout options followed, yet the moldy oldies still dominate in mainstream publishing—not because of any inherent superiority but because mainstream publishers are used to them, and loathe to change.

Finally, as any graphic designer will tell you, fonts and layout can be used to convey something about their content. Anyone who's ever chosen a font for a sign, greeting card, banner or scrapbook knows this is true. Look at the various fonts on the next page, and see if each one doesn't inspire a different mood.

ALGERIAN	Comic Sans MS	Goudy Old Style	Modern No. 20
Andy	Curlz MT	Jokerman	Papyrus
Bauhaus 93	Euphemia	Kristen ITC	Segoe Print
Beesknees ITC	Garamond	Maiandra GD	Tempus Sans ITC

Not all of the examples in the table are appropriate for use in a book, they're shown to illustrate a point. However, if you want to use Euphemia for your futuristic sci-fi book, Garamond for your romance, or Goudy Old Style for your circa 1880's mystery, why shouldn't you? If you want to use Bauhaus 93 just for the chapter headings of your 1970's era chick-lit, why not?

Where your mainstream-published peers are stuck with boring Times New Roman and the like, as an indie author you can utilize fonts to enhance the reader's overall experience. As long as the font is easy to read and not so busy or design-heavy that it will fatigue the eyes when laid out in paragraphs (like Algerian, Bauhaus 93 and Beesknees ITC in the table above), there's no reason *not* to choose a font that evokes the mood you're after.

Similarly, your chosen font may be too small in a standard, 10-point size, or easier to read with line spacing slightly greater than industry standards dictate. Many readers find the usual 10-point, narrowly-spaced lines of the typical mass-market paperback hard on the eyes, but don't really need a large-print edition. I generally work with non-standard fonts in a size larger than industry standard with 1.5 line spacing, and readers have specifically complimented the superior readability of my books. If you are publishing to an eBook format other than pdf however, you should only use HTML-compliant fonts (see HTML Primer chapter).

5.2 BUILD A MANUSCRIPT SHELL

A manuscript shell is to your manuscript what framing is to a house: it provides a consistent structure to the overall project. The shell is where you set up all the necessary formatting options for text and the manuscript in general. It's a lengthy pain setting up the manuscript shell, but you only have to do it once and manuscripts created in the shell will automatically be properly formatted for POD as you work. After the shell is created, save it for use as a template: each time you begin a manuscript, open the shell and "Save As" under a new filename.

Begin by opening a new, blank document and doing a "Save As" with your desired filename. Save frequently as you work on setting up the shell.

5.2.1 CREATE CUSTOM STYLES

Make a list of the Styles you will need, select a name for each one, and create them as described previously.

5.2.2 MODIFY PAGE SETUP

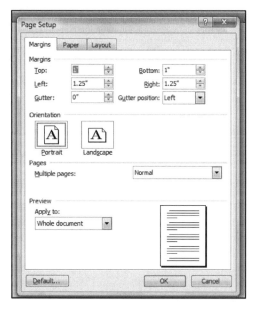

Go to File > Page Setup to access the Page Setup dialog. The screen shot at left shows how the dialog looks when you first open it, with default values filled in.

The dialog has three tabs: Margins, Paper and Layout. When setting your top and bottom margins, bear headers and footers in mind. If you will have headers and footers—and most books do, even if only for page numbering—be sure to make headers and footers wide enough to allow for spacing between the header/footer and adjacent text. Your text should not butt right up against your headers or footers.

Before changing anything else, in the Pages section select "Mirror margins" (highlighted in screen shot at right). This will make the margins on facing pages mirror images of one another, and alters some options in the dialog. Left and Right margin names are changed to Inside and Outside respectively, the Gutter position drop-down is locked, and instead of one page, the dialog displays two facing pages at the bottom.

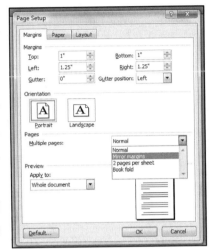

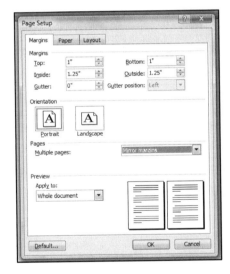

Now you can set your inside and outside margins. Take a book of the same dimensions and type as your intended book (i.e., trade paperback novel, training manual, etc.) off your shelf and measure its margins. Note that margins are sized up or down incrementally for different page sizes. This book has 1" margins, but that would be much too wide for a mass-market paperback-sized book. In trade paperbacks, I set margins of ½".

Inside and outside margins are generally set to the same width. Don't worry about making the inside margin wider to account for the binding, because the Gutter setting will handle that.

Because hardcover and paperback books do not lie flat when they're opened, a certain amount of empty space is needed between the book's spine and the text on each page, to account for the part of the page that's hidden by the binding. The Gutter setting allows you to specify how much empty space you want in that area of each page, between the spine and the inside margin.

The dimensions, page count and purpose of your book will determine the appropriate Gutter width. A large-format book will open a little bit wider than a small-format book, exposing more of the Gutter area to the reader. A thin book will open wider than a thick one as well, also exposing more of the Gutter.

Get a book of the same approximate size and thickness as your intended book and open it to a page somewhere near the middle, as if to read. Tilt the top of the book down so you can see the top edge of the spine, and measure the distance between the spine and visible inner edge of the printed pages—in other words, measure how much of each page is invisible because it's curved inward, toward the spine. That distance is the width of the Gutter, and in mainstream books with glued bindings, it's often too narrow.

If you've ever had to forcibly flatten an open book in order to more easily see the text closest to the spine, you know how annoying it is to the reader when Gutters are too narrow. Moreover, flattening a book in such a way can crack a glued binding, resulting in loose or even lost pages. If you want to make the reader comfortable and increase the chance your book will survive its first reading, be generous with your Gutters.

The purpose of your book comes into play when you imagine how the book is most likely to be positioned when the buyer is reading it. Books that are read for pleasure will be held in the reader's hands, but in a how-to book like this one, the reader will frequently need to lay the book open on a desk or table and refer to it as she follows a step-by-step procedure. Knowing this, I set the Gutter for this book to 1". This, together with my 1" inner margin, makes the distance from the spine to the inner edge of my text a whopping 2". The book still won't lay flat on a desk or table, but the reader should have no difficulty reading right up to the inner margin when she glances up from her computer to look at it.

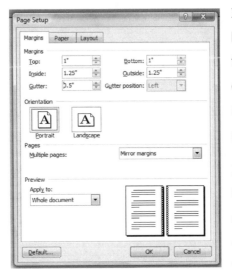

In the example shown at left, the Gutter has been set to .5, or ½". Notice that the facing-pages image at the bottom of the dialog displays the gutter as shaded margins along the inner edge of each page.

In the Preview section at the bottom of the dialog, leave the 'Apply to' dialog box set to its default value of 'Whole document'. Click the 'Paper' tab to open the Paper options dialog.

All you need to set on this tab is 'Paper size', at the top of the dialog, by manually entering your desired page height and width. If your book will be a 'perfect bound' paperback, in which the pages of the book are flush with the edges of the cover, set the paper size to your intended book's dimensions (i.e., 6x9" for trade paperback).

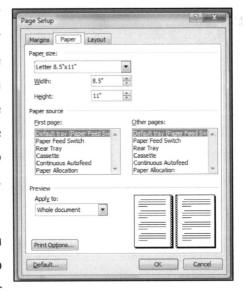

If your book will be a hardcover, you will need to consult your publisher to learn the correct paper size for your book's dimensions.

The facing-pages preview at the bottom of the dialog will display a rough approximation of how your margin and gutter options will be applied to pages of the size you've specified, so if something looks screwy in that little picture you may need to go back to the Margins tab and make adjustments. When you're satisfied with the preview image, click the Layout tab.

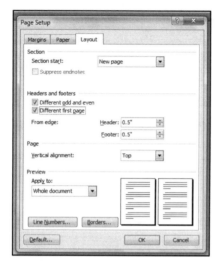

For most books, the only settings to be altered here are in the Headers and Footers section. Click on the checkboxes next to 'Different odd and even' and 'Different first page' to select them.

If yours is a poetry book, cartoon collection or other type of book with 'alternative' page layout, you may want to set 'Vertical alignment' in the Page section to Center instead of its default value of Top.

Click the OK button, and you're done with the Page Setup dialog.

5.2.3 SET UP FRONT SECTION

Your book should have all the same front matter as a mainstream-published book. That means a copyright page, dedication page, title page, and table of contents. The page facing the reader when he opens the front cover should be blank. Set a placeholder on the first page of your word processing document for

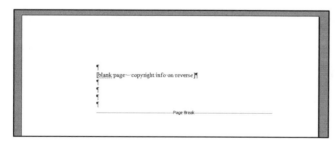

this page, followed by some carriage returns and a page break.

To insert the page break, under the Insert menu on the toolbar, select 'Break'. In the Insert Break dialog, select 'Page break' and click OK. To insert a page break using the keyboard shortcut, hold down the Ctrl key while pressing the Enter key.

This brings you to page two of your word processing file, which is actually the reverse of that blank page the reader sees when he opens the cover of the book. This is where you will put your copyright information, in the format shown below.

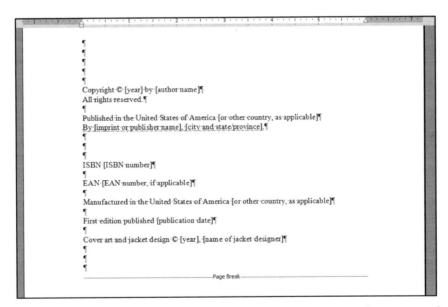

You will notice that the left-hand margin on this page is much narrower than the left-hand margin on the previous page. This is because the left-hand margin on the first page consisted of a Gutter plus a margin, since on that page the left-hand side is where the page will be glued or sewn into the book's spine. On this page, which will be the reverse of the first page in the printed book, the Gutter is on the right-hand side.

The effect can be jarring when viewed onscreen. Remember that each page of the finished book will consist of two pages from your word processing document. The blank page directly beneath the front cover is page one of the book, an odd-numbered page. Its reverse is page two of the book, an even-numbered page. When the book is open, pages on the left will always be even-numbered (because they are always the backs of odd-numbered pages) and pages on the right will always be odd.

 Recall the facing-pages preview in the Page Setup dialog box. If these were two facing pages bound into a book, the one on the left side would be even-numbered and the one on the right would be odd-numbered. The Gutter will always appear on the left on odd-numbered pages, and on the right on even-numbered pages.

If you do not have all of the information needed for your copyright page (i.e., ISBN, EAN, etc.), leave placeholders as necessary. Just don't forget to go back and update your copyright page when all the needed information is available. If your book mentions brand names of products or services, add copyright and trademark information about those items to your copyright page, following the format shown on the copyright page of this book. Finally, select all the text on the page and apply your custom copyright Style to it. Insert a few carriage returns and another page break.

Now you're on page three of your word processing file, which is the front of the second page in the book. This will be your title page. Enter your title, subtitle (if applicable), and author byline as desired, then apply the correct custom Style to each item. Enter a few carriage returns and a page break.

This brings you to page four of your file, which will be the reverse of the title page in your book. It may be blank or display titles of your other published books in an Also By [author name] list, according to your preference. Enter a placeholder, carriage returns and page break as shown below.

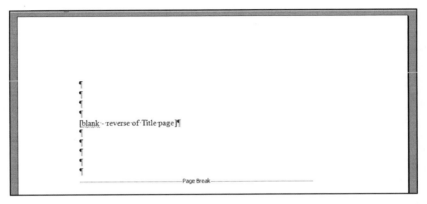

Now you're on page five of your word processing file, or the front of the third page in your eventual book. This is your dedication page. Enter your dedication message about 1/3 of the way down from the top of the page, then select all of its text and apply your custom dedication Style to it. Enter a few carriage returns and a page break.

Page six of your word processing file is the back of the dedication page in your book. Enter a placeholder, carriage returns and a page break, following the prior examples of blank pages.

The next page, page seven of your word processing file, is where the table of contents goes. Enter a 'Table of Contents' header and apply your custom formatting Style to it, then the usual carriage returns and page break. The actual table of contents will be inserted much later, when the book is being prepared for print.

Now you've reached page eight, the reverse of your table of contents page. This page may or may not have text on it in the printed book, depending on the length of your table of contents. For now, set it up like the other blank placeholder pages, but instead of inserting a page break after the carriage returns, insert a Next Page Section Break.

This is done via the Break menu, as described previously. You're inserting a section break instead of a page break to create a new 'section' for chapter one of your book. This is necessary because headers, footers and page numbers aren't typically displayed on 'front matter' pages (copyright page, title page, dedication page, table of contents) but *are* displayed on the pages making up the main body of the book. Since headers and footers are applied on a per-section basis, if you want headers and footers on some pages but not others, you must set up separate document sections for each instance of changed formatting. Going forward, each chapter will be set up as a new section in the document.

5.2.4   A NOTE ABOUT COPYRIGHT

Per the United States Copyright Office, "Your work is under copyright protection the moment it is created and fixed in a tangible form that it is perceptible either directly or with the aid of a machine or device."

In response to the question of whether or not copyright registration with the U.S. Copyright Office is mandatory in order to receive copyright protection in the U.S., the Office responds, "No. In general, registration is voluntary. Copyright exists from the moment the work is created. You will have to register, however, if you wish to bring a lawsuit for infringement of a U.S. work."

In response to the question of why a copyright should be registered at all if copyright already exists, the Office answers, "Registration is recommended for a number of reasons. Many choose to register their works because they wish to have the facts of their copyright on the public record and have a certificate of registration. Registered works may be eligible for statutory damages and attorney's fees in successful litigation. Finally, if registration occurs within 5 years of publication, it is considered prima facie evidence in a court of law."

In other words, a registered copyright affords an author maximum protection in a court of law if he or she should ever need to bring a case of copyright infringement.

Having said that, legal matters are outside the scope of this book and nothing herein should be construed as legal advice. If you are uncertain whether or not to obtain a registered copyright for your work in the U.S., I encourage you to obtain Circular 1, Copyright Basics, from the U.S. Copyright Office website (http://www.copyright.gov/), and confer with an attorney for further guidance. For information about copyright law and enforcement outside the U.S., confer with an attorney versed in international copyright law.

5.2.5   SET UP HEADERS AND FOOTERS

Headers and footers will appear on your chapter pages, but not on the first page of each chapter. This is why you selected the 'Different first page' option for headers and footers in the Page Setup section.

In this book, text in the header is right-aligned on odd-numbered pages and left-aligned on even-numbered pages. This ensures the header is always aligned to the outer margin of each page, not the inner margin, near the Gutter. Likewise, in the footer page numbers are right-aligned on odd-numbered pages and left-aligned on even-numbered pages. This is why the "Different odd and even" option exists for headers and footers in the Page Setup section.

If you want the text and page numbers in your headers *or* footers to be differently-aligned on odd- and even-numbered pages, as they are in this book, you need to insert four placeholder pages in your manuscript shell, as shown in the table on the following page. If your header *and* footer content will be centered on every page, you still need to insert one placeholder page for the first page of the chapter (which won't have a header), and a second placeholder page to represent how headers and footers should be formatted on every other page of the chapter. In that event, you can go back and de-select the 'Different odd and even' checkbox in the Page Setup dialog.

Chapter Page	Header Content	Footer Content
1	No header	Right-aligned page number
2	Left-aligned header text	Left-aligned page number
3	Right-aligned header text	Right-aligned page number
4	Left-aligned header text	Left-aligned page number

Begin by inserting placeholder pages, without headers or footers. Page nine is the first page of your first chapter. Enter the name or number of the chapter and apply your custom chapter heading Style to it. Enter a few carriage returns and a page break.

For header and footer formatting with differently-aligned odd- and even-numbered pages, you must set up three more placeholder pages. On pages ten and eleven, enter a few carriage returns and a page break. On page twelve, enter a few carriage returns and a Next Page Section Break, as described previously. For books with identically-aligned headers and footers, you only need to have one additional placeholder page (page ten) with a few carriage returns and a Next Page Section Break on it.

Set Up Headers

Go back to page nine and select the Header and Footer option of the View menu.

The cursor jumps up into the header section, and the Header and Footer toolbar is displayed.

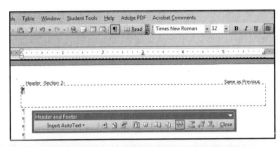

Notice the highlighted button on the toolbar (you can also mouse over the toolbar to see each button's name). That's the Link to Previous button, and it's always selected at the start of a new section by default. Its current setting is displayed in the header or footer onscreen as well. This option should never be selected for your headers, even if you intend to use centered headers, because the first page of each chapter won't have a header but subsequent pages will.

You don't want a header on the first page of any chapter. Leave the header blank. The far right button, next to the Close button, is the Show Next button. Click it to go to the header on the second page of your chapter.

The second page of your chapter is an even-numbered page. If the Link to Previous button is selected, click it to de-select it. In a book with centered headers, the header on this page should be center-aligned. In a book with headers aligned like this book, the header on this page should be left-aligned so it will appear near the outside margin of the page. Enter your desired text (book title or chapter title) in the header. Apply formatting options as desired, including desired text alignment. Click the Show Next button.

If your page headers are all center-aligned, you don't have any more page headers to set up. Click the Previous button to get back to page nine of your manuscript, then skip ahead to the Set Up Footers section on the following page. Otherwise, read on to complete your header formatting.

The third page of your chapter is an odd-numbered page, which means its header should be right-aligned. De-select the Link to Previous button if applicable. Enter the same header text as on the previous page and apply the same formatting, but make the text right-aligned. Click the Show Next button.

The fourth page of your chapter is an even-numbered page, which means its header should be left-aligned. If the Link to Previous button is selected, click it to de-select it. Enter the same header text as on the previous page and apply the same formatting, but make the text right-aligned.

Instead of the Show Next button, this time click the Show Previous button, located immediately left of the Show Next button. Click it two more times to get back to the blank header on the first page of your chapter.

Set Up Footers

Click the Switch Between Header and Footer button, to the immediate right of the Link to Previous button, to switch to the footer.

Again, by default, the Same as Next button is selected. Click it to de-select it. Insert the page number (and any other desired text) in the footer. Apply desired formatting, including desired alignment. Page numbers will be either centered or right-aligned.

By default, page numbering will display the actual page number of the word processing document. If you want page numbering to begin with "1", click the Format Page Number button (highlighted above) to display the Page Number Format dialog box.

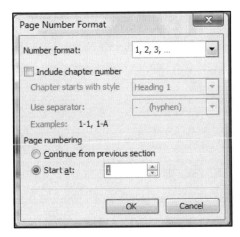

In the Page Number Format dialog box, click the Start At option to select it and accept the default number setting of "1". Leave all other options in the dialog set to their defaults and click OK.

On the Header and Footer toolbar, click the Show Next button to go to the footer on the second page of your chapter. Insert the page number (and other desired text, if applicable) and apply desired formatting, including left-alignment of the page number.

That's all there is to footer setup, regardless of whether or not your footers will be differently-aligned on odd and even pages. Since all chapter pages will have footers, all even-page footers will be formatted the same as one another, all odd-page footers will be formatted the same as one another, and Link to Previous is always selected for a new section by default, you don't need to do any footer setup for subsequent chapters/sections. Word will automatically continue inserting the correct odd- and even-page footers as pages are added to the manuscript.

As for headers, Word will continue to insert the correct odd- and even-page headers as you add pages to your chapter, but because you don't want a header on the first page of any subsequent chapters/sections you will have to repeat the header setup steps for each chapter/section in your manuscript.

An even number of pages (two or four, depending on whether or not you want differently-aligned headers and/or footers) are inserted as placeholders for each chapter/section to ensure the first page of each *new* chapter/section will always be an odd-numbered, or right-hand, page. This is pretty standard in mainstream-published books, and while I don't generally kowtow to mainstream conventions this is one case where I do, simply because it's what readers are used to and have come to expect. Later on, as you type or paste chapter text into your manuscript, you may find the chapter/section ends on an odd-numbered page. If that's the case, insert a page break to create a blank even-numbered page at the end of the chapter.

The last page of each chapter/section should always be an even-numbered page, and should always end with a Next Page Section Break. After you're finished typing or pasting in chapter text later, if you find some of your original placeholder pages are still there at the end of the chapter/section, delete any extra, blank pages—but again, make sure the last page of the chapter is an even-numbered page, and that it ends with a Next Page Section Break.

Set up a second chapter/section as you did the first one, inserting and formatting desired headers and footers the same as for the first chapter/section. Two placeholder chapters are enough for the manuscript shell, so let's move on to the back matter of the book.

5.2.6 SET UP BACK SECTION

The last page of your manuscript shell is the beginning of a new section, but instead of setting it up as another chapter you'll be using it for back matter. The back matter of a book consists of all the pages at the end of the book that have nothing to do with the contents of the book. An About the Author page, and an Also From [author name] page containing cross-sell descriptions of the author's other books are two typical examples. Definitely add an About the Author page in every one of your books, and include a link to your author website or blog (see Promotion chapter) in it. Keep the bio brief, as you'll want to use it online as well and most websites place limitations on the 'About Me' or 'Biography' section in members' profiles. See my bio at the end of this book for an example.

If you have other books similar to the one you're working on in print, include descriptions for one or two of them on a cross-sell page. If the book is part of a series, you can include cross-sell descriptions for every other book in the series. Otherwise, more than two cross-sell descriptions may seem tacky.

Just as with the front matter section, the back matter section doesn't typically include headers or footers.

5.3   CREATE A SEPARATE, CHAPTER SHELL

You should now have a complete manuscript shell with all your custom Styles, a front matter section, two chapter sections and a back matter section. Save it with your desired manuscript shell name.

The manuscript shell will be used to assemble your final manuscript, but as you work through drafts of chapters it's best to store, and work on, each chapter as a separate file. This is because you want to be able to make full use of your word processor's spell check and grammar check tools (see Editing chapter). These tools run in the background as you work, constantly scanning every word on every page for errors. As page count increases, performance gets more and more sluggish. Eventually you'll hit the point where the file is so large it crashes your word processor altogether, and from then on you won't be able to open the file at all. That's why you need to create a separate, chapter shell.

Do a "Save As' to create a copy of the manuscript shell, saving it with a name specific to a chapter shell. Delete the front matter section, the second chapter section and the back matter section, and save again. There you have it, your chapter shell is complete.

5.3.1 USING THE CHAPTER SHELL

To write a new chapter, open the chapter shell and do a "Save As" to create a copy. Type the chapter into the word processing file as you normally would, but applying your custom Styles from the Style list.

Don't Fake It

You went through all the trouble of setting up a shell so that formatting would be applied consistently, using the word processor's formatting tools, so there will be no unpleasant surprises after file conversion. Don't undermine all that effort with 'fake' formatting tricks while using the shell.

Use the tab key to indent at the beginning of a new paragraph, not the space bar. Use the left and right indent tools to inset blocks of text, not the space bar. Use the borders and shading tool to insert horizontal lines, not a row of dashes. When creating a long dash in a sentence for emphasis—like this—, insert an em dash (accessed via Insert > Symbol > Special Characters, or Alt+Ctrl+[minus sign]) instead of typing three short dashes from the keyboard.

What About Pre-Existing Chapters?

If you already have a chapter written, copy its contents and paste it into a copy of the chapter shell as unformatted text. This feature is accessed via the Paste

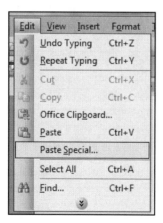

Special option under the Edit menu on the main toolbar.

In the Paste Special dialog, select Unformatted Text. When your text is added to the chapter shell document, it will acquire the custom Styles you've set up in the shell.

Note that you can leave the chapter heading out, since it will already be in place in the manuscript shell when you're ready to assemble all your chapters into a single document.

5.4   USING THE MANUSCRIPT SHELL

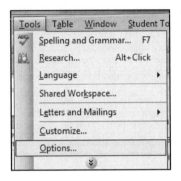 Open the manuscript shell and do a "Save As" to create a copy. Under the Tools menu, select Options.

In the Options dialog, select the Spelling and Grammar tab (shown at right). In the Spelling section, de-select Check Spelling As You Type. In the Grammar section, de-select Check Grammar As You Type. Click OK to save your changes.

Copy and paste the contents of your separate chapters into the document, creating new chapter sections as needed. If you're copying and pasting from a corresponding chapter shell, you don't have to use the Paste Special command because the text should already be formatted with the same Styles as those in the manuscript shell. If you're copying and pasting from a different source, use the Paste Special function, as described in the previous section.

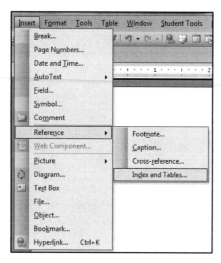

When all your content is present in the manuscript, go to the placeholder page for the table of contents. Delete the placeholder text. Place your cursor where you want the table of contents to begin, a line or two beneath the table of contents header, and select Index and Tables from the Reference list under the Insert menu on the main toolbar.

In the Index and Tables dialog, click the Table of Contents tab. De-select the 'Use hyperlinks instead of page numbers' option on the right-hand side. Set other options as desired and click OK to insert the table of contents on your page. Its font most likely will not match

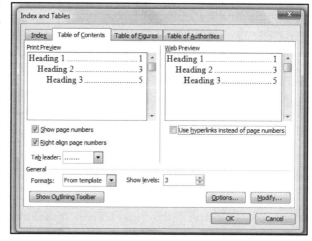

the rest of your document. If this is the case, select all the text contained in the table of contents and manually change the font and point size according to your preference. If your table of contents is longer than one page, make sure the last page of the front matter section is still an even-numbered page ending in a Next Page Section Break. Insert a blank page after the table of contents to accomplish this, if necessary.

5.4.1 DO A FINAL REVIEW

Update the copyright information page if needed to eliminate any placeholders remaining there. Delete placeholder text on pages that will be blank in the printed book. Go through the completed manuscript to verify your headers are correct, any extraneous placeholder pages have been removed, page numbering is correct and graphics are properly positioned (if applicable).

If you've moved chapters around or inserted new chapters or sections between pre-existing ones in the manuscript shell, you may find the relocated or inserted sections have inherited the same headers as the sections preceding them due to that pesky Link to Previous default. Edit such headers as needed. Also note, since the back of the last page in a printed book is an even-numbered page, the manuscript file must end with an even-numbered page. Insert a blank page at the end if necessary.

5.5 READY FOR THE PUBLISHER

When you're done, you've got a manuscript that's properly formatted to meet the basic requirements of any POD publisher, though you should check your own publisher's specific formatting guidelines (available on the publisher's website) to see if there are any additional requirements specific to that publisher. However, if your publisher will accept a pdf file I strongly recommend you convert the file to pdf format instead. A pdf file won't require further conversion or manipulation at the publisher's end, so you can feel confident that the file you send them is exactly what you'll see in print when you receive your proof copy of the book. Be sure to do a thorough review of the pdf file before you send it to the publisher, since pdf converters don't work perfectly every time, or for every file.

6 EDITING AND REVISING

Under the general heading of "Editing," there are actually two types: 'copyediting', and just plain old 'editing'. Copyediting concerns itself with the nuts and bolts of correct language: grammar, spelling, punctuation and the like. Editing, in the more general sense, is about flow, readability, and showing stylistic choices in their best light.

Consider an example in which three sentences in a row begin with the phrase, "He was all alone". Because there's nothing grammatically wrong with the three sentences, a copyeditor would sign off on them. As to the other editor, his response depends on whether the three appear to reflect a purposeful, stylistic choice on the part of the author, or seem merely to be an oversight on the author's part. In the following passage, the usage seems purposeful:

He was all alone, he sensed it. He was all alone, he felt it. He was all alone, he knew it.

Clearly, the author intended to repeat the opening phrase for effect, intending a certain rhythm. Now look at this passage:

He was all alone, so now it would be up to him to complete the mission. He was all alone, Harold and Jessica wouldn't be there to show him the way anymore. He was all alone, and the next week was looking like it would be a lot harder than he first imagined.

In this case, it doesn't seem as if the repetitive usage of the phrase was a purposeful stylistic choice, and even if it was, it's not effective. An editor would likely suggest these changes:

He was all alone, so now it would be up to him to complete the mission. Harold and Jessica wouldn't be there to show him the way anymore. The next week was looking like it would be a lot harder than he first imagined.

You can see that deleting the second and third usages of the phrase actually punches up the prose considerably. Even so, notice that I said the editor would *suggest* deleting the phrases. When copyeditors and editors mark up your manuscript, they are suggesting changes, not actually making changes.

While grammar, spelling and punctuation rules are fairly constant, sometimes authors make the stylistic choice to go with usage that's technically incorrect but works for the sentence or passage in question. The word "library" may be purposely misspelled as "liberry" to convey a character's mispronunciation of the word. In the second "he was all alone" passage, even though the suggested edits seem to improve the flow of the prose, because it's a matter of taste and opinion the editor will leave it up to the author to decide. Likewise, treat the contents of this chapter as a guide, not a set of rules. In the end it will be up to you, the author, to decide what's right for your book.

6.1 DIY COPYEDITING

You can probably catch 80 – 90% of your spelling and grammar errors with the proper use of the tools and techniques in this section, but you can't expect to do the job as completely or thoroughly as a professional copyeditor. Even so, an 80 – 90% copyedited draft probably does not require the services of a professional copyeditor. Moreover, hiring a copyeditor after most of the work is done doesn't make financial sense because they charge by the page or hour, regardless of error count.

If you're using MS Word 2003 or higher, or any competing word processor from that year or later, you should be able to manage most of your copyediting by yourself, using your word processor's built-in copyediting tools. If you're not using such a word processor, you can buy one for the same or less than what you'd typically pay a professional copyeditor to do the job for you. Even if you're totally broke, you can download a free copy of Open Office, an open-source competitor to Microsoft Office, that is fully compatible with Office and includes a powerful word processor. Go to http://www.openoffice.org to get it.

The tools are very robust, but they use a lot of system resources and memory. The larger your file is, the more resources and memory are required. For that reason, you will want to save each chapter of your manuscript in a separate file as you work, then combine them into a single file when you're confident you're finished with copyediting.

In MS Word 2003, click on Tools > Spelling and Grammar > Options to access the Spelling and Grammar options dialog box, shown on the following page. The location for this tool varies with the version of MS Word and with different word processors. If you don't know how to access it in your program, consult your program's Help files and search on "Spelling and Grammar," or alternatively, search for each item separately: "spelling" and "grammar".

In the screen shot at left, the most commonly-used options are selected.

"Check spelling as you type" means the program will check your spelling on the fly, as you type, and immediately provide visual or auditory feedback to let you know when it detects a misspelled word.

"Always suggest corrections" means that when you run a spell check and/or grammar check, the program will suggest corrections for any items it has found to be misspelled or grammatically incorrect.

"Suggest from main dictionary only" means spelling will be checked only against the main dictionary, not any custom or user-populated dictionary files. The dictionary is discussed further below.

Leave "Hide spelling errors in this document" unselected, to display spelling errors.

"Ignore words in UPPERCASE" ensures acronyms will be ignored by the spellchecker. "Ignore words with numbers" makes the spell checker ignore special words you may have made up as part of the world of your story, i.e., a nightclub called "Area61". "Ignore internet and file addresses" is self-explanatory.

In the Grammar section, "Check grammar as you type" and "Hide grammatical errors in this document" work the same as for spelling.

If "Check grammar with spelling" is selected, when you run a spell check your program will also check your grammar.

"Display readability statistics" is an option to display the calculated reading level of the writing after the spell check and grammar check are complete. This is a useful tool for authors writing books aimed at a specific reader grade level.

Under "Writing Style" you can select "Grammar only" or "Grammar and style", and then click the "Settings" button to specify what types of things you want corrected.

Now let's look at how these tools work. As you type, the program highlights the errors you've selected under "Options" and "Settings."

Look at the screen shot below.

Her·and·him·went·to·the·mall·on·yesstirday.¶

Red, squiggly underlining means the word processor has detected a misspelling. Green, squiggly underlining means the world processor has detected a grammar error. When I select the text and run a spelling/grammar check, here's what I see.

First, the spell checker will go through each misspelled word one at a time and suggest corrections.

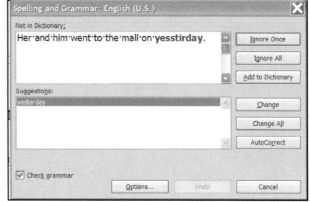

I won't go into detail about how spell checkers work since their specific use varies from program to program and I assume anyone reading this already knows how to use them, but I do want to highlight the "Add to Dictionary" button. Your word processor may allow access to the dictionary elsewhere; if you don't know where it is, go to your program's Help files and search on "dictionary".

Use the "Add to Dictionary" function to add any proper names, made-up words and words not already included in your word processor to the program's dictionary so it will ignore them in future spell checks. Writers of fantasy, science fiction and possibly literary fiction will find this feature to be very useful. You can also choose to "Ignore" specific instances of misspelling.

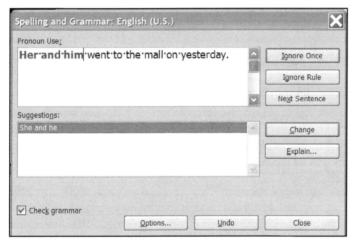

When all misspellings have been reviewed, the grammar check shows its suggestions. Note that while you can calibrate the grammar checker's rules and sensitivity with the "Settings" checkboxes, because the English language is so complex the grammar checker will never catch every single mistake. In this case, it caught the incorrect pronoun usage but did not indicate that "on yesterday" is also incorrect.

Most word processors have an autocorrect feature, which automatically corrects common typographical errors on the fly (i.e., changing "the" to "the"). In MS Word 2003, autocorrect is accessed via Tools > AutoCorrect Options. There, you can specify the things you want the program to correct on the fly, and how you want them corrected.

When workshopping the manuscript later on, you can ask your readers to mark up any errors they find as they read, confident in the knowledge there shouldn't be so many grammatical or spelling errors as to be burdensome or interfere with the read overall. Fresh eyes—eyes other than your own—are the only way you'll catch misspellings that result in different words that are correctly spelled, and therefore overlooked by your spell-checker. For example, you want your character to "read" a book, but due to misspelling he will "reed" a book.

6.2   DIY EDITING

Your manuscript should now be pretty clean in terms of grammar and usage, but there are still some problems you most likely won't have picked up on yet. This is where you hit the finer points.

Overused Words And Phrases

Use your word processor's search function to locate and eliminate overused words and expressions. You are probably aware of certain words or phrases you tend to use as transition crutches or standby openers, but there are plenty of other 'go to' words and expressions you may not even realize you're using too often. While you may know you're supposed to avoid over reliance on –ly, –ing and –tion words, it's easy to lose track of how often they find their way into your prose while you're concentrating on plot and characterization.

As you do a search for the upcoming words, make note of their frequency. If it's low, the words may be fine as-is. But if you're seeing the same word or expression more than once in the same page or even the same ten pages, it's time to do some ruthless editing. Since overuse of certain words also exposes overuse of certain sentence structures, the best tack when eliminating those words is to rework the sentence. Turn to the thesaurus as a last resort.

An excellent resource for this type of copyediting is *The Dimwit's Dictionary: More Than 5,000 Overused Words and Phrases and Alternatives to Them* by Robert Hartwell Fiske. Look for:

actual	get	okay	sudden
actually	getting	only	suddenly
almost	goes	partly	surely
apparently	going	perfectly	that
as if	got	race	then
basically	gotten	raced	totally
beautiful	hard	racing	try
beautifully	hardly	raging	trying
began	hope	realize	use
begin	hopefully	realized	usually
beginning	hoping	realizing	very
but	important	really	virtually
careful	importantly	safely	well
carefully	like	say	what
completely	likely	scenario	whatever
doing	making	simply	yet
even	meaningful	so	
evenly	meaningfully	stunned	

Tricky Grammar And Punctuation

There are many instances of incorrect grammar and punctuation that will be missed by your word processor's grammar checker because they're areas of nuance, or situations in which correct usage is dictated by context. Unless you intend to become a career grammarian, the best cure is prevention.

First, get a copy of the book *Eats, Shoots and Leaves: A Zero Tolerance Approach to Punctuation* by Lynne Truss. It's a small book, not very expensive or time-consuming. Read through it to acquaint yourself with the most common punctuation mistakes, then go on a search-and-destroy mission through your manuscript just as you did with overused words and phrases.

Next, when in doubt about grammar, try some online research. The following sites are excellent, free resources for grammar help:

Grammar Girl: http://grammar.quickanddirtytips.com/

Using English: http://www.usingenglish.com

Guide to Grammar & Writing: http://grammar.ccc.commnet.edu/grammar/

Finally, when in doubt, cut it out. If you can't find adequate clarification on your grammar or punctuation quandary, change the sentence to eliminate the questionable thing or things.

Check Your Jargon

If your manuscript uses a lot of technical, historical, or idiomatic jargon, you will want to be sure you're using that language properly. Inevitably, there will be someone out there reading your book who just happens to be an expert in whatever it is you're writing about, and when the time comes he won't hesitate to criticize your ignorance in his Amazon review.

For specific terms, try http://www.glossarist.com. For more general inquiries on a specific subject or time period, do an internet search (i.e., "15th century clothing," "computer terms," "human anatomy," "12th century food," etc.).

Improve Readability

View your manuscript in full-page, or facing-pages, print preview mode to spot lengthy blocks of unbroken text and awkward page transitions.

Break up paragraphs to improve readability. In general, no paragraph should take up more than half a standard, trade paperback (6x9") page; ideally, none should take up more than one third of a page.

Look for instances of only one or two words on a line at the end of a paragraph, and see if you can't rework the sentences to eliminate these danglers.

Do some widow and orphan control. In copyediting, the term "widow" is used to describe the last line of a paragraph which appears at the top of a new page. An "orphan" is the first line of a new paragraph that appears at the bottom of the previous page. Look at the following example from www.textcontrol.com:

The real evils, indeed, of Emma's situation were the power of having rather too much her own way, and a disposition to think a little too well of herself; these were the disadvantages which threatened alloy to her many enjoyments. The danger, however, was at present so unperceived, that they did not by any means rank as	misfortunes with her. *widow* Sorrow came - a gentle sorrow - but not at all in the shape of any disagreeable consciousness. Miss Taylor married. It was Miss Taylor's loss which first brought grief. *orphan* It was on the wedding-day of this	beloved friend that Emma first sat in mournful thought of any continuance. The wedding over, and the bride-people gone, her father and herself were left to dine together, with no prospect of a third to cheer a long evening. Her father composed himself to sleep after dinner, as usual, and

Source: *Emma* by Jane Austen. Courtesy Project Gutenberg.

If you really don't want to alter your sentences to eliminate widows and orphans, consider judicious application of page breaks.

6.3   CONTENT RIGHTS

If your manuscript quotes commercial material originated by another person, living or dead, unless that material is in the public domain you cannot include it in your manuscript without securing the rights to do so first. Common examples are song lyrics, bits of poetry, excerpts from essays and product jingles from advertising.

Song Lyrics

If you have a character singing along to a song and feel it's an important action on the part of that character, the easiest solution is to switch whatever lyrics you've got for lyrics from a song in the public domain. Do an internet search on "public domain lyrics" and "public domain songs" to find alternatives.

If the song in question is not in the public domain but isn't a current hit, it may be worthwhile to contact whoever owns the rights and ask permission to quote from the lyrics. In many cases, owners of older lyrics will allow you to use them at no charge so long as you provide proper credit on your copyright page or in a 'notes' section of your manuscript. If permission is only given for a fee, you will have to decide if use of the lyric is worth the asking price. Go to the American Society of Composers, Authors and Performers (ASCAP) and run a search of their database for the song by title, composer or performer:

http://www.ascap.com/ace/search.cfm?mode=search

The search results will provide contact information for the current owner. Politely ask if you may quote the lyrics in question, and specify that when the book is printed, you will provide a copy of it to the rights owner at no charge; this is a standard condition of rights permissions. Also provide the full context in which the quotation will appear.

If the quotation serves as a chapter opener, specify that the quotation will stand alone and will not take the form of character dialog. Conversely, if the quotation will take the form of a character quoting or singing the lyrics, provide a description of the character, a brief description of the setting and circumstances in which the lyric will be quoted, and an excerpt from the manuscript containing the proposed lyric quotation in the context of the scene in which it appears.

This is important, because the rights owner may give permission for a hero character to sing along to the song as he's rushing in to rescue the fair maiden, but might feel very differently about the story's villain singing along to the song as he's committing murders.

Published Material

You can quote from public-domain published material without securing rights. To locate public domain material, do an internet search on "public domain

_____," filling in the blank with the type of material for which you're searching (i.e., poetry, books, stories, plays, essays, etc.). You can also search sites that contain nothing but public domain material, such as Project Gutenberg (http://www.gutenberg.org).

In cases where the copyright has not expired, you will have to contact the publisher which currently holds the rights to the material and ask their permission to quote from it. As with the song lyric example above, you will want to provide as much information as possible about how the quoted material will be used, and you must be prepared to send a free copy of the published book to the rights holder. Again, if permission can only be had for a fee, you'll have to decide whether or not it's worth the cost.

Commercial Jingles

Generally, jingles for companies and products that no longer exist are safe to quote without permission, simply because there is no longer anyone to provide that permission. Otherwise, you will need to contact the Public Relations department of the company in question, or the company that manufactures the product in question.

Public Figure Names And Likenesses

As a rule, it's a bad idea to make references to contemporary public figures by name in your manuscript if you intend to have a character or narrator voice any opinion whatsoever of that public figure. Apart from the risk of being slapped with a slander or libel lawsuit, the more practical reason is that such references will date your manuscript.

In the case of historical fiction you still must tread lightly around living public figures, as well as deceased public figures with surviving relatives. It's fine to say, "Joe was looking forward to the debate between Gore and Bush," because you're only making reference to the fact that such a debate took place, which is already a matter of public record. However, it's very risky to say, "Joe was hoping [blank] would win the debate, because he knew the other guy had always been a two-bit, lying hustler in a designer suit." In the latter sentence, your character is expressing an opinion about a public figure with which that public figure or his living relatives might take issue.

Believe it or not, even a reference you think is highly complimentary may not pass muster with the public figure in question, or his/her surviving relatives. There could be a pop singer who's particularly well-known for her 8-octave range, but if your narrator or one of your characters speaks of admiring that facet of the singer it's possible the singer (or her surviving relatives) could be miffed that you didn't also mention the singer's ability with composing her own songs and dancing. When in doubt, ask permission. When you can't get (or can't afford) permission, eliminate the reference completely.

6.4   WORKSHOPPING

It's somewhat misleading to use the term "DIY" in reference to revising, because the truth is, you cannot fully revise your manuscript yourself. Obviously, if you had noticed the areas where your prose could be improved, you would've improved them. You need an outside, unbiased opinion, but this doesn't mean you must fork over the big bucks to a professional editor or book doctor. In fact, paying for such services will not necessarily get the best results.

Seasoned, professional editors and book doctors are used to editing toward the goal of pleasing a major publisher. But that isn't *your* goal, since you're an independent. Your goal is to please the eventual reader. To that end, collection and consideration of input from multiple, informed readers can serve your needs as well, or even better, than the opinion of a single, paid professional.

6.4.1 CAN YOU HANDLE THE TRUTH?

Before going on, you need to be brutally honest with yourself in answering this question: can you receive constructive criticism gracefully? I'm sure you just answered 'yes' as a reflex, but really stop and think about it because this is a crucial juncture for the independent author, even more so than for mainstream authors. A mainstream author's agent or manager will solicit feedback from a professional editor and then share that feedback with the author in the most tactful, sensitive manner possible. When you solicit feedback, those notes and comments will be coming directly back to you in their raw, unfiltered form.

Imagine your most beloved, carefully crafted character; now imagine an incoming note that says the reader especially disliked that character, or found that character to be poorly written. How will you react to this news? Think about a cherished scene or dialog exchange in your manuscript; will you go ballistic if your reader suggests you summarily drop the passage because it doesn't add significantly to the plot or tone?

Finally, no matter how ill-advised or even downright crazy a given note seems to you, are you capable of simply absorbing it, appreciating the time and effort your reader has given and sincerely thanking him or her? Can you resist the overwhelming urge to correct the reader, or defend the choices you made to which the reader took exception? Books are a matter of taste, but you must also remember that very often, if you have to explain something to the reader it's a sign that you didn't write it well enough to be easily understood in the first place. After all, you won't be sitting there next to each person who will someday buy your finished book, ready to explain and defend every questionable item.

However careful you are in selecting readers, occasionally you will still find yourself the victim of someone who doesn't know how to give truly constructive criticism, and may even seem to get a bit of a thrill from hurling insults at your work in the most personal and inappropriate terms possible. Even in this extreme situation, you must be able to politely thank the reader for his or her time and effort, and make no further attempt to respond to the notes; it's pointless to try reasoning with an unreasonable person. But do remove that reader's name from consideration in any future rounds of note-collecting.

If you can't maintain an air of detachment when the notes come rolling in, your best option is to pay for the services of a professional editor or book doctor. You can be certain a professional editor or book doctor has no personal investment in your success or failure, because you are paying for his or her services and the price doesn't go up or down based on the reader's opinion. Therefore, you will be much more likely to accept the notes given in the impersonal, dispassionate tone they are intended.

6.4.2   FINDING FEEDBACK

Many aspiring writers will turn to their writing group at this point, to exchange manuscripts and share notes with one another. There is some value in that approach, but in my opinion it's primarily value based in bonding and mutual support. When you agree to such an exchange, you don't necessarily know the other author's skill level or style. Notes from someone who's just written the first chapter of a first manuscript probably won't be as useful to you as notes from a more seasoned writer. Likewise, if you write sensitive, coming of age dramas, notes from a writer of gory horror stories probably won't be too meaningful to you. Carefully targeted readers will yield much more useful feedback.

You need to find three writers whose work you admire, whose preferred styles and genres are in line with your own, and who are working at a level of the craft either at or above your level. These people do not have to be professional writers, though. You want three so the vote on a given note will never be split.

Start your search on the internet. Many, many aspiring authors have blogs and websites with excerpts of their work on display, and you can find some to match your needs by using keyword searches. For example, if you want to find authors of comic fiction, search on: writer + "comic fiction". You can search for writers in other genres the same way. Also try searching for writers' groups, as many of them include a showcase area for their members' work.

When you find some likely candidates, email three of them. Briefly introduce yourself (just your name, rough location in the world and the fact that you're an aspiring writer is enough), then explain where you found their work and what you liked about it. Finally, ask each writer if he or she would be willing to do a manuscript exchange for notes with you, and if not, whether he or she could suggest someone else for the task. Very clearly state your desire for constructive criticism, and MEAN it. Attach a chapter or excerpt from the work for which you're seeking help, so that the candidate will have some idea of what he or she is getting into before agreeing to the arrangement.

If the answer is no, graciously accept that answer and write back to thank the writer for responding to your message anyway. You never know when your paths may cross again, and you can't know for certain why the person turned you down. It may be that they didn't like your excerpt, but it could also be that they only do exchanges within their writing group or they're simply too busy at the moment to help you.

I guarantee if you keep trying you will eventually succeed in finding three like-minded writers with whom to exchange manuscripts. One of the advantages of this approach is that the writers with whom you connect will be virtual strangers, so you don't need to worry too much that they'll hold back on their constructive criticisms for the sake of your feelings.

6.4.3   WHAT TO DO WITH THE FEEDBACK

You've solicited feedback and graciously, profusely thanked everyone who's given it. Now, what do you do with it? Above all other considerations are the facts that it will ultimately be your name on the cover, and the finished book should reflect your unique sensibilities and writer's voice. Having said that, I have a few rules of thumb you may find useful in deciding what to change and what to leave alone.

First, when you sent the manuscript out there were undoubtedly some items or areas in it about which you yourself felt a bit iffy. If two or more of your three readers are likewise iffy on them, those things probably need to be changed.

Second, let the majority guide you. If the same change is suggested by two out of three readers, I seriously consider making the change. If it's suggested by all three readers, I make that change without much further consideration. Remember, these are all writers whose work you admire; their opinions are not to be lightly dismissed.

Third, anytime a change is suggested which strongly resonates with me, I make that change even if only one reader made the suggestion.

Beyond this, there are no other easy-to-follow, all-inclusive rules I can suggest. Even the three rules of thumb above are entirely up to your discretion.

If you write the sort of material that tends to divide readers, eliciting only very positive or very negative reactions, your editing task is much harder because something one reader found particularly objectionable could be the exact thing another reader particularly loves about the work. Typically, this is the constructive criticism experience for authors of literary fiction; if you write literary fiction that will likely polarize readers, you're probably best served by a paid, professional book editor or book doctor.

Otherwise, you want to incorporate all the revisions that make sense to you, then go out for the next round of constructive criticism. Some of your readers probably expressed interest in reading the revised copy, but you will need to contact the others and politely ask if they are willing to read it also. If not, you will need to solicit some new readers to get your group of three. Rinse and repeat through additional iterations of review until you, and the majority of your readers, feel the manuscript is ready for a wider audience.

Then, seek out three new readers who've never seen a single draft of the work. If their reaction is substantially positive, you're ready to mark that draft "final". This is where connecting with like-minded writers pays off, in that there should be some consistency across the feedback. Nevertheless, remember that even published bestsellers are not uniformly well-liked by all readers, so it's not reasonable to expect that you can eventually reach a point where every reader you can find will love the draft. You can reach a point where virtually every reader agrees the draft is well-written, however.

If this sounds like a lengthy and challenging process, that's because it is. Remember that as in indie author, you're facing the bias that all self-published books are dreck. It's not fair, but your book must be a whole lot better than 'not dreck' to overcome that bias.

7   DESIGNING YOUR OWN BOOK COVER

If you have a photo editing or graphics editing program and know how to use it, you can create your own book cover without much difficulty. You can find plenty of free templates online by doing an internet search on "book cover template", and some self-publishing outfits also offer free templates for use with their services. The only trick with these ready-made templates is that they must be manually customized to fit your book. Specifically, you must figure out how wide to make the spine section of your cover, since its width depends on the number of pages in your book as well as page thickness, and then re-size the spine section of the template to fit. Sites that offer templates will usually have instructions for doing the necessary calculations, but they're a bother.

I prefer to use the free templates offered by CreateSpace (CS), the on-demand publisher which is wholly owned by Amazon.com. The CS templates are offered in a 'wizard' format, such that all you need do is fill in a form with details about your desired book dimensions. CS runs calculations on the information and generates a custom book cover template that already includes a properly-sized spine. As of this writing, the templates are readily available to any site visitor, you don't have to be a CS customer to access the templates or use them.

This chapter will take you through the process of creating a custom book cover for a trade paperback edition using the CS template, but apart from instructions specific to the CS template wizard, the steps presented here are applicable for use with any template.

7.1   WRITE A BOOK DESCRIPTION

You will need a description of your book, to appear on its back cover as well as for use in marketing materials and on product pages when the book is released. You're going for a synopsis that says enough about the story to lure a reader in, but doesn't give away too much. Keep it brief to closely match your Amazon prodcut description (if applicable), which is limited to 200 words or less. Create a separate word processor or .txt document for the description, and work and rework it until it's exactly what you want.

I set up a single .txt file for each book, containing my description/back cover text, any one-liner reviews I may want to quote on the book, my brief 'About the Author' biography, and a cross-sell one-liner for another of my books. I can copy and paste from this .txt file as needed when editing the book cover template or creating promotional materials like posters or press releases.

7.2 GATHER BLURBS

Remember, you want your finished book to be indistinguishable from a professionally-produced book. Professionally-produced books tend to have review blurbs on their back covers, and so should yours.

You can quote a blurb from anyone who has given you permission to do so. That means people from your writing group, a college professor, a blogger, or anyone else who has read your book and has something nice to say about it. Even on mainstream books, blurbs don't always come from famous critics or well-known publications.

To the person perusing your book jacket, assuming that person isn't familiar with either of the two critics quoted, either of these two blurbs will accomplish the same degree of 'sell' as the blurbs on mainstream book covers:

Don't buy this book unless you can stay up all night reading it, with the lights on!
- Candace Meyers, Bookish

Creepy and atmospheric...a page-turner.
- Trent Willoughby, Times Herald

It's not apparent in the first blurb that "Bookish" is the name of Candace Meyers' blog, nor is it apparent in the second blurb that the "Times Herald" is a small quarterly distributed only within your local community. Nevertheless, there's nothing dishonest or misleading about the blurbs, so long as you are accurately quoting your sources and have obtained their permission to do so.

Solicit for manuscript reviews, and if those requests net you some complimentary, quotable one-liners, ask the reviewer if you may quote them on your book cover. Most are flattered by the request and will happily agree.

Many Amazon Top Reviewers accept review requests, so long as you're willing to send them a free, review copy of your book. An electronic version is acceptable to many prior to your book's publication, but they will still want a copy of the actual book as soon it's available. You'll need to check each reviewer's profile to see first of all if he or she provides a contact email address, secondly to see if he or she accepts review requests, and finally to see if your work suits his or her tastes. If you get a good one-liner from your efforts, you can credit the blurb as: [Name], Amazon Top [number] Reviewer (i.e., Amazon Top 10 Reviewer, Amazon Top 50 Reviewer, etc.). Use this link for a listing of all Amazon Top Reviewers, from which you can access their individual profiles:

http://www.amazon.com/review/top-reviewers.html

If Amazon makes some changes that render the link broken, you can find the listing in a more roundabout way. Go to any product page with reviews and click on the username of any reviewer to get to their profile page. Scroll down the page to the Reviews section.

Click the "See all [#] reviews' link at the bottom of the section to access a page with all of the user's product reviews.

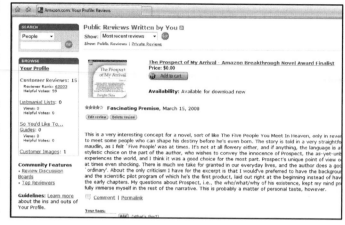

On the 'all reviews' page, at the left-hand side, under Community Features, there's a link for Top Reviewers. That link will take you to the current version of the Amazon Top Reviewers page.

Another good source is LibraryThing (http://www.librarything.com), where readers keep online, virtual bookshelves and engage in discussions about books and the publishing industry. You can view member profiles to look for contact email addresses and do the same kind of due diligence as that described above for Amazon Top Reviewers.

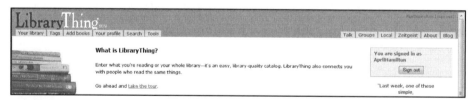

On the LibraryThing home page, click the Groups tab on the right-hand side. This will take you to a page listing LibraryThing discussion groups.

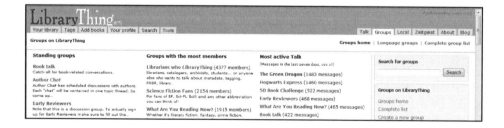

Scan through the groups to find any dedicated to your type of book, or reviewing in general. Click the group's link to access its home page.

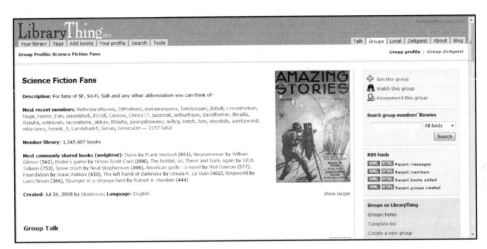

On the group's page, a description of the group is listed at the top, then recent members, followed by most commonly shared books, and beneath that is the Group Talk discussion board. You can click on any username at the top of the page or in the discussion group threads to view that user's profile.

Just as on Amazon, there will be enough information in the profile to give you some idea of whether a given member might like your book. In fact, there's even more information than Amazon because on LibraryThing, you can look at each member's virtual library and see how that member rated or reviewed each book. As on Amazon profiles, many members list their email addresses or outside website addresses. LT members may not require you to send them a copy of the finished book, but it's good form to offer one anyway. Credit LT reviews like this: [Name], LibraryThing.

Try searching blogs for anything related to books, the publishing industry, or subjects related to the subject of your book. Look for a contact email address on the blog owner's profile page, or if none is available, post a comment to the blog asking the owner to contact you.

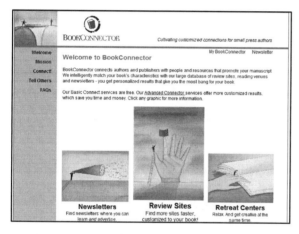

For a wealth of possible sources that will likely take a little longer to yield results, sign up for a free account at http://www.bookconnector.com to do a search of all outlets which have expressed interest in giving reviews of your type of book.

Don't be reticent about soliciting for reviews, as most avid readers are happy to get their hands on pre-publication manuscripts so long as there's some reasonable expectation that the manuscript is of high quality and of a type they typically enjoy. Consider attaching a brief excerpt from your book to your emailed solicitations, and inviting the recipient to read the excerpt before deciding whether or not to review the full manuscript. This gives the person on the receiving end a quick and easy way to tell what they're getting into, and the means to a graceful exit with no hard feelings if they don't find the excerpt to their liking. Many of your prospects will be amenable to reviewing an electronic copy of your manuscript, but be prepared to print one out in hard copy for snail-mailing (at your own expense, of course) if requested.

See the Editorial Reviews section of the Promotion chapter for more specific details of how to write a solicitation for a review.

7.3 DOWNLOAD A BOOK COVER TEMPLATE

Go to the CS site (http://www.createspace.com) and click the "Help" link to reach the page shown below.

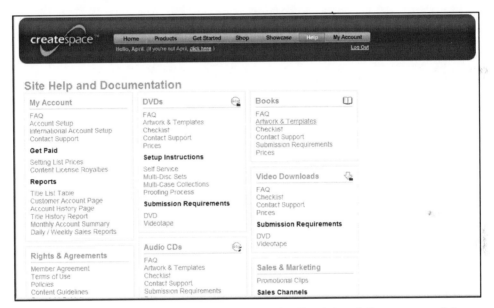

Under "Books", at the top of the column at the far right of the screen, click on the link for "Artwork & Templates" (indicated by underline in screen shot) to get to the Artwork & Templates screen, shown on the next page. If CS has done any site redesign that changes the location of these items, just scan the help page for book topics to find the Artwork & Templates area.

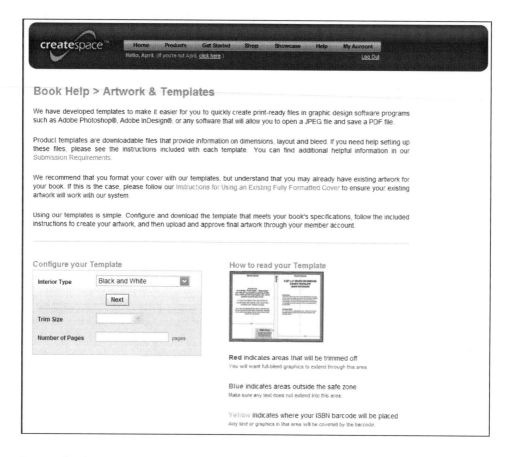

Leave the 'interior type' set to its default value, "black and white". Click the 'Next' button to accept this value and unlock the other fields on the page. For 'trim size', select the size of your book project. For 'number of pages', enter the page count of your completed manuscript.

This number must be an even number; remember that the book will be printed on both sides of each page, so if your word processor says your manuscript has 300 pages, when it's printed the number of bound paper pages will be 150. It's very important that the manuscript is complete and 'locked' against future changes, since any edits you make to it may increase or decrease page count, rendering your book cover design useless. Enter the page count shown by your word processor, but if that page count is odd, add one to it. The template will do the math to figure the number of bound paper pages.

Note that a new field, 'Paper Color', and a new button, 'Build Template' were added to the form when you clicked the 'Next' button. If you're creating a cover for use other than with a CS book, it doesn't matter which paper color you select. If you do intend to use this cover for a CS book, choose 'White' or 'Cream' according to your preference and make a note of your choice as you will need to indicate the same paper color in the CS book project setup screens later on. Click 'Build Template', and the download box shown below is displayed.

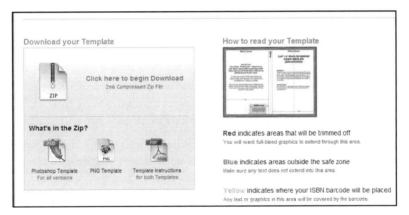

Click on the 'Click here to begin Download' link, and save the zipped file to your desired location on your computer's hard drive. The zipped file contains a customized template in .psd version for Photoshop users and .png format for users of other graphics programs, as well as a .pdf 'Template Instructions' file.

When you navigate to the zipped file, it will appear in your Windows Explorer file manager  window with a zipped folder icon, as shown at right. If you're using Windows XP or Mac OS X (or higher), you don't need any special software to unzip the files.

On older Macs, you'll need an unzip utility such as Stuffit or Maczip. Do an internet search to locate downloads of these utilities.

Double-click the zipped folder icon. In Windows, you will see the contents of the folder, illustrated below. On a Mac, the folder will 'unzip' automatically and the enclosed files will be displayed.

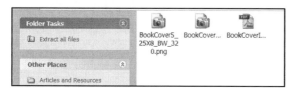

On a PC, click the link labeled 'Extract all files' under Folder Tasks, at the left-hand side of your screen.

This will open the 'Compressed (zipped) Folders Extraction Wizard'. Click the 'Next' button.

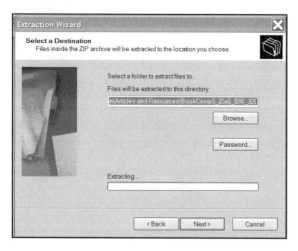

Specify a location for the files and click 'Next' again.

When the extraction is complete, you will see the confirmation screen.

Leave the 'Show extracted files' checkbox checked and click 'Finish'.

The extracted files are shown.

If you use an Adobe Photoshop-based graphics editor, you will use the .psd file. Otherwise, you will use the .png file. But before you do anything with the applicable graphics file, open the Instructions file and read it carefully.

7.4   A NOTE ABOUT COVER ART RIGHTS

You can use any public-domain or purchased clip art in your cover image, but you may not use graphics copied off the internet. Also be aware that, apart from photos in purchased clip art and stock photo collections, if you intend to use a photo in which anyone's face is recognizable, you must have a written and signed release from every living person who is recognizable in the photo. If any of those people are celebrities, even if the person is dead you may have to obtain a written and signed release from surviving family members. It's best to avoid these hassles entirely by sticking to purchased clip art and stock photos.

7.5 ADD ART AND TEXT

For purposes of this chapter I will give instructions specific to Microsoft Digital Image Pro 10, but the functions demonstrated here should all be present in your specific graphics program as well. If you're unsure where a given editor tool is located in your program, or how to use it, refer to your program's Help files.

To begin, open the .psd or .png file in your graphics editor program. In Digital Image Pro, you will use the .png file. When you open the file, you'll be looking at the template 'layer', shown below, which will be deleted when you're finished creating your book cover. It's there to assist with placement of art and text.

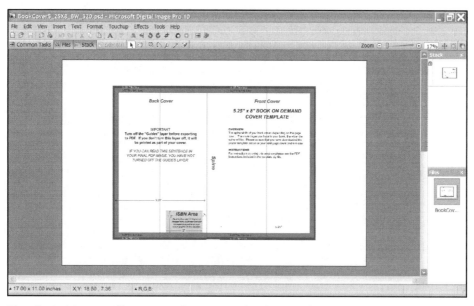

The first thing you'll want to do is set a background for your book cover. You can use a background image or a solid color. In my opinion, use of a background image gives the finished book a more polished, professional look so that's what I'll demonstrate here.

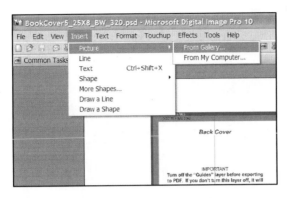

Try to choose images that convey some of the meaning or tone of your book. In this example, let's say the book is about a Depression-era farming town. Go to Insert > Picture > From Gallery to access the program's clip art. If you have other backgrounds or clipart on your computer you'd prefer to use, select 'From My Computer' instead of 'From Gallery' and navigate to the desired image.

In this case, I'll be selecting the 'Green Star' image from 'Backgounds' > 'designs/patterns' in the program's pre-loaded clipart, because it features a pattern and colors appropriate to the historical setting of the story.

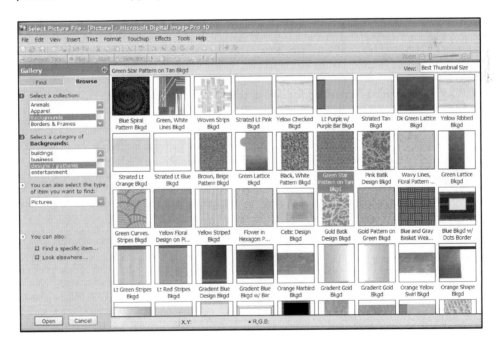

This is what is shown after I click 'Open' to insert the selected image:

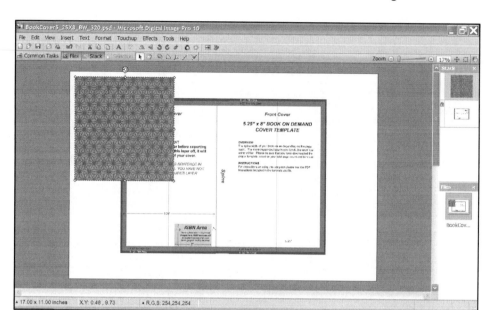

Resize the image and drag it onto the template, as shown below. Note that the image extends a tiny bit into the inner 'buffer' border of the template. This is because the book cover will eventually be cut at the inside edge of the blue border, and allowing the background to extend into the buffer ensures there will

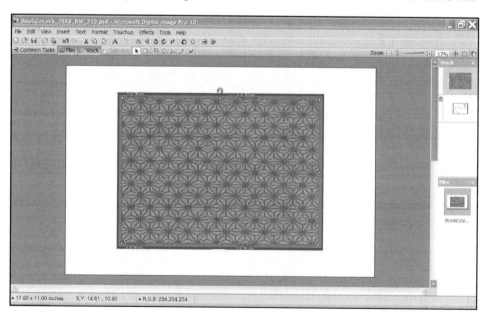

be no white space at the edges of your printed book covers.

Now you need to make the background partially transparent, partly so that you can still see the template beneath it, and partly because you will be placing text and images on top of it and want those items to be easily legible.

In Digital Image Pro 10, transparency is one of the options under the Effects menu. If you're not sure where the option is set in your program, search your program's help files for "transparency". In the image shown below, I've set the transparency to 50%.

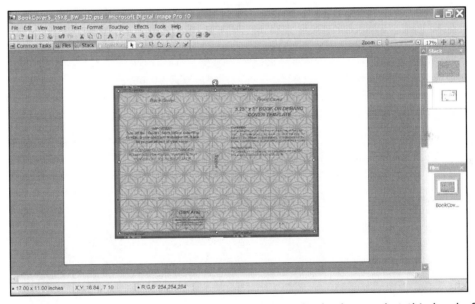

If it appears text may still be difficult to read on the background at this level of transparency, increase it. In the screenshot shown on the following page, I've increased it to 75%.

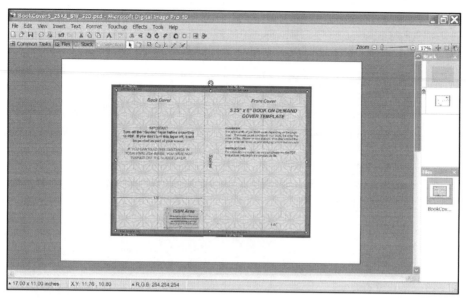

Click outside the template frame to de-select the background image.

Now you can insert some additional clip art to dress up the cover. In keeping with the historical setting and subject matter of our example book, I search for images related to farming, small town life, the 1930's, etc.

The goofy, fisheye view of a bull would be great for a book that's comic in tone, but let's say that this book is serious. The second image may be perfect if sisters are featured in the story, but I don't want the word 'sisters' in the image because it seems heavy-handed. The third picture shows a farm, but it's a tidy farm that doesn't look at all like it's struggling, so that one's probably not a good choice. The last photo could work if horses figure in my story at all, and since most Depression-era farms employed horses, they're probably a safe bet. Let's say that my story does feature two sisters. First, I insert the desired art.

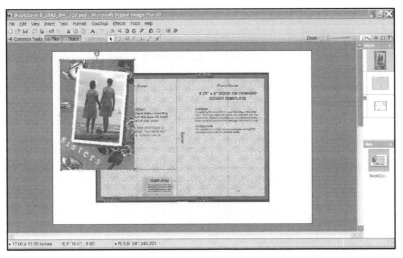

To separate the photo of the sisters from the background I don't want, first I rotate the entire image to the left until the photo of the sisters is level.

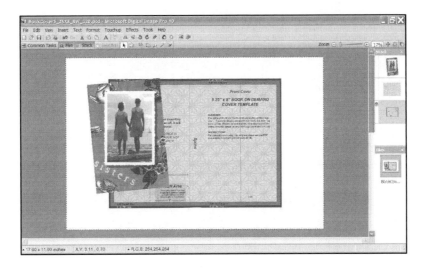

Now I can crop the image to cut away everything I don't want.

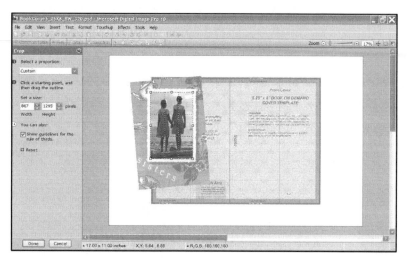

The resulting image is shown below.

The image looks good, the sepia tone is great for the period look I want, but there's one problem: the sisters are standing on a beach and appear to be looking at a sailboat. I crop the image further to cut the boat out of the picture.

With the boat gone, it's no longer clear that these girls are standing on a beach with driftwood at their feet. They could just as easily be standing at the edge of the patch of dirt that was once their family's crop. They're no longer gazing at a boat, now they appear to be gazing off into the distance, toward the setting (or rising?) sun.

For a novel, it's a good idea to keep your cover art evocative, but in a general way. Think in terms of symbols, moods and tone as you select and edit your cover art; imagine how the reader can connect the selected image(s) to your story and characters. If possible, let the art hint at an important event or relationship in the story.

In working with clipart and photos, experiment with all the different tools available in your editing program to get a custom look that will instantly communicate something about your book.

By making some adjustments to color, contrast and brightness settings, I can 'age' the photo further, and tint it to match the dustbowl era.

Insert your edited clipart where you want it on the template, using the blue template guidelines for centering.

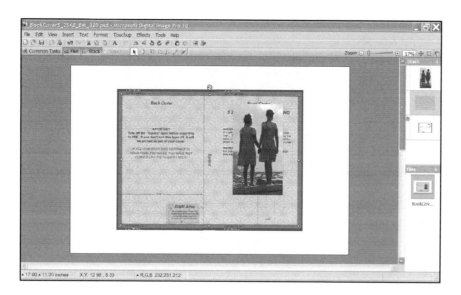

Now add your title and author name by inserting text boxes, again being careful to select a fitting font and font color. Note that the author name text is smaller than the title text.

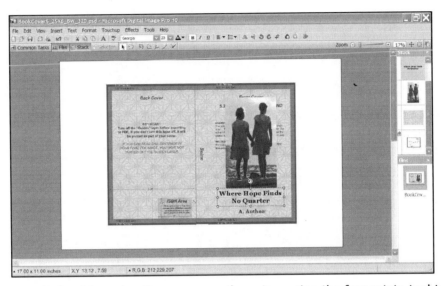

Repeat the title and author name on the spine, using the free-rotate tool to turn it perpendicular to the bottom edge of the template.

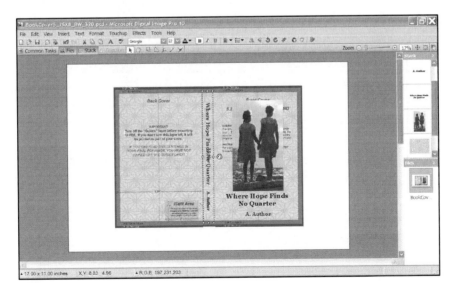

Next, insert another text box for your back cover teaser. I use the same text for my back cover teaser as I do for the book description which appears in online store listings, for two reasons: first, it keeps things consistent, and second, it keeps things brief. If you've followed the directions in this chapter up to now, you should already have a separate word processor or text file containing your book description. Just copy its contents and paste into the text box.

Make sure that when you insert the back cover text, you use either a smaller version of the same font you used for the title or a similar, but more legible font.

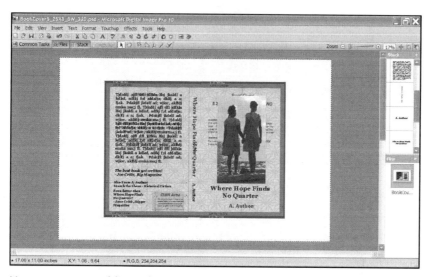

Here are some additional tips on back-cover layout:

- Use 'justified' alignment for the description/teaser

- Subtly highlight blurbs by left-aligning, italicizing, and using a different (but complementary) color

- Allow a margin of empty space around all your text boxes to ensure they won't be cut off when the book cover is cut

- If you will be publishing through CS, be sure to leave the yellow ISBN block empty—this is where CS will add your book's barcode and ISBN

- If you're publishing elsewhere, refer to your publisher's directions for placement of the ISBN block

- Use the empty space next to the ISBN block to cross-sell another title if you have one available for sale; otherwise fill it with a blurb

- If you use a cross-sell text box, set its font size one level smaller than that used in the other, main text boxes

- Use separate text boxes for each back-cover text element, to simplify custom formatting for each element

7.6   DELETE THE TEMPLATE GUIDE LAYER

Select the Template Guide Layer and delete it. In Microsoft Digital image Pro 10, the easiest way to do this is to click on the desired layer in the 'Stack' window at the far right. In the screen shot shown below, the Template layer has a padlock icon because the layer itself cannot be modified by the user. When you click on this layer to select it, it will become shaded, as shown in the screen shot below (right-hand side).

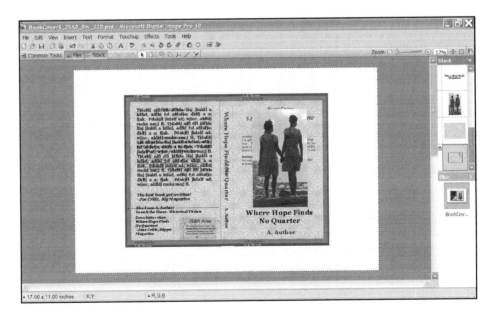

With the Template layer selected, press the 'Delete' key to delete the Template layer. The final book cover is shown below.

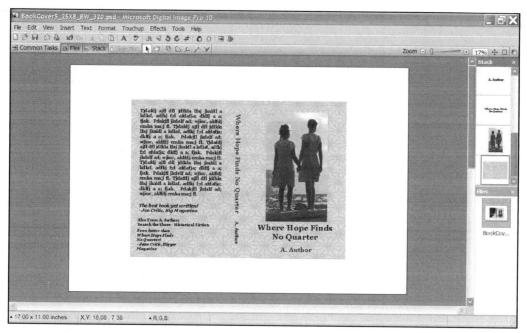

7.7   SAVE YOUR FILE

If you are saving the file for use with a CS book, you will need to save it in pdf format according to the specifications given in the Template Instructions document. Otherwise, you can 'save as' whatever format you like, within the limitations imposed by your graphics editing program and the requirements of your publisher.

I suggest you save the original file in its original, .png or .psd format, then 'save as' as many different formats as possible. You will also want to save a cropped version of the file, displaying only the front cover of the book, to use as a thumbnail image on web pages, promotional materials and in emails.

7.8 FINAL TIPS AND NOTES

If you revise your manuscript such that page count is altered, you will need to start all over with a new template because the template is customized to match your page count. Page count affects the thickness of your book, and therefore the width of your book's spine. It's a good idea to save each element of your cover as a separate file (i.e., transparent background image, cropped and edited clipart image, text from each text box used on back cover), just in case. It's much easier to re-compose the book cover if all you need do is drag the prepared elements into the right places on the new template.

8   PUBLISHING THROUGH CREATESPACE

There are differences among POD publishers, but the overall process of working with them is essentially the same.

You format your manuscript and cover art files according to the publisher's requirements (available on each publisher's website), and convert them to a file type acceptable to the publisher if necessary. Next, you create an account at the publisher's website, paying any membership or upfront fees if required, and enter details about your book. Following that, you upload your files to the publisher, wait for their confirmation that the files are acceptable for print and order a proof copy of the printed, bound book. When the proof arrives, you review it thoroughly—it's an exact replica of the book your customers will receive. If there are problems with the proof, you make changes to your files and re-upload, wait for confirmation of acceptance and order a new proof copy. When you're happy with the proof, you approve it for publication and sale. Optionally, if your publisher offers its own online store, you may be able to customize your book's product page in the store.

In this chapter, I'll go through the process in detail with CreateSpace (CS) as the publisher. CS is an on-demand media publication company which is wholly owned by Amazon.com. I say 'media publication' because books aren't the only things they publish. This chapter is specific to their POD service for books.

As Of This Writing...

The formatting and file type requirements may be slightly different for different publishers, and I can't address the specific requirements of every publisher here. The formatting instructions in the DIY Formatting For POD chapter of this book will produce a manuscript file that's acceptable as-is for either CS or Lulu (http://www.lulu.com). iUniverse (http://www.iuniverse.com) requires only one space between sentences instead of the usual two, but provides a macro you can use to automate the process. Other than that one change, formatting per the instructions in the formatting chapter will be correct for iUniverse as well. However, because books are static whereas the web changes daily, be sure to check the formatting requirements of your chosen publisher before you submit, as they may have changed since the time this book was printed.

8.1 ADVANTAGES OF POD

Print on Demand (POD) technologies allow a publisher to keep a digital copy of a work on file, and then create physical copies of that work only as needed to fill individual orders. This is a departure from the old business model of publishing, in which the publisher would try to estimate how many copies of a given title would sell, pay tens to hundreds of thousands of dollars to have that many copies manufactured in advance of the title going on sale, then fulfill orders for the title from a large, warehoused stockpile of copies. For most titles, inevitably a certain amount of the stockpile would not sell and the publisher would have to dispose of them. That waste is part of the reason why traditional publishers have such high overhead costs.

8.2 WHAT'S THE DIFFERENCE BETWEEN CREATESPACE AND BOOKSURGE?

CS is only a content publisher. CS does not offer editorial, art or promotional services. Whatever you give them to publish will be published, but you're on your own in getting the work into publishable condition and you're also on your own to promote that work after it's published.

BookSurge is another content publication company, also owned by Amazon, which specializes in books and takes a more 'cradle to grave' approach. BookSurge offers tailored services for every step of the process for authors who prefer to focus solely on writing and are willing to pay for all other services (i.e., manuscript formatting, editing, artwork, creation of promotional materials, etc.).

One other noteworthy difference is that with BookSurge you have the option to publish hardcover books, whereas CS only offers soft covers.

8.3   QUESTIONS AND ANSWERS ABOUT CREATESPACE

Do I Need Any Special Tools To Use CS?

You need a word processing program to create your manuscript, a graphics editing program to create your cover art, and a program that can convert both your completed manuscript and your cover art into .pdf files. In this chapter, I'll be using MS Word 2003, Microsoft Digital Image Pro, and Adobe Acrobat. See section 1.6.1, Tools Of The Indie Author Trade, for more details.

In General, How Does It Work?

CS uses a heavily-automated staging system to manage your project. You begin by setting up an account and creating a project. After entering and saving details about your book, such as title, category, author name(s), keywords, description, etc., you upload your manuscript and cover art in pdf format. If you don't already have cover art prepared, you can download a free, customized CS template that greatly simplifies the process of creating your own cover art.

Following file uploads, CS staffers review them to ensure the files meet with their specifications for your chosen project type. If the files are acceptable, you receive an email confirmation inviting you to order a proof copy of the book. If not, you receive an email detailing any problems with the files, inviting you to make corrections and upload new .pdf files as needed.

Once you've received confirmation that your files are acceptable, you can order a proof copy of the book. After you've received your proof copy, you review it to ensure it meets with your approval prior to formal release of the book for sale on CS's site and on Amazon.com. If you find any problems, you can make corrections to your files, generate new .pdfs, re-upload the files, wait for the confirmation email and order a new, corrected proof.

When you've received a proof with which you're satisfied, you approve the proof for release. If you've specified a desire to offer the book for sale when you first set up the project, the book shows up for sale on the CS site immediately, on a personalized product page to which you can link from your own website or blog, and which you can publicize by emailing or posting its URL wherever you like. It takes approximately 15 business days to show up on Amazon's site.

What Does It Cost?

There is no cost to open a CS account, nor to set up a 'Basic' package book, which at this time includes free ISBN and EAN-13 number assignment if you haven't already purchased your own. If you go with the Basic package, the first time you're asked to pay anything is when you order a proof copy of your book.

If you elect to upgrade your book to the 'Pro Plan' you pay a flat fee at setup and an additional, annual fee per year for the project. See the CS website (http://www.createspace.com) for more information about pricing. Additional details of what the 'Pro Plan' has to offer are provided later in this chapter.

If there are problems with your first proof and you elect to make changes, you will have to order and pay for a new proof after your new files have been received and confirmed by CS. After you've approved the proof, the book immediately becomes available for sale in the CS online store, and you can order author copies of the book at a price reflecting production costs only. A listing is submitted to Amazon, and your book's Amazon page will appear from 5 – 15 business days later.

There is no minimum number of author copies you must buy, and in fact, apart from the proof(s), you don't have to buy any copies at all. The CS store listing and Amazon listing are free.

How Long Does It Take?

It takes about 15 minutes to set up a CS account. Assuming your manuscript is complete and properly formatted per the instructions in this book, it takes another 5-10 minutes to enter the specific details of your project and upload the manuscript. Assuming your cover art is complete and properly formatted per the instructions in this book, it takes only a few minutes to upload that file.

The delays introduced into the process are a result of waiting for CS staffers to confirm receipt and acceptance of your files, and then waiting for receipt of your snail-mailed proof copy.

What Rights Do I Give Up With CS Publication?

None. CS is essentially manufacturing a book on your behalf, and you are the publisher.

Does My Book Need To Have A Pre-Assigned ISBN?

No. As stated above, whether you go with the free, Basic package or upgrade to Pro, if you don't supply an ISBN you've purchased on your own, one will automatically be assigned to your book at no charge. An internal Amazon Store Identification Number (ASIN) will automatically be assigned to your book when it's released to the store as well, assuming you've opted to sell the finished book through Amazon.

What Is My Author Royalty On My CS Book?

Your author royalty is determined by four factors: 1) the number of pages in the book, 2) whether or not you've upgraded to the Pro Plan, 3) whether a given copy of your book is sold via Amazon/Borders or through your CS product page, and 4) the list price you set. Basically, the formula works like this:

Author Royalty = List Price − CS Share

You set the list price for your book. The CS Share is comprised of the following:

CS Share = Base Price Per Book + Cost Per Page + Vendor Sales Percentage

See section 8.5.6, Determine Your Pricing, for more details on how CS price structures work and how your author royalties are calculated. The following tables, copied from the CS website, show pricing in effect as of this writing. Refer to the CS website for the most up-to-date base pricing information.

Charges for Black & White Books
All trim sizes

	Standard	☆ Pro
Books with fewer than 108 pages Fixed Charge	$3.66 per book	$2.25 per book
Charge per Page	None	None
Books with more than 108 pages Fixed Charge	$1.50 per book	$0.85 per book
Charge per Page	+ $0.02 per page	+ $0.013 per page

Charges for Color Books
All trim sizes

	Standard	☆ Pro
Books with fewer than 40 pages Fixed Charge	$6.55 per book	$4.45 per book
Charge per Page	None	None
Books with more than 40 pages Fixed Charge	$1.75 per book	$0.85 per book
Charge per Page	+ $0.12 per page	+ $0.09 per page

Note that a "color book" is a book that has a full-color cover and includes color on its interior pages. A "black and white" book has a full-color cover and interior pages that are black and white.

How Hard Is It, Really?

The more and better your computer skills, the easier it is to do a really professional-looking job of things. Even with only intermediate word procssor skills and beginner skills in your graphics or photo editing program (to create cover art), using this guide you will be able to manage without much difficulty.

Can You Answer My Ten Million Other Questions?

No, but the folks at CS can. Go to http://www.createspace.com, click the 'Help' link, and click on the FAQ link under the Books heading.

8.4 PREPARING YOUR MANUSCRIPT FOR CS

This chapter assumes you have a complete, final copy of your manuscript formatted according to the instructions in the Formatting For POD chapter. Open your manuscript and do a "Save As" to create a copy of the manuscript just for CS.

8.4.1 SAVE IN PDF FORMAT

Use your pdf-maker program or utility to save a pdf version of the file. Open the pdf version and look through it to ensure it's complete and all your desired formatting has been preserved.

Verify that the page numbers shown in the table of contents match up with the page numbers printed on the corresponding pages of the pdf file. Bear in mind that the document page numbers reflect the page count, but will not match the page numbers printed on your book's pages because none of the pages in Section 1 of your manuscript are numbered.

If you are satisfied with the pdf version, make a note of the document page count (which includes unnumbered front and back section pages), save the file and close it. If not, delete the pdf version, make any desired changes in the word processing version of the file, update the Table of Contents if needed, save as a pdf, and again make note of the document page count.

8.4.2 CRAFT YOUR BOOK DESCRIPTION & AUTHOR BIO

If you designed your cover using the Designing Your Own Book Cover chapter, you should already have a book description of the appropriate length. If not, refer to directions in that chapter. You should also already have an author bio prepared from the Formatting For POD chapter.

8.5 SET UP YOUR BOOK AT CS

Now that you've got your manuscript shipshape for publication, you need to register a CS account and enter all the details about yourself and your project. Go to http://www.createspace.com and click the "create a new account" link in the top, dark blue banner.

When you click on that link, you will be taken to a screen where you're asked to provide your email address and first and last name, and are also asked to create a password. Click the "Create My Account" button to create your account. Your account is created and you're taken to your member 'dashboard'.

In the future, anytime you login or click the 'My Account' link at CS, you will be taken to this member dashboard page. The dashboard page has four main sections.

The "My Account" link box at the upper left of the screen contains shortcuts to jump to specific areas of the dashboard.

The "Recent Messages" section, immediately beneath the "My Account" heading at the top center of the page, contains copies of recent email communications between yourself and CS support. Note that there is no internal messaging system within CS, what's shown in the "Recent Messages" box are copies of emails sent from you to CS and vice-versa. You can click on any message to open and read it.

The "My Products" section contains details about projects you've set up for publication and sale through CS. In this section you can view at-a-glance information about the current status of in-progress projects, as well as sales figures for completed projects. Completed projects appear in a tabular list, as my books "Snow Ball" and "Adelaide Einstein" do in the screen shot. You can click on a project title in the table to view the detail page for the project. Click the pencil icon next to a project to edit that project's details. Click the graph icon to view a sales report for that project. Click the price tag icon to visit your e-store page for that project. Click the shopping cart to order author copies of that project.

The "My Account Information" section contains details about you and your account. This is where you enter, and can later edit if necessary, your profiles: Account Profile, Royalty Payment Profile, Shipping Profile and Billing Profile. There's also a link in this section to view a summary report of your purchases, which includes not only purchases of author copies but proof purchases as well.

8.5.1 COMPLETE YOUR PROFILES

Click on each Profile link to access the Profile pages and complete the required fields on each one.

The Account Profile contains your name, email address, password and advertising preferences checkbox.

The Royalty Payment Profile contains your tax I.D. number, which is required in order for CS to pay your author royalties on copies of your books sold through the CS e-store and through Amazon.com, as well as to report those royalties to the IRS. If you elect to receive royalty payments via direct deposit (at no cost to you), you can enter bank information in the Royalty Payment Profile. You can elect to have your royalties mailed to you in the form of a check instead, but there's an $8 handling fee per check.

The Shipping Profile contains your default shipping address, for receipt of author copy orders, and the Billing Profile contains information about the last credit/debit card you used to pay for CS purchases. Note that you can always change the stored information, to substitute a different credit/debit card as desired.

8.5.2 ADD A NEW TITLE

After you're finished setting up your account and Profiles, click "Add A New Title"

in the link box at the upper left-hand corner of the dashboard page to access the Product Selection page (at left). Click on the link for "Paperback Book", at the lower right, to access the Title Setup screen, shown on the following page. Most of the fields are self-explanatory, and those that aren't self-explanatory generally have a blue 'about' link you can click to get more information about what to put in the field. However, there are certain fields that require special attention.

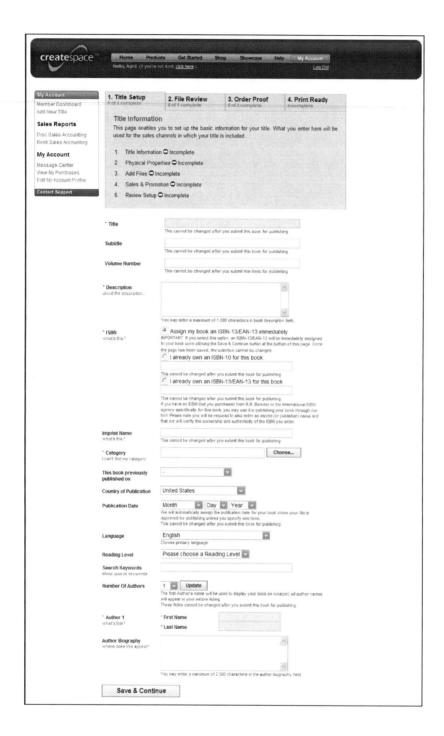

Several of the fields are marked, "cannot be changed after you submit the book for publication." Recall that after you've uploaded your content and cover art you will receive an email from CS indicating whether or not your files meet their specifications; if your files are approved, your next step is to order a proof copy of the book for review. When you order the proof copy, you are submitting the book for publication. In other words, the contents of the specially-marked fields can be changed any time up until you order your proof. When you order a proof, those fields will be locked.

Also pay particular attention to the Title and Author First Name/Last Name fields. Remember, your book may eventually come to be published in multiple editions (i.e., trade paperback, Kindle eBook, audiobook, etc.) and you must be certain the Title you enter here is consistent across all editions so that Amazon and other retailers will recognize them as different editions of the same book. In my case, I published Kindle editions prior to trade paperback editions, so I was careful to copy my titles exactly as I'd entered them for the Kindle editions. This may seem like a no-brainer, but in my case I'd used the subtitle, "A Novel By April L. Hamilton" for both of my Kindle editions and had to make sure I used the same subtitle for the trade paperbacks.

Author name must also be consistent, not only across all editions of a given book, but across all books you want to be associated with the author name you're using. Some writers use a single pen name for all their works, some use different pen names for different types of works, and still others use some version of their real name. See the Creating Your Brand chapter for more information about author name.

The "Description" field is where you will want to paste in the description you developed in the Designing Your Own Book Cover chapter, as this is the description that will appear in online store listings for your book. The "Author Biography" field contents will be displayed on your CS e-store page.

8.5.3   ENTER PHYSICAL PROPERTIES

When you click the "Save and Continue" button at the bottom of the Title Information screen you will be taken to the Physical Properties screen, where you need to provide the following:

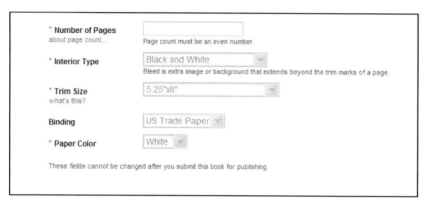

If you've followed all the formatting instructions in this book carefully, you should have a very accurate page count for the pdf file you created at the end of the Formatting For POD chapter. Recall from that chapter, because each page of a book has a front and back side, CS will only accept an even page count. If your count was originally odd, you should have already inserted a blank page at the end to make your page count even.

"Black and White" is the default selection for Interior Type, and this chapter assumes that's the type of book you're publishing. The default Trim Size (shown above) is 5.25"x8", but you'll choose the trim size matching the book dimensions specified by your formatted manuscript.

Binding Type should be left at the default value of "US Trade Paper". You can choose either White or Cream for paper color, according to your preference; there is no cost difference to you or your customers.

8.5.4 ADD FILES

After saving your physical properties, the next page allows you to upload your Book Interior and Book Cover files. You will upload the .pdf file you created in in the formatting chapter for the book's interior, and a .pdf version of the cover file you created in the Design Your Own Book Cover chapter. In a day or two, you will receive a confirmation email for each uploaded file received by CS.

8.5.5 SALES AND PROMOTION

The last screen you must complete is Sales and Promotion. Here's where you specify your publishing plan (Basic or Pro, see next section for more information), your book's list price, your main search keyword, your choice of whether or not to list your published book for sale in Amazon's store, your CS e-store type (more information) and your e-store sales region (U.S. only, or International). If you select "U.S. only" for e-store sales region, only U.S.-based customers will be allowed to purchase your book from your CS e-store. Since CS will handle any currency conversion needed, unless you have a specific reason to limit e-store sales to U.S. customers it's probably best to accept the default value of "U.S. and international".

8.5.6 DETERMINE YOUR PRICING

The decision of how to price your book should take two major considerations into account: what's typical for a book like yours, and how much do you want to earn in author royalties?

First, what is the typical list price for a mainstream book of the same approximate length, in roughly the same dimensions, as your book? As of this writing a 6"x9" mainstream trade paperback retails for $14-$16, so I priced my 5.25"x8" trade paperbacks at the low end of that scale: $14.

Now, calculate what your author royalty will be and adjust up or down to suit your needs. Recall the formula for calculating author royalties:

Author Royalty = List Price – CS Share

CS Share = Base Price Per Book + Cost Per Page + Vendor Sales Percentage

In this example, List Price is $14. Under the Basic plan (as of this writing), the base price for books with more than 108pp is $1.50 per book + .02 per page. Let's say your book has 360pp. The base price for your book is $1.50 + (.02x360), for a total of $8.70. Note that this is also the price you will be charged to order author copies of your book; basically, you're paying for the production costs only.

Vendor Sales Percentage is 40% of the list price for each copy sold through Amazon and 20% of the list price for each copy sold through your CS e-store. In the current example, the Amazon sales percentage would be $5.60 and the CS e-store sales percentage would be $2.80. Looking back at the royalty formula, your author royalty for this example would be:

Amazon Sales: $14 – ($8.70 + $5.60) = -$.30

CS e-store Sales: $14 – ($8.70 + $2.80) = $2.50

You probably noticed right away that you'd actually be losing money on each Amazon sale, and that fact doesn't escape CS's notice either. This is why CS calculates a minimum required list price for your book to break even (based on your stated preference for CS e-store and/or Amazon sales) and won't allow a list price lower than what they've calculated. It's easy enough to keep adjusting your list price upward until you're getting at least a little money back on each sale, but don't forget that the higher you set your price, the more likely you are to turn off potential buyers.

If you intend to sell exclusively through the CS e-store (which can also encompass sales from a personal website with links that go directly to the CS e-store), the Basic Plan is probably fine for you because the $2.50 author royalty you'll earn on each copy sold is still more than twice the typical author royalty on mainstream trade paperbacks. However, if you intend to sell through Amazon and other retailers, or if you intend to order more than just a few author copies, you should consider upgrading to the Pro plan.

Decide Whether Or Not To Go 'Pro'

With the Pro Plan, you pay a flat upfront fee plus a nominal annual fee for your project, and in exchange you get approximately 50% off the base price per book and per page cost. The result is a much higher author royalty per copy sold and a greatly reduced price for ordering author copies. As of this writing, the per-book base price for black and white Pro Plan books with greater than 108pp is $.85 and the per-page cost is $.013. In the current example:

Base Price/Author Copy Price = $.85 + (.013x360) = $5.53

Amazon Sales = $14 - $5.53 - $5.60 = $2.87

CS e-store Sales = $14 - $5.53 - $2.80 = $5.67

As you can see, by upgrading to Pro you will earn a 20.5% author royalty on each Amazon sale and a whopping 40.5% royalty on each CS e-store sale.

As of this writing it costs $50 upfront plus an additional $5 per year to upgrade to the Pro Plan. Even if your sales are through Amazon exclusively, you need only sell 18 copies in your first year to earn your $50 upfront investment back, and only two copies per year after that to cover the ongoing Pro Plan expense.

Another factor to consider is whether or not you plan to order many author copies. Under the Pro Plan, you pay $3.17 less per author copy than you would pay under the Basic Plan. 20 author copies with this current example will cost you $174 under the Basic Plan, but only $110.60 under the Pro Plan. Given those numbers, the Pro Plan pays for itself in author copy savings alone.

Note that if you do elect to upgrade to Pro you must pay the upfront fee immediately upon making that choice, so have your debit or credit card ready.

8.6   REVIEW SETUP

After you're done entering Sales and Promotion information, the last step is to review your setup. You'll be shown a screen that summarizes everything you entered for your book, and the graphic summary of your setup steps will show a green light next to each completed step.

Review everything very carefully. If you've entered all of the information in a single sitting, consider taking a break for an hour or more before doing this final review. After you're satisfied that everything is correct and to your liking, click "Submit for Publication".

Verification Email From CS

CS will review your uploaded files and other information. If they find everything has been entered correctly and your uploaded files meet their specifications, you will receive an email inviting you to order a proof copy of your book.

CS's staging process seems to be tied into their email notification system. The status of your project might appear to be updated to the next stage when you visit the CS site, but you must wait until after you've received the appropriate email before going to the next step. If you find a problem with your files after uploading them, and upload new files *before* receiving the 'thanks for uploading your files' email, staging for your project will be off-kilter and you'll have to contact CS support to fix the problem. Since CS support is email-only, this can introduce a delay of several days.

If There Are Problems...

If CS finds any problems with the information you entered or with your uploaded files, they will send an email detailing what problems exist and what steps you need to take to correct the problems. When you're done, you will need to "Submit for Publication" again.

8.7   THE REVIEW PROOF

If CS has approved your files and you are also satisfied that all the information you entered is correct, the next step is to order a proof copy of your book. Since the purpose of a proof copy is to verify that the book meets with your approval, you only need to order one copy. You will be asked to pay for this order immediately and there will also be tax and shipping costs, just as if you were ordering a regular book from any retailer.

When you receive your proof, inspect it very, very carefully. Remember that if you approve this proof, the book your customers receive will be an identical copy of the proof. Examine every page, check the alignment of the cover art and cover text, and if possible, have someone else examine the proof very carefully as well since a fresh pair of eyes will catch things that have escaped your notice. After you ordered the proof, CS sent you an email with instructions for how to approve the proof if you find it to be acceptable. If you are happy with the proof, follow the directions in that email to approve the proof, thereby approving your book for release.

8.7.1 IF THERE ARE PROBLEMS...

If there are any problems with your proof copy, you will need to log back in to your CS dashboard to make any necessary corrections, upload new files if the problems were in the body of your manuscript or the body of your cover, submit for publication, wait for the CS confirmation email, and "Submit for Publication" again. When you're done, you will need to order a new proof.

However, CS "locked" all the details of your book when you submitted it for publication last time. You will have to "unlock" the title from your dashboard by clicking the "Make Changes" button before you will be allowed to make changes:

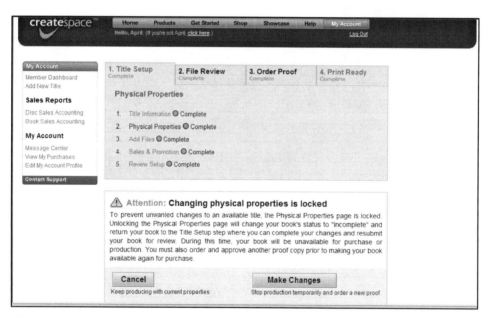

When you receive your new proof, go over it just as carefully as you did the first one.   If you are happy with the new proof, follow the directions in the "Instructions to Approve Proof" email from CS to approve the proof, thereby approving your book for release.

The moment you approve your proof, your book becomes available for sale in your CS e-store (see next section) and you can order author copies. It takes anywhere from 5 – 15 business days for your book to show up in Amazon's listings, at which point it will also show up in any Amazon affiliate store listings.

8.8 CUSTOMIZE YOUR CS E-STORE PAGE

Whether you went with the Basic Plan or the Pro Plan, CS provides you with a customized product page ("e-store") on their site from which to sell your book. Each book you publish through CS will get its own, separate e-store. As you can see in the example screen shot below, the default e-store page is pretty bland. It displays your book title, description and author bio, but nothing else.

Back at your Dashboard, when you click on the title of your published book there's an "E-store (edit)" link near the bottom of your book's detail page: E-Store | Edit. Click it to open the CS e-store page for that book.

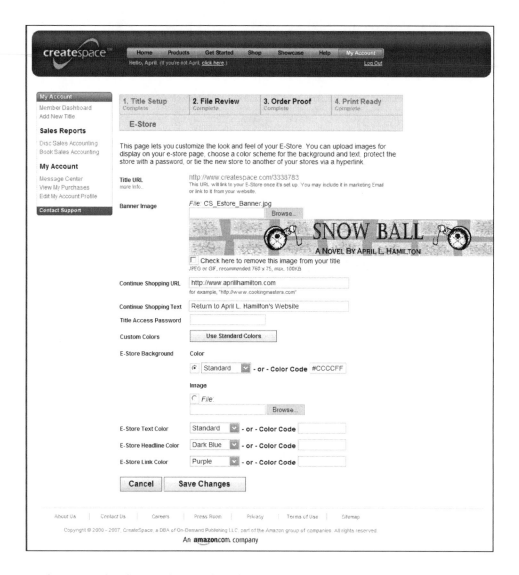

In the example shown above, I've already customized my e-store page for my novel "Snow Ball" by uploading a custom banner, setting custom background and font colors, and substituting a link back to my author website for the default "Continue Shopping" link. You're supposed to be able to upload a thumbnail image of your book cover on this form as well, but as of this writing that functionality seems to be missing. I got a thumbnail image loaded by sending a message to CS support (the support request form can be accessed via the Help link at the upper right-hand corner of all CS pages), asking them to add my thumbnail to my e-store and Amazon listing, and including a copy of the

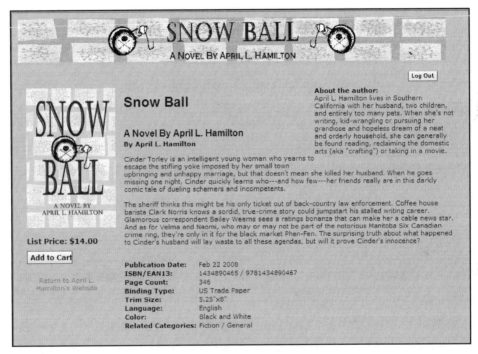

thumbnail in .jpg format as an attachment to that message. Below, you can see how my customized e-store page looks.

It's still pretty rinky-dink compared to an Amazon store page, but it's a great improvement over the default e-store page.

If you wish to add a thumbnail you can create one by saving a cropped version of the book cover you created in the Design Your Own Book Cover chapter. Make sure the cropped image meets Amazon's product image specifications: JPEG (.jpeg/.jpg) format, at least 500 pixels on the longest side (recommended minimum: 1200 pixels on the longest side). See section 9.14 in the Publishing For The Kindle chapter for more information about thumbnails.

Even if you only intend to sell through your e-store, these are good guidelines to follow for the best possible image resolution and proportions. I size my thumbnails at 1200 pixels tall by 700 pixels wide to ensure I meet Amazon's guidelines while still keeping my file size low.

A custom banner can be created in your graphics editing program. The recommended banner dimensions are 760x75 pixels, so all you need to do is set your 'canvas' or 'page' size to 760x75 pixels and proceed to add your graphic and text elements. If those dimensions are too small to work with in your graphics editor program, start with a 'canvas' or 'page' size 100 times larger, 7600x750 pixels, and then size it down to 760x75 pixels when saving the final file.

Your banner should echo your book cover. Use the same background image or color as that used on your book cover, as well as the same font and text color. If possible, also incorporate a graphic element from your book cover, as I've done in my banner.

When you're finished creating the banner, save it in the native file format of your graphics editor (usually .psd or .png). If you intend to size the banner down, be sure to save this 'native' copy before you downsize the file. You'll need the native copy for any future edits or changes if you're not completely happy with the banner once you've seen it in place on your e-store page. Now use the 'Save for Email or Web' option in your graphics editor program to save a .jpg version of the file with dimensions of 760x75 pixels. Saving 'for Email or Web' compresses the file to reduce its byte size, and since CS will only accept banners of 100KB or less, you need that compression.

By default, CS includes a "Continue Shopping" link on each e-store page. If you don't customize the link in any way, it will take your customer to the general category heading for your type of book in the CS store (i.e., General Fiction, Mystery, etc.). Bear in mind, customers will only be clicking on this link if they've decided not to click the "Add to Cart" button on your e-store page. If a customer clicks the "Add to Cart" button, he or she will be taken to the CS checkout process.

Assuming you intend to direct customers to your e-store page from a personal website, you will want to customize the "Continue Shopping" link to take your customers back to that website if they've decided not to buy your book. In the example above, I've changed the link to take customers back to my author website and changed the link wording to, "Return to April L. Hamilton's Website."

The Title Access Password field is used to password-protect the e-store page. This is for cases where the author/publisher wants to make the title available for sale through a password-protected page, but not to the general public.

In the Custom Colors area, you can accept the standard (default) CS e-store colors for various items on your book's sale page or specify your own. A few colors are provided for selection through the drop-down boxes, but you can specify any hexadecimal color code as well. See the HTML Primer chapter for more information about color codes. With respect to the background, you can specify a solid color or a patterned background from an uploaded image file. Given that major online bookstores use a solid-color background, or just a white background, I recommend indie authors do the same.

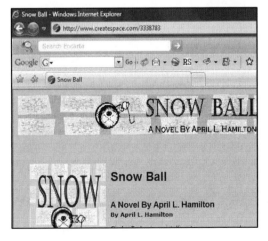

When you've got your e-store page customized to your liking, you can start using its link to direct family, friends and customers to it. You can copy your e-store page link from the detail page that's displayed when you click on your book's title from your main dashboard page. Scroll down to the "E-store" section, and copy the e-store URL displayed there. Notice that the URL takes the form of "http://www.createspace.com/[your project #]".

8.9 WATCH FOR YOUR AMAZON LISTING

If you've opted to sell your book through Amazon, beginning 5 business days after you approved your proof start checking your dashboard every day to see if your Amazon store listing is up. It can take up to 15 business days for your listing to appear. Click on your book's title on the main dashboard page to get to the detail page, and scroll down to check the "Sales and Promotion" section.

Sales & Promotion (Complete) Edit	
Pro	Yes
List Price	$14.00
Sell via Amazon Retail Sales	Yes
Amazon Retail Sales status	Live on Amazon
Sell via E-Store Sales	Yes
Type of E-Store	Public
Sales Region	US and international sales

When your book goes 'live' on Amazon, "Amazon Retail Sales Status" will display "Live on Amazon." At that point you can go to Amazon, look up your book, copy the URL for your book's product page and start using it to sell and promote your book the same as you've done with the e-store link.

8.10 AFTER YOUR BOOK IS PUBLISHED

You can log back into your CS dashboard anytime you want and click on the Reports icon next to your book title to see how many copies of your book have sold through Amazon, how many have sold through the CS e-store, and what your cumulative author royalty total is to date. You can also order author copies at any time.

8.10.1 GETTING PAID

Here's what CS has to say in its FAQ regarding the payment of author royalties.

When do I get paid for sales of my title?

CreateSpace pays your royalty for a given month's sales at the end of the following month. For example, you will receive your royalty payment at the end of March covering all the sales you made in February. The lag time of approximately 30 days covers any sales revenue collections, customer returns, and payment processing.

How do I get paid for sales of my title?

Members living inside the United States will receive their royalty payment via direct deposit into their bank account. This service is free. Enter bank account information by the 20th of the month to begin direct deposits in that same month. Information entered after the 20th will be used for the following month. By written request, a member could choose to be paid by check, but an $8 dollar handling fee applies.

We don't make deposits for amounts less than $20. Instead, we'll keep a running total and once the amount exceeds $20, we'll make a deposit at the end of that month. For members residing outside the United States, royalty payment checks will be mailed. This service is free. By written request, a member could choose to be paid via wire transfer directly into their foreign bank account. A $25 dollar service fee applies per transaction for this wire transfer service. Before we can send any content license royalties, you will need to provide your tax identification number: social security number, employer identification number, or individual tax identification number. A payment record is provided on your Account History Report. For additional information, please see Content License Royalties.

"Content License Royalties" is another help topic in the FAQ.

8.11 STILL UNCLEAR ON SOMETHING?

First, go to the CS site and click the Help link at the upper-right hand corner of any page on the site. On the Help page, click the FAQ link under the Books section, as shown below:

This will take you to a fairly thorough FAQ page that covers most of the topics for which you might need help or clarification. If you can't find your answer there, return to the main Help page and click the "Contact Support" link under the Books section to access the member support form, below.

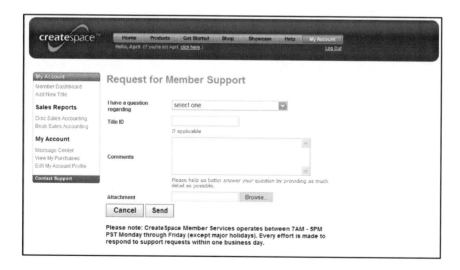

9 PUBLISHING FOR THE KINDLE

Amazon's Digital Text Platform, or DTP, is a conversion tool used to create content for the Kindle eBook reader device and put that content up for sale in the Amazon Kindle Store. You cannot use the DTP to create Kindle editions of your work for your own personal use, the content creation process automatically generates an accompanying Amazon product page.

9.1 WHY PUBLISH FOR THE KINDLE?

Since you've already made the decision to self-publish, there are three very good reasons to publish for the Kindle via Amazon's DTP: it's easy, it's free, and it gets your work onto the virtual shelves at Amazon in a matter of days. While it's true that only Kindle owners will be able to buy your DTP book, and they are a relatively small group compared to the general public, these are the very circumstances that offer distinct advantages over other forms of self-publishing.

First, because Kindle owners are a small and specific population, it's easy to target your promotional efforts by seeking out their blogs and discussion groups. Second, because the Kindle book store has a much more limited inventory than the 'regular' Amazon book store, you don't have to sell many copies of your DTP book to quickly rise into the Kindle store bestseller ranks. Finally, because Amazon book listings combine reviews and sales figures from all available editions of a given book, you can use your DTP edition to accumulate sales and reviews to support a POD release in the 'regular' book store: the day your POD book goes on sale, it can already have sales and positive reviews associated with it from the Kindle book store.

9.2   QUESTIONS AND ANSWERS ABOUT THE DTP

Who Can Use The DTP?

As of this writing, anyone with an Amazon account can use the DTP to create and sell Kindle editions of anything from short fiction to doorstop-sized tomes.

In General, How Does It Work?

You begin by entering details about your book, such as title, category, author name(s), keywords, description, etc. Next, you upload your manuscript in HTML format (don't panic, Word and most other word processors can convert to .html for you automatically) and optionally upload cover art as a .jpg or .gif image. When the upload is complete, you can preview what your manuscript will look like on the Kindle from your web browser screen. If all looks correct, the final step is to set your price, save your changes, and then 'Publish' with one final button click.

What Does It Cost?

There is no cost to set your book up for sale as a Kindle edition via the DTP.

How Long Does It Take?

It takes anywhere from 20-45 minutes to fill in the necessary online forms, upload and preview your DTP edition. From the time you click the 'Publish' button, signifying your approval of your book, its details and the associated cover art, it takes approximately 3 business days for your book to show up in the Kindle book store.

What Rights Do I Give Up With Dtp?

First, the usual caveat: legal advice is outside the scope of this book, and full disclosure on the matter can be found in the DTP Terms and Conditions, which can be accessed in the Forums and Support area of the Amazon DTP site (http://forums.digitaltextplatform.com/dtpforums/) under Additional Information > Legal. If the document should be moved at some point in the future, rendering the above link broken, just go to http://dtp.amazon.com, click the Support link, and do a search on "Terms & Conditions" in the support area.

Having said that, in agreeing to the Terms & Conditions you're granting Amazon sole right to sell, distribute and promote the Kindle edition of your work, as created by the DTP, in whatever manner they see fit. You're agreeing to let them share free digital excerpts and images of your work taken from the Kindle edition (i.e., 'Search Inside the Book,' 'Read A Free Excerpt,' etc.), as well as to discount, bundle or cross-sell your Kindle edition work as they wish.

However, your percentage of the profit from each sale is always based on the list price you set, regardless of the price at which Amazon ultimately sells the book---more on that later. You're also granting them the right to release the work to customers who buy it, store the work on their servers or the servers of their designee(s), and store the work on behalf of purchasers in each purchaser's 'digital locker'.

You are not giving up any other rights to publish any other editions of your work, not even other eBook editions. Given that the Kindle file format is proprietary and specific to the Amazon DTP, it's not as if standalone DTP/Kindle rights could ever be sold to another entity anyway. Still, it's worth mentioning that publishers will tend to view the entire thing just as negatively as they do any form of self-publishing, and are therefore likely to be turned off to any manuscript you release via DTP regardless of your largely intact rights.

There are more details in the Terms & Conditions, and I urge you to read it in its entirety, and even consult with an attorney about it if you have any doubts, before you decide whether or not to use the DTP.

Does My Book Need To Have A Pre-Assigned ISBN?

No, and you don't have to purchase one for your DTP book, either. Note that generally, where ISBNs are used each different edition of a book (i.e., audiobook, hardcover, trade paperback, eBook) is assigned a unique ISBN. This means that you cannot assign the ISBN used for some other edition of your book to the DTP edition. However, since the DTP does not require an ISBN you also don't have to buy a new one just for the DTP edition of your book. An internal Amazon Store Identification Number (ASIN) will automatically be assigned to your DTP book when it's released to the store.

What Is My Author Royalty On My Kindle Book?

As of this writing, your author royalty is 35% of the list price you set when you enter the details for your Kindle book. For example, if you price your book at $4.99, your royalty on each copy sold is $1.75. Even if Amazon discounts your book and sells it for 20% off the list price, you still get $1.75 for each copy sold.

How Hard Is It, Really?

As you might expect, the more and better your computer skills, the easier it is to do a really professional-looking job. Even with only intermediate word processing skills and beginner skills with your graphics or photo editing program (to create cover art), so long as your manuscript doesn't have illustrations or other graphics in it, you will be able to manage without much difficulty.

Directions for converting manuscripts that have illustrations or graphics are provided herein, but as of this writing the DTP isn't really set up to handle graphics all that well. If your book is heavily dependent on illustrations, I do not recommend publishing a Kindle edition.

Can You Answer My Ten Million Other Questions?

No, but the folks at Amazon DTP can. Go to http://dtp.amazon.com, click the 'Getting Started' link, and avail yourself of the Getting Started Guide, Formatting Guide, FAQ and Additional Information links. Also feel free to peruse the Ask The Community user forums, as many specific questions, concerns, tricks and tips are also discussed there.

Getting Ready For The DTP

First things first: as mentioned above, it's a very good idea to go to http://dtp.amazon.com, click the 'Help' link, and avail yourself of the Getting Started Guide, Formatting Guide, FAQ and Additional Information links. The links will take you to help pages where you can download pdf guides, tutorials, and a quick start guide. Grab a copy of everything available, and read all of it. Then come back to this document for a simpler set of instructions that also cover some tips, tricks and gotchas not included in Amazon's materials.

You will have to provide a tax ID number (i.e., social security number) and bank information in order for Amazon to pay you your author royalties. Don't get all paranoid about this, because any author must provide a tax ID number to his or her publisher, and the bank information is only needed so that Amazon can electronically transfer your royalties directly to your bank account instead of cutting and mailing a check.

Don't Use Anything Less Than A Final, 'Locked' Draft

Remember, once you click that 'Publish' button your work is on its way to the Kindle store shelves for the whole world to see. Do not publish anything via DTP that you would not feel comfortable seeing on the shelf at your local brick-and-mortar bookstore with your name on the cover. This is not the time or place for anything less than a final, completely polished draft that you've 'locked' against more revisions.

9.3 PREPARING YOUR MANUSCRIPT FOR THE DTP

While it is possible to upload any manuscript formatted as HTML to the DTP, this article assumes you have a complete, final copy of your manuscript formatted according to the instructions in the Formatting For POD chapter. Open your manuscript and do a "Save As" to create a copy of the manuscript just for DTP.

Prior to upload to the DTP, you will be saving your manuscript as an HTML file in which most of your formatting options will be lost, along with any embedded graphics and special characters such as Webding symbols. Therefore, to save yourself from unwelcome formatting surprises after you upload to DTP, you want your text to be as minimally-formatted as possible before saving as HTML. When you're done, the HTML version of your manuscript should be virtually identical to the word processing file you used to create it.

The DTP guides all talk about making changes to your HTML file to correct formatting problems, but it's much easier to make all the changes you possibly can in your word processor, a program you know well, than to go trudging through lines of HTML code trying to figure out how to make it look the way you want. If you follow the directions in this chapter, you should have a pretty clean file when you're ready to save as HTML and should not have to go through multiple iterations of uploading to DTP, previewing, making changes and uploading again to resolve formatting issues. As you go through these steps, save frequently (still in your word processor's normal format---you won't 'Save As' HTML until all changes and corrections have been made).

9.4 DELETE THE EXTRANEOUS

Delete any blank pages that were inserted into the original manuscript for purposes of 'facing pages' formatting. Delete all headers and footers, because they'll be lost in the conversion process anyway. Don't worry about losing your page numbers, as the Kindle automatically regenerates digital page numbers each time it loads a file.

9.5   ALTER PAGE SETUP

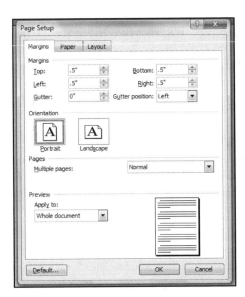

In the Margins tab of the Page Setup dialog (see Formatting for POD chapter), change the 'Multiple Pages' drop-down box back to its default value of "Normal". Set 'Top', 'Bottom', 'Left' and 'Right' margins to ".5". Set the 'Gutter' to "0". Leave the 'Gutter position' set to its default value of "Left". Select "Portrait" for 'Orientation'. In the Preview section, set 'Apply to' to "Whole Document".

In the Paper tab (not shown), set paper size back to its default of 8.5x11".

The Layout tab should look like the screen shot at right. If it doesn't, make any necessary changes: in the Header and footers section, de-select the checkboxes for 'Different odd and even' and 'Different first page', and ensure 'Vertical alignment' in the Page section is set to "Top".

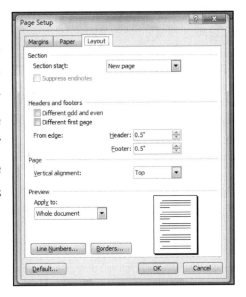

9.6   REARRANGE FRONT MATTER PAGES

In eBooks, the order of information in the 'front matter' is a little different than in a printed book. The title page comes first, followed by copyright information, dedication, then table of contents. Cut and paste to rearrange your front pages. On your copyright page, delete references to any ISBN or EAN, and change the publisher name to "Amazon DTP", with a location of "Seattle, WA".

9.7   VERIFY STYLES

If you've followed the directions in the Formatting chapter, your manuscript should not be littered with duplicate Styles (and you should know why duplicate Styles are to be avoided). Nevertheless, in the course of writing you may have inadvertently created new Styles. Ensure that all like-formatted sections of text have the same Style applied to them.

An easy way to spot superfluous Styles is to open the Styles listbox and scan through them. If you see one you don't recognize, or that appears to be a duplicate, mouse over it to activate its drop-down option box. In the screen shot at left, the drop-down option box has been activated for Heading 1, as indicated by the appearance of a downward-pointing arrow at the right of the Style name.

If you keep the mouse pointer in place over the selected Style, a box with all the format settings for the Style will display just below the mouse pointer. Read through the settings to see if one of your purposely-created custom Styles can substitute for

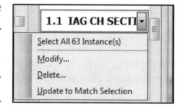

the unwanted Style. If so, click on the 'Select All [number] Instances' item to locate and select every instance of the unwanted Style in your document. Locate the desired custom Style in the list and click it to apply it to all the selected instances.

Go back to the unwanted Style name in the list and check its drop-down option box again. Where number of instances appeared previously, you should now see that the Style is marked 'not in use'. If so, click the Delete option in the drop-down list to eliminate the unwanted Style from your document. If not, repeat the correction procedure.

Click the arrow to open the option box, as shown at right. The top line shows how many times, or in how many 'instances', the selected Style has been used in the document.

9.8   MODIFY STYLES

To update a Style, mouse over it in the Styles list, then click its downward-pointing arrow to open its option list. In the option list, select Modify.

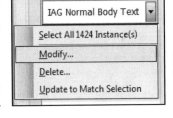

Make your desired changes in the Modify Style dialog (shown below). Click the "Add to template" box at the lower left of the dialog to apply your changes to all instances of the

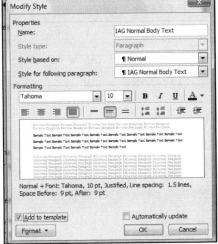

selected Style in the document, then click OK to save your changes.

9.8.1   GENERAL FORMATTING

HTML can render up to six levels of headers, body text, indented text blocks, numbered or bulleted lists, and simple tables, as well as italics, boldface, underlined and enlarged text. If any of your Styles employ formatting that's more complex than these few options, you will need to either modify those Styles to simplify them or apply different, simpler Styles to text that's too heavily-formatted.

In all your Styles used for for body text, under Format > Paragraph, set line spacing to 1.5. Wider-spaced text takes up an annoying amount of screen real estate on an eBook reader, and all that extra white space doesn't actually improve its readability.

9.8.2   FONTS

The default font for HTML is Times New Roman, and the few other fonts considered standard for use in HTML are Andale Mono, Arial, Comic Sans MS, Courier New, Georgia, Impact, Trebuchet MS, and Verdana. If you're using a font in your Styles that isn't on that list, it will be changed to Times New Roman during conversion to HTML. To avoid this, select one of the HTML-standard fonts and update all your Styles with it.

Set the font size for body text Styles to 10 or 11. Font sizes up to 14 will convert to HTML, but it's not necessary to use a large font size because eBook readers have a 'zoom' or 'enlarge' function for use if the onscreen text appears too small.

9.9   REMOVE BREAKS AND RETURNS

Section breaks will not be recognized in the HTML conversion, but page breaks will. It's appropriate to use page breaks at the end of each chapter, but delete any that were used for any other reason, such as for widow or orphan control.

Also delete carriage returns which may have been used to offset differently-formatted sections of text, but are no longer necessary now that your formatting is being greatly simplified. HTML will interpret each carriage return as the start of a new paragraph, and may insert unwanted blank lines between those paragraphs (see HTML Primer chapter).

Special Characters

Use Search and Replace to locate and delete or replace any special characters. For example, if you've used a bullet icon such as a star or snowflake as a graphic element to create dividers between sections of text, you will need to delete those bullets or replace them with a regular character, such as an asterisk or dash.

HTML has its own set of supported special characters, some of which are listed in the 'ANSI Codes' table in the HTML Primer chapter, but since these must be entered into the HTML file after conversion, it's safer and easier to just fall back on standard keyboard characters.

Subscripts and superscripts are also not likely to translate properly; locate all such instances and reformat accordingly.

9.10 DEALING WITH GRAPHICS

If your manuscript includes illustrations, diagrams or other graphics, you must store each one as an individual file outside of your document, in .jpg, .gif, .tiff or ideally, .png format, and replace them with HTML pointers in the document. Finally, you must save the manuscript and graphics files together in a single, .zip file for upload to the DTP system.

If you can't extract (or copy) the pictures to be saved separately, you don't have a graphics editor program, you aren't familiar with how to change the file size and dimensions of graphics in your graphics editor program, or the graphics can't be saved in .gif, .jpg or .png format, you won't be able to include your graphics in your Kindle book. Also, although instructions will be provided for how to set pointers in the HTML file after conversion, if you're not comfortable editing an HTML file you will struggle with the task. As stated previously, I do not recommend publishing manuscripts containing graphics for the Kindle.

Moderate to advanced HTML skills are required if you need to tightly control the location of each graphic/picture on the page, or the way your text 'wraps' around the graphic in a page; such HTML instruction is beyond the scope of this book, so the instructions here assume you do not need or want that level of control.

9.10.1 EXTRACT GRAPHICS

Create a folder to hold your manuscript and all your graphics files and move the DTP-formatting copy of the manuscript into the new folder.

With your word processor open in one window and your graphics-editor program open in a second window, right-click the first graphic in your manuscript and select Copy, then switch to your graphics program. In the graphics program, select File > New and paste the copied graphic into the new file.

9.10.2 EDIT GRAPHICS

Edit the graphic so that its dimensions are no larger than 450 x 550 pixels, its file size is no larger than 64kb, and its aspect ratio is 9:11. You may need to alter the 'canvas' size to get the aspect ratio right without distorting your image.

Save the graphic file in .gif, .jpg, .tiff, or .png format, in the same folder as your manuscript—do not set up any subfolders within the main folder. The preferred format is .png, as that format converts most easily. Give the file a name that will make it easy for you to match the file to its location in the manuscript.

After the file has been saved, close it and re-open it in the graphics program to make sure it looks all right. If there are any problems, you can start over by copying the graphic from the manuscript and repeating the editing steps.

Switch to the word processor window. Delete the graphic and leave placeholder text in its place to indicate where the picture should appear in the manuscript. Include the filename of the extracted graphic in the placeholder text, and begin the text with a word or characters you can easily search for when editing the

HTML file to insert pointers later. Repeat these steps for every graphic in your manuscript file.

Do not attempt to set any HTML pointers yet; this step will occur after you've finished with all other formatting changes and have saved the file as HTML.

9.11 INSERT A HYPERLINKED TABLE OF CONTENTS

EBook users have come to expect a hyperlinked table of contents, and this is one of the criteria they use to cut the non-professionals from the herd in judging which books are, or are not, worth their time and money. Fortunately, it's very easy to create a hyperlinked Table of Contents in any modern word processor, and when you 'Save As' HTML the hyperlinks will be preserved.

The following instructions are specific to Word 2003; to locate the same feature in a different word processing program, consult your program's Help files.

Ensure each chapter of your manuscript has a chapter number or title on its first page, and that the number or title is formatted as a Heading Style with an outline level of 1 (see Formatting for POD chapter, Creating Custom Styles section). If your original manuscript didn't have chapter headings, you will need to create them now. Remember to stick to formatting that will be HTML-friendly.

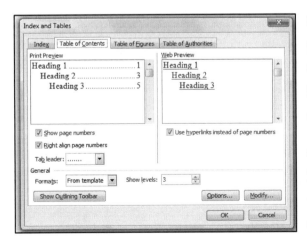

Go to the table of contents page. Leave the table of contents title header in place, but select the table of contents itself and delete it.

Click Insert > Reference > Index and Tables and select the Table of Contents tab. Click the boxes for 'Show

Page Numbers', 'Right-Align Page Numbers' and 'Use Hyperlinks Instead of Page Numbers'.

Set the 'Show Levels' drop-down to the number of different heading Styles you want to appear in the table of contents. If your chapters have chapter headings, but no subheadings within chapters, set 'Show Levels' to "1".

You can include a level in your table of contents for every level of heading in use in your manuscript, but with the exception of textbooks and technical manuals, it's typical to limit the table of contents to outline level 1 headings. That way, only the main chapter headings are shown.

The inserted table of contents will employ the Times New Roman font by default, which most likely will not match the rest of your document. If this is the case, select all the text contained in the table of contents and manually change the font and point size to match the rest of your document.

9.12 'SAVE AS' HTML

Do one last save of the manuscript in your word processor's usual format before proceeding. Remember, if the uploaded file needs further corrections or changes, you will want to modify the word processor file, not the HTML version.

Now 'Save As', selecting "Web Page (*.htm, *.html)" as the file type and setting the file extension to ".html". You may want to give this version a distinct name, but it's not really necessary. Since its file extension is ".html", it won't be hard to tell this file apart from the word processing file later.

After you click 'Save' you'll be looking at the HTML version of the file. If you've properly corrected and simplified all your formatting, other than any graphics you've replaced with placeholders, there shouldn't be any significant differences between this HTML version and the word processor file.

9.13 INSERT GRAPHICS POINTERS, IF APPLICABLE

Close the HTML file and close your word processor. Open a simple text editor program, such as Notepad (located in the Accessories folder of Windows). Make sure the Word Wrap or Text Wrap option is turned off. In Notepad, do this by de-selecting the Word Wrap option in the Format menu.

Open your HTML file in the text editor. It will look seriously messed up to you, not at all like your original manuscript file, but don't worry: that's how HTML is supposed to look when viewed in a text editor. See the HTML Primer chapter for more information about HTML source code files.

Use the Edit > Find function to locate each graphics placeholder in your file and replace it with the text shown below to create an HTML pointer to the appropriate, reformatted, separately-saved graphics file:

<IMG SRC="[myimagefilename].[myimagefileformat]">

For example, if you saved a graphic with the name "Chap2Fig2" in .png format, your HTML pointer would look like this:

<IMG SRC="Chap2Fig2.png">

WARNING: Do not alter a single character of any text in the HTML file other than your graphics placeholders. A single extraneous character or character out of place in an HTML file can ruin your formatting, or even make the HTML fail to display at all. Don't worry if text wraps oddly, line or page breaks seem to be missing, or anything else looks wrong in the text editor. You're looking at HTML source code, not a word processing file.

Be careful, but remember that even in the event of a total disaster, you can just delete the damaged HTML file, re-open the word processor file, and re-do the "Save As HTML" step to create a new HTML file.

When you're done, save the file in the text editor program. Make sure that when you save, the file extension/type shown is ".html", not ".txt".

9.13.1 VERIFY GRAPHICS POINTERS

Inserting an HTML pointer will not make the associated graphic appear in the text file as you're viewing it in the text editor. You must view the HTML in a browser to verify your graphics pointers are working properly.

Locate your saved .html file on your computer and double-click it. Since the file type is .html, your computer will recognize it as a web page and open it in your usual web browser program (i.e., Internet Explorer, Mozilla Firefox, etc.).

You will be looking at an approximation of how your content will look on the Kindle, but not a very good one. This is because the Kindle screen displays everything in a 9:11 aspect ratio—roughly the same shape and overall dimensions as a page from a large-format trade paperback book, whereas most computer screens are wider than they are tall. Pages of your book will look a lot wider on your computer screen than they will on the Kindle screen. You'll be able to view a much more accurate approximation of how your book will look on the Kindle later, after uploading your finished content to the DTP. This first preview is only being done to ensure your graphics are all displaying in the correct locations, which indicates your graphics pointers are working.

If any of your graphics are missing, go back to the Insert Graphics Pointers steps above to double-check the pointers you inserted. HTML is finicky, so just one character, quotation mark or period out of place will mess up a pointer. If your pointers all seem to be correct, verify that every graphics file is located in the same folder as your manuscript file, not in a sub-folder or any other location.

If the graphics are all there but you don't like the way text is wrapping around them, unfortunately, you can't do anything about it. If the HTML file is just plain messed up, however, see the If There Are Problems section at the end of this chapter for instructions on how to create a new HTML file.

9.13.2 SAVE FILES IN A .ZIP ARCHIVE

Manuscripts with graphics must be uploaded to the DTP in the form of a .zip archive file which contains the manuscript file and all associated graphics files. In Windows XP or higher, you can simply right-click on the folder and select "Send To > Compressed (zipped) folder" to create the .zip file. On Mac computers running OS X or later, Ctrl-click the folder and select "Create Archive". If your computer doesn't offer this option, you will need to run the appropriate zipping program to complete this task. If you don't already have such a program, do an internet search on "zip file" + [Mac or Windows] to locate a free download of a zipping program online.

9.14 PREPARE YOUR COVER ART

Kindle store customers judge the lack of cover art, or the presence of stock-photo cover art, to be a hallmark of the non-professional. You definitely want some nice cover art for your DTP book, and you want it to match the cover art of all other editions of your book for consistency's sake. Even if you don't have any other editions available yet, don't skimp on the time or effort here because whatever you create for DTP will have to serve for possible future POD books.

See the Designing Your Own Book Cover chapter for detailed instructions on how to create a book cover design for use both here and on a trade paperback edition of your book. If you don't intend to ever publish your book in a trade paperback edition, just skip the portions of the chapter dealing with art and formatting on the spine and back cover—leave those portions of the cover blank.

When your cover design is complete, copy just the front cover portion of the image and paste it into a new file under a different name. This file will be the image displayed on Amazon in your Kindle book's product page.

Your cover art must meet Amazon product image standards: TIFF (.tif/.tiff) or JPEG (.jpeg/.jpg) file format, with image pixel dimensions of at least 1000 pixels on the longest side. Most graphics editors have a 'save for web' option under the file menu, in which you can specify pixel dimensions. Set pixel dimensions based on the standard dimensions of a trade paperback book, which is 6x9". This means that for every 6 pixels in width, there should be 9 pixels in height. As an easy shortcut, just set pixel dimensions to 600 wide by 900 high.

Color mode must be "sRGB" (this is the default for most graphics programs), not "CMYK". Refer to your graphics program documentation or help files for more information on how to edit your file to meet these requirements.

9.15 CRAFT YOUR BOOK DESCRIPTION

You are only given 200 words for your book description, which will appear on your Amazon product page when the book is released. Look at a few such descriptions for books in the Kindle store to get some idea of how to approach this. You're going for a synopsis that says enough about the story to lure a reader in, but doesn't give away too much. Create a separate Word or .txt document just for the description, so you can spend some quality time working and reworking it until it's exactly what you want.

9.16 MAKE A FREE EXCERPT AVAILABLE

When you upload your content to the DTP the first 10% of the file will be made available for the "Look Inside the Book" feature. However, 10% is not a very large excerpt. Because the availability of a free excerpt to try-before-you-buy is of critical importance to Kindle owners who might not otherwise take a risk on an unknown author, and a more lengthy excerpt will be more likely to pull readers in, it's worth the effort to make a longer excerpt available outside of Amazon. See the Make a Free Excerpt Available section in the Promotion chapter for details of how to do this.

On the last page of your excerpt, you will be inserting a blurb to the effect of, "Thank you for reading this excerpt. If you would like to continue reading [book title], you may purchase it from the Kindle book store at Amazon.com." In your word processing program, select that last part of the text ("Kindle book store at Amazon.com") and select Insert > Hyperlink to set a link to the Kindle store, currently at this URL:

http://www.amazon.com/b?ie=UTF8&node=133141011

Later, after your DTP book is live, you can replace this link with a link to your actual product page by editing the excerpt file and re-uploading it to the web if desired.

Now you must go back to your book description file, created in section 9.15, and add the line, "Read a free, more lengthy excerpt at [URL of your .pdf excerpt]." at the end of your book description. Note that you can insert a blank line between the book description and this one-liner, and it's generally a good idea to do so. Shoppers can see at a glance there's a free excerpt available, they don't have to read the entire description to get to the excerpt notice.

You may have to do some editing to make this fit into your description if you've used all 200 words, but it's important, so make it work.

9.17 READY, SET, DTP!

The details of how to fill out the required fields for DTP processing are already covered in the Amazon DTP guides I've mentioned previously, and I will not rehash them here. Just note that only fields marked with a red asterisk are required, so don't feel obligated to make up a Publisher Name, or a Series Name if it's really not applicable to your book. A screen shot of the main DTP 'dashboard' is shown on the following page.

For my DTP books, I left the ISBN, Publisher Name, Series Title and Series Volume all blank. Remember that ISBNs are not required for eBooks, and where ISBNs *are* required, every edition of a book must have its own, unique ISBN. You should not enter an ISBN previously assigned to another edition of your book (i.e., trade paperback) here, nor should you waste a purchased ISBN on the Kindle edition of your book.

I entered "1" for Edition Number, and I entered as many search keywords (i.e., comic fiction, mystery, Midwest, womens fiction, etc.) as I could possibly think of that would fit in the space provided. The keywords will help customers find your book when they search the store, so don't be afraid to really go nuts with them. More keywords = more people finding your book. Also note that when it comes to filling in your Book Description field, all you have to do is copy the description you created previously and paste it into the field.

Follow the instructions to "Enter Product Details" and "Upload & Review Book" as outlined in the Amazon DTP guides, and meet me back here after you've uploaded your cover image and your HTML file. Remember that if your manuscript has graphics, you will be uploading a .zip file, not just the HTML version of your manuscript file (see section 9.13.2).

9.18 LOOKING AT YOUR DTP PREVIEW

When the file is finished uploading, click the Preview button to go to a page where you can preview the file roughly how it will look on the Kindle. Don't just check the first few pages, jump around throughout the file by using the "Go To Page" box at the top of the preview screen. Look at the back pages, to be sure your 'About the Author' and other back-material stuff came through okay. Do some spot-checking of the pages where new chapters begin.

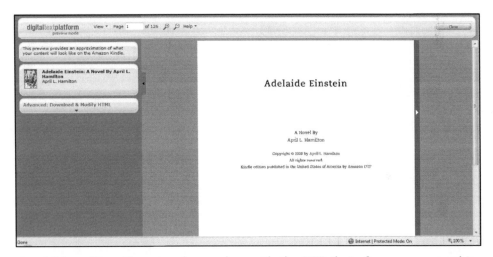

As of this writing, there is a known bug with the DTP that often causes graphics to display smaller than they really are, or oriented incorrectly (i.e., in landscape instead of portrait) when you view your file in preview mode. Unfortunately, there's nothing you can do about this. According to the DTP Administrator on the DTP Help boards, if your graphics are displayed at all you should just trust that they will display correctly when viewed on a Kindle screen. By the time you're reading this, the problem may have been corrected.

Note that it will appear as if your text goes right to the edge of the screen on the right-hand side, but this is deceptive. In reality, the Kindle will provide a white-space margin there on its screen.

Also, your hyperlinked table of contents will have had its page numbers removed and may seem non-functional. Page numbers are removed because Kindle re-paginates and re-numbers the pages of each file it loads, but the hyperlinks in the table of contents are updated to reflect the newly-generated page numbers at the same time. The links in this new table of contents will seem 'broken', but that's only because hyperlink functionality is not available in the preview screen. So long as your table of contents entries are blue and underlined, signifying hyperlinks, you can rest assured they will work.

9.19 IF THERE ARE PROBLEMS...

DO NOT open the HTML version of your file to make edits or corrections, as the DTP guides suggest. Instead, follow these steps:

Delete the HTML version of your file from your computer; don't worry, you'll be replacing it with a new one.

Open the edited-for-DTP word processing manuscript---the one you saved right before doing the 'Save As' HTML.

Make any desired changes and save the file, still in word processing format.

Update the hyperlinked table of contents. In Word, you do this by clicking anywhere inside the table of contents and pressing the F9 key. When prompted, select "Update Entire Table' and click OK. You will have to re-apply desired font formatting if you don't want your table of contents to display in 10-point Times New Roman.

Save the file one last time in its usual word processing format, then do a 'Save As' in HTML format, following the same directions from section 9.12 as you did previously.

If there were graphics in your manuscript, repeat the steps in section 9.13.

9.20 IF IT LOOKS GOOD, SET YOUR PRICE AND PUBLISH!

Back at your DTP dashboard, click on that lowermost tab: Enter Price. The checkbox next to "Kindle store" should already be marked. If it isn't, place a checkmark in it by clicking on it.

Bestsellers that are only available in hardcover in the 'regular' book store tend to be priced at $9.99 in the Kindle store, and those available as trade paperbacks in the 'regular' bookstore usually run between $6.99 - $8. I price my Kindle-edition novels at $4.99, partly in recognition of the fact that I'm not a bestselling author and partly because I personally feel eBooks should always cost less than their paper-pulp counterparts. You will have to use your own best judgment in deciding where to set the price point for your books, but remember that your author royalty will be 35% of the price you set here, regardless of the price at which Amazon ultimately sells each copy (see section 9.2).

Click 'Save Entries' on the 'Enter Price' tab. Go back and check all the entries in the first two tabs one last time, just to be absolutely sure it's all accurate and the way you want it. When you're ready, take a deep breath and click "Publish".

Log back into your DTP dashboard in about three days to see if your book is marked "Live" yet. First it will go "Live", but not all the details will show up on the product page and it will be listed as "not yet available" while Amazon works to get your book's details added to all their various databases. By the end of 5 business days at most, your book should be live, complete and available for sale in the Kindle store. It will take up to 15 weeks for the 'Search Inside the Book' feature to become available for your book.

9.21 AFTER YOUR BOOK IS PUBLISHED

You can log back into your DTP dashboard anytime you want and click on the "My Reports" tab to see how many copies of your book have sold, and what your cumulative author royalty total is to date. You can also re-upload and re-publish revised versions of your files at any time, but if you've done everything according to this guide, it shouldn't be necessary.

10 PUBLISHING TO OTHER EBOOK FORMATS

There are many other eBook formats in addition to Kindle books, and people who read eBooks will tend to have their favorites. The more formats in which you can offer your book, the more readers you stand to reach.

10.1 DIFFERENT FILE FORMATS

Among the most popular eBook formats are Palm Doc (pdb), DropBook/eReader/Palm Markup Language (PML), Mobipocket (prc), Sony Reader (lrf), Rich Text Format (rtf) and HTML. Some publishers are working on a new, open format called epub, which they hope to make the industry standard file format for all eBooks.

10.2 FILE CONVERSION TOOLS

HTML and rtf can be output by any modern word processor using the 'Save As' command and altering the file type accordingly. You can use the HTML file created in the previous chapter as an eBook file in and of itself, but if you do so, save it under a unique file name. Graphics in the file will pose problems, since rtf doesn't support them at all and HTML supports them via the use of pointers.

You can download a free PML converter program and view help files for its use at the eReader site (http://www.ereader.com), through the 'Make eBooks' link on the bottom of its home page. If the link location has changed, search the site for "make eBooks".

There are free downloads available online for converter software to create prc, pdb and epub formats. Do an internet search on "[file format] converter + free" to find them. For example, you could search on "pdb converter + free". Each program will come with its own directions and help files, but any of them should be able to accept either your formatted word processing document or the HTML

---

file created in the previous chapter for the Kindle. Again, embedded graphics will not be supported by most formats.

Thus far, I've found the lrf format, for Sony's Reader, to be problematic. I've yet to find a free converter for lrf that works well. If you want to release your books in lrf format, continue to search the internet for a converter from time to time, as new programs are being created every day.

10.3 EBOOK STORES

There are lots of eBook stores online. Some carry eBooks in various formats and others are specific to a single format. EBook stores that carry mainstream titles and indie titles in various formats are the online equivalent of independent booksellers, not tied to any big corporations. There are some sites that specialize in indie eBooks exclusively. Do an internet search on "eBook store" to find all these types of stores.

10.3.1 TYPICAL STORES

The Kindle Store on Amazon only carries Kindle books, the Sony Reader store (http://ebookstore.sony.com) only carries lrf books, the Mobipocket store (http://www.mobipocket.com) only carries prc books and the eReader store only carries PML books. Each of these stores offers different terms to authors and publishers for the display and sale of their books, with the exception of the Sony Reader store, which doesn't currently have any mechanism for authors to upload eBooks for sale.

Authors wishing to offer their books for sale in the Kindle, eReader and Mobipocket stores must agree to the site's terms and conditions, and sign up for an account with the site. See each site's terms and conditions for information about fees and royalties.

Just as the Kindle Store has its DTP for creating Kindle books, Mobipocket and eReader's stores offer free file conversion tools to create eBooks in their respective formats. The eReader converter is a downloadable program, so eBooks created with the eReader converter can be uploaded to the eReader store for sale, sold on your own website or through an independent online bookseller. As for the Kindle and Mobipocket stores, their conversion tools are online-only and are only intended for use by authors and publishers who intend to list their converted eBooks for sale on those sites. However, recall that free, self-contained prc converter programs are available online as well.

You will have to contact 'independent bookseller' –type stores individually to learn how to list your books with them, and what fees and royalties to expect.

10.4 SMASHWORDS

A recently-launched alternative to eBook stores like those discussed previously is Smashwords (http://www.smashwords.com). Smashwords only carries indie eBooks, and its mission has as much to do with growing the indie author movement as with making money on eBook sales, which is why I don't group it with other eBook stores. It's free to sign up for a Smashwords account, free to list your eBooks on the site, and there's a free, online file converter tool that will convert your .doc, .html, .rtf or .txt file to pdf, rtf, pdb, txt, or prc format (according to your preferences) all at the same time. As with Kindle books, you get to set your own selling price, but as of this writing the Smashwords store only keeps 15% of the profit from each book sold.

Furthermore, unlike the Kindle store, Smashwords allows authors and publishers to offer their eBooks for free on the site, and also can create an optional excerpt from your eBook (up to 50% of the book) for display to potential customers right in the store, so you don't have to create a separate excerpt and arrange to host it on your own. The process is considerably simpler than the Amazon DTP, too.

10.5 AUTHOR WEBSITE SALES

You can offer your eBooks for sale directly from your author website, though you'll need considerable web skills to do so since you'll have to build webpages and incorporate shopping cart functionality. If you have those skills, you already know how to do this. If not, the instructions for how to do it are outside the scope of this book.

ADELAIDE EINSTEIN - TRADE PAPERBACK, $14
❖ AMAZON - STANDARD AUTHOR ROYALTY
❖ CREATESPACE - 20% HIGHER AUTHOR ROYALTY

ADELAIDE EINSTEIN - KINDLE FORMAT, $4.99 (OR LESS - CLICK LINK TO SEE TODAY'S PRICE)
❖ AMAZON

ADELAIDE EINSTEIN - PDF, RTF, PDB, TXT, OR MOBIPOCKET, $4.99
❖ SMASHWORDS

SNOW BALL - TRADE PAPERBACK, $14
❖ AMAZON - STANDARD AUTHOR ROYALTY
❖ CREATESPACE - 20% HIGHER AUTHOR ROYALTY

SNOW BALL - KINDLE FORMAT, $5.99 (OR LESS - CLICK LINK TO SEE TODAY'S PRICE)
❖ AMAZON

SNOW BALL - PDF, RTF, PDB, TXT, OR MOBIPOCKET - $4.99
❖ SMASHWORDS

A much simpler approach is to get your eBooks set up for sale in various online stores and just link to those product pages from your author website. That's what I do on my own website, with a "Buy My Books" page containing links to all available formats.

(http://www.aprillhamilton.com/buybooks.html)

11 PROMOTION

Once upon a time, when an author sold a manuscript to a publisher, the publisher had a promotional plan and marketing budget in mind. These days the majority of authors, including those published by big, mainstream houses, are on their own to promote their books. The bad news is, promotion takes a lot of time and effort. The good news is, there are two pieces of good news. First, promotion works; so long as you're actively promoting them, your books will sell. Second, thanks to the internet, authors today have far more tools and techniques available for promotion than ever before—many of which are free.

While it's true that most mainstream-published authors are on the hook for promotion every bit as much as their indie author peers, indies still have a slightly more difficult task. For one thing, major publishers' recognized, respected brand names can be door-openers in and of themselves. For another, most brick-and-mortar bookstores will not stock books by indie authors. Finally, indie authors' work is largely excluded from the mainstream media, which is the primary source of publicity for mainstream books.

Fortunately for today's authors, it's possible to mount a successful marketing campaign completely outside of mainstream media outlets. Better still, such a marketing campaign will cost you less, and be more effective, than a traditional, mainstream media blitz.

11.1 WHAT'S THE BEST WAY TO PROMOTE?

The answer to the question, "What's the best way to promote my books?" depends on four things: time, money, skills and confidence. To be more specific, how much of each one do you have to give? In the algebra of marketing, the more you have of any one of these four commodities, the less you need of the other three. An author with lots of time and confidence will need far less money and skills than an author who's extremely shy and can't spare more than a half

---

hour a day on promotion. Ideally you should have at least a little of all four, or have enough flexibility to acquire a little bit of each.

11.2 ARE YOU CUT OUT FOR THIS?

In all honesty, for most of the Do-It-Yourself (DIY) ideas presented in this chapter you need at least basic computer and internet skills. You don't have to be able to build your own website, write software or know how to program your Tivo from your cell phone, but should be at least competent with some of the advanced features of your word processor (i.e., how to insert pictures, format tables, create flyers, etc.), familiar with how online discussion groups work, comfortable using email (including sending/receiving attachments), and able to use basic photo editing software. If your computer skills are weak or you're not very internet-literate, the majority of this chapter will be useless to you. In that case you have two options: hire a publicist, or improve your skills.

TIME

Don't assume that having a fulltime job or college courseload means you don't have enough time to effectively market your work. If you can spare just one hour a day, seven hours a week, you'll be fine. If you can scrape together ten to fifteen hours a week, you'll do great. And if you've got twenty or more hours to devote to marketing, even if you've got little money or confidence, you can still be very successful.

If you've got no time whatsoever to spare, the only way you can hope to promote your work is by hiring someone else to do it. Unless you've got a professional publicist in the family, those services will cost you, and cost you dearly. An author with no time and no money at present would probably do well to delay publication of his book until a later date, when either time or money aren't so tight.

MONEY $

It may surprise you to learn that money isn't an absolute necessity for marketing success, but just like good looks and well-connected relatives, it does tend to make things easier. Still, even if you've got no cash to spare for marketing you'll find you can use many of the promotional strategies in this Guide. If you've got around fifty bucks to invest, you'll be able to use most of the promotional strategies presented here. Only two of the techniques covered in the Guide will definitely cost you more than a hundred dollars, but there are many techniques for which it's up to you to decide how much you want to spend.

SKILLS ✗

The general heading of "skills" covers a broad range of knowledge and abilities. For purposes of this chapter, the most valuable skills you can have are those involving the computer and internet, copywriting, research, graphic art, public speaking and organization. However, with a little out-of-the-box thinking, you'll find virtually any special skills you have can become part of your promotional efforts, whether you sing, cook or rope cattle.

CONFIDENCE ✓

"Confidence," for purposes of this chapter, encompasses three things: confidence in yourself, confidence in your work, and social confidence: being comfortable in social situations involving strangers—in some cases, whole rooms full of strangers. Authors who are good at public speaking have little to worry about in this category, but even an author who's downright introverted in public social situations will be all right so long as she can interact comfortably with others online. Remember that most people expect writers to be a little shy and awkward, so don't worry you're doomed to failure if you can't be a dynamo.

11.3 A SIGNATURE LOOK

First things first: it's important to cultivate a signature look across all your promotional materials. This means using the same font(s), color scheme, and graphic elements wherever possible in everything from your business cards to your website. It doesn't mean all your book covers should look alike, however. The consistency you're after is like that employed by McDonald's, where you can tell at a glance that all their print ads, TV ads, food wrappers and even employee uniforms came from the same place.

Choose a font that's easy to read both onscreen and in print, all the way down to the 9-pt size you'll need on business cards. Choose classic or muted colors, nothing faddish. You hope to be working with your chosen font and colors for decades to come, so don't select anything that could look dated, or that you'll be sick of, in just a few years.

If you intend to have an author website—something I strongly recommend—it's a good idea to let the site set the tone for your signature look. This is because only a limited number of fonts, graphics file types, and even colors can be used on websites, whereas the possibilities in print are virtually limitless. If you start by setting up promotional materials for print and then find your chosen font, graphics or colors don't readily transfer to the web, you'll have to start all over again. Beginning with the website is even more crucial if you'll be using templates to build your site, since the fonts, colors and graphic elements will be dictated by the templates.

11.4 SYMBOL KEY

Going forward, this chapter will indicate the amount of time, money, skills and confidence required for each promotional item or technique using the clock, money bag, tool and lightning bolt symbols, as described in the table below.

COUNT	TIME 🕐	MONEY $	SKILLS 🛠	CONFIDENCE ⟋
0	N/A – at least a little time is always needed	Free!	Amish person can do it	Agoraphobic hermit can do it
1	≤ 1 hour	≤ $10 US	Person who knows what a computer, the internet and a word processor are can do it	Mildly insecure, but curious, loner can do it
2	≤ 2 hours	≤ $20 US	A person with basic computer, internet & word processing skills can do it	Person with average written and verbal communication skills who feels OK about self can do it
3	≤ 3 hours	≤ $30 US	Person with moderate computer, internet & word processing skills can do it	Person with above-average written and verbal communication skills and strong self-esteem can do it
4	≤ 4 hours	≤ $40 US	Person with advanced computer, internet & word processing skills can do it	Person comfortable with public speaking can do it
5	> 4 hours	> $40 US	Bill Gates can do it	Donald Trump can do it

Where amount of time, money, skills or confidence required can vary, a range is provided.

11.5 TRADITIONAL TACTICS

Even in today's technology-driven world, some of the tried and true marketing strategies of the past can still be the most effective, depending on your individual needs and circumstances.

11.5.1 THE PRESS KIT

A press kit is a collection of information about you and your work, intended to cast both in the most positive, interesting light possible. A press kit intended to promote a book may include one-sheets, press releases, editorial review reprints, article reprints, an enlarged copy of the book cover printed on glossy paper stock, promotional giveways (i.e., bookmarks, pencils, mugs, etc. with the name of the book printed on them), and/or a printed excerpt from the book. It will be up to you to decide which items make the most sense for you to include in your own press kits, based on the amount of time, money, skills and confidence you have. Some of the items are self-explanatory, and others are covered individually in this chapter.

When a mainstream author with a large marketing budget has a new book to promote, a press kit will be sent, along with a review copy of the book, to every major media outlet in an effort to generate buzz and editorial reviews. This approach would be a huge waste for an indie author, since the great majority of mainstream media outlets won't even consider reviewing your book or publicizing its author. Nevertheless, a targeted press kit will come in handy when you line up a review, article or interview because it cuts down on the interviewer/journalist's work by providing a stack of reference material, quotes, etc. about you and your work. Sending a press kit in advance allows you to influence the information that will be served up for public consumption.

Be careful not to overstuff your press kits. Keep them specific, to the extent possible, and include only the most relevant and recent items. You may have accumulated thirty press releases over the past few years, but that doesn't mean you should include all of them. Remember to tailor each press kit to the wants and needs of the recipient, to provide only the most useful or desirable content. You don't want the recipient to open up your kit and feel so overwhelmed by the sheer volume of it that she tosses it directly into the recycle bin.

As a rule of thumb, you can assume a basic press kit will include your author one-sheet, a one-sheet for your most recent book in print, your most recent press release (or two, if both are dated within the past 6 months), and if desired, one promotional item. Article reprints and book excerpts can be included if the recipient has expressed specific interest in them, but should otherwise be left out because they most likely won't be read anyway.

11.5.2 THE "ONE-SHEET"

🕐🕐🕐	$	⚒⚒ - ⚒⚒⚒	No Confidence!

A "one-sheet" is a single sheet of paper, printed on one side only, that summarizes a person, product or service for marketing purposes. The one-sheet is the backbone of a press kit, so if you're going to send out press kits, read this section carefully.

You'll need some time and basic computer skills to create your own one-sheets, more advanced skills if you want to do anything fancy, but the only expense involved is for paper and ink when you print them. You don't need much in the way of confidence either, since you'll just be copying and pasting in pre-existing text and picture items.

In terms of layout there are no hard-and-fast rules, but it's common practice to position text and pictures in the same way typically seen in newsletters. The content depends on what you're promoting. A one-sheet can be used to promote you as an author in the general sense, or as a promotional tool for an individual book you've published. It's a good idea to create a separate one-sheet for each of your books and one more for you as an author. Don't use one-sheets to publicize publication of a poem, piece of short fiction or the like, as there's not enough to say about such a piece to fill out a whole one-sheet.

The example at left is a dummy one-sheet for promotion of a specific book, and it was created using a newsletter template in Microsoft Publisher. Microsoft Word and most other word processing programs also have newsletter templates you can use as a starting point, and any desktop publishing program will have such templates as well.

The book's title and author's name appear in the large block at the top left of the page. An image of the book's cover would be inserted below the title block, followed by a large text block about the book. The large text block will generally contain the same text as your book cover jacket copy, and if there's room, other promotional details such as review blurbs, available sales figures, etc. One review blurb can be highlighted in the large text block, or if you don't have review blurbs yet, you can quote your best line from the jacket copy.

Information about where to buy the book, and if desired, a copy of your ISBN bar code and number, appear in a separate block at the end of the large text block. The ISBN bar code is there for retailers who want to order your book in quantities for resale. Even if you don't intend to send one-sheets to booksellers, remember that you want your one-sheets to look every bit as legitimate as those prepared by professional publicists, so keeping the ISBN block is a good idea if there's any way you can manage it. You can capture an image of the ISBN barcode by scanning it off your book, then cropping the image and saving the file as a .jpg or .gif image on your computer. To the right is a sidebar block for the author's biography, with the author's photo at the top, brief biography in the middle, and contact/website information at the bottom.

The same basic layout can be used for a one-sheet intended to promote an author in general, not a specific book, by reversing the content and eliminating the ISBN/where to buy block. In that case, you'd use the large text block at the left to provide a more detailed author biography and the sidebar to list some titles of your published work (books, short stories, articles, etc.). The picture above the large text block would be your author photo, and the one above the sidebar would be eliminated.

You can get a little creative with color and fonts in your one-sheet, but don't go crazy. The purpose of your one-sheet is not to dazzle the viewer with your awesome artistic skills, but to clearly, concisely describe yourself or your book. Resist the urge to insert a bunch of clip art on the page, and remember to stick with the 'signature look' you're trying to establish.

There's a general rule of three in graphic art: no more than three different fonts or three different color elements should be used on the same page. Since you should already be working with a single, signature font, limit yourself to fonts from the same font family, or at least fonts that are very similar in appearance to your signature font. Try using your signature font formatted in two or three different ways (i.e., italicized, different sizes, shadowed, embossed, etc.). With respect to color elements, such as the watermarks in the dummy one-sheet, it's safest to limit yourself to just one color. If you want to go with more than one color, choose complementary colors (opposites on the color wheel, i.e., yellow and purple) or different shades of the same color (i.e., sky blue, denim blue, navy blue, etc), again, in keeping with your signature look.

When you find a layout you like, stick with that layout for all your one-sheets. Remember: consistency is key to your marketing success.

11.5.3 AUTHOR PHOTO

☺☺	Free! - $$$$$	No Skills! - ✗✗✗	✐ ✐

An author photo is needed not only for one-sheets in your press kit, but pretty much anywhere you want or need your likeness to appear: flyers, book covers, website, blog, online profiles, etc. etc. It's a good idea to get one picture you're happy with and use it for everything, as most well-known, mainstream authors do. This lends that all-important consistency to your promotional efforts and helps to establish your likeness as a recognizable presence in readers' minds.

This gets two lightning bolts for confidence because you need to feel comfortable before the camera. A self-conscious author is a nervous author, and not likely to take a good picture. If you have average skills with a digital camera and know how to use photo editing software, you can go totally DIY, for free. So long as you've got a mirror in a room with good lighting, or know how to use your digital camera's timer function, you can even take the picture yourself.

The author photo that appears on my website and in most of my online profiles is a picture I took myself, aiming the camera into a mirror. I loaded the photo to my computer, cropped it, adjusted its color and contrast settings, then saved it in various formats for use online and in print. You can get a friend or family member to help with taking the picture or editing it also. Remember to save a smaller, 'compressed' version for use online, in .jpg or .gif format, with a file size of no more than 100KB.

If you're not so strong in the camera or photo editing areas, and you don't have any friends or family to help, you will have to pay a professional photographer to take the picture for you. Even so, it doesn't have to cost a fortune. Sears, JC Penney, and even WalMart have portrait services at affordable prices. At the other end of the pricing scale are boutique photographers, whose services can run into the thousands of dollars.

As you make your calls to get pricing information, make sure the photographer or studio will provide a copy of the portrait in digital format (.jpg or .gif file provided on a CD, DVD or via email). Also ensure the photographer or studio will provide a 'compressed' copy of your chosen pose for use on web pages: a smaller version of the picture in a .jpg or .gif file no larger than 100KB.

If you're paying for the photos, go through your books and find an appealing photo of an author to show the photographer, to give him or her some idea of the look and pose you're going for. This will save time and money on rejected poses later.

One last thing...here's a tip I've heard for anyone who worries about the "wattle" effect (loose neck skin) in a portrait. Try posing with your chin on your hands, or with one fist supporting your chin or jaw, so that your hands or arm conceal your neck.

11.5.4 PRESS RELEASES

🕔 - 🕔🕔	$-$$$$$	⚒⚒	ϟϟϟ

Press releases add information about your recent activities and accolades to the press kit, and can also be featured on your author website. A press release is an announcement distributed to media outlets as a means of quickly passing along information from a single, controlled channel. The variability in cost reflected above comes in press release distribution: you can use a free distribution service or a paid service. Tour dates, airline luggage restrictions, CEO hirings and firings, celebrity child adoptions, corporate bankruptcies, and much, much more come to the public's attention via press releases. Those deemed most newsworthy get 'picked up' by the Associated Press (AP), and from there are reported in newspapers, magazines and on websites all over the world.

Press releases can be an easy, low-cost way to publicize your work, but it takes confidence and above-average written communication skills to craft a good one. You may write amazing prose, but the type of writing called for in this instance is more journalistic and on the face of it, there's nothing very newsworthy about books or authors. Books are written and published every day, there's nothing Earth-shattering, or even interesting, about that.

For an author, press release success requires an angle: you must be saying something interesting, relevant, surprising or even shocking in your press release if you want any news outlets to report on it. This doesn't mean you should lie or fill your press release with empty hype, however. In fact, doing so will not only not help with your publicity campaign, it will damage your credibility and make it that much harder to get any press coverage in the future. Rather, you must wait until you've got something genuinely interesting, relevant, surprising or shocking to say about yourself or your book. Don't worry, this isn't as hopeless as it sounds.

There are five main junctures at which it's common to put out a press release about a book: when the publishing contract is signed, when the book is published, when there are impressive sales figures to report, when the book or author wins an award, and when the book or author does something interesting. As an indie author you will lose out on juncture #1 because there are no contracts involved in the publication of your books, but the other four junctures are wide open to you. The 'book is published' press release doesn't require further clarification, but the last three do.

The Impressive Sales Press Release

Sales figures on indie books are typically modest at best, nonexistent at worst. However, if your book is being sold by Amazon.com, impressive sales figures aren't entirely out of reach. Amazon lists its books under hundreds of categories, and maintains 'bestseller' lists in every one of those categories, constantly updating sales rankings as books are sold. While it may be absolute pie in the sky for you to think your indie book will make the New York Times bestseller list, it's not all that farfetched to imagine your book earning a slot in the top 100 of one of Amazon's many specific book categories. The publishing industry literati are cognizant of the fact that Amazon's bestseller lists are very specific, and therefore being #1 in one of those specific categories is a far cry from being #1 on the New York Times bestseller list for overall fiction or nonfiction, but this isn't so apparent to the general public.

As of this writing my novel Adelaide Einstein is ranked at #778,432 in overall sales of books at Amazon, which is nothing to merit a press release. In the Kindle store it's ranked considerably higher in overall book sales, at #23,039, but this is still nothing to brag about. However, in 'Motherhood' it's #26:

> **Amazon.com Sales Rank:** #23,039 in Kindle Store (See <u>Bestsellers in Kindle Store</u>)
> Popular in this category: (<u>What's this?</u>)
> #26 in <u>Kindle Store</u> > <u>Books</u> > <u>Parenting & Families</u> > <u>Family Relationships</u> > <u>Motherhood</u>

The #26 sales slot still isn't quite impressive enough to build a press release on, but when Adelaide occupied the #10 spot, I definitely seized the opportunity to trumpet my success. It's newsworthy when any book gets up into the top 10 on bestseller lists, but even more so for an indie book because indie books have a notorious reputation for slow sales and difficulty in reaching an audience. Any indie book that makes it into an Amazon top 10 bestseller list is deemed exceptional, and its presence in that list is likewise deemed newsworthy.

If it's possible for you to work in some kind of surprising or interesting angle that makes the sales figure even more impressive, so much the better. In the case of my Adelaide press release, I reported that the manuscript had advanced no further than the semifinal round in the Amazon Breakthrough Novel Award contest, yet went on to become an Amazon #10 bestseller after I published it independently.

In order to take advantage of Amazon sales rankings your book must be available for sale on Amazon.com. Also, as you've no doubt guessed, the more categories in which your book is listed, the more chances you have at hitting the upper reaches of one or more Amazon bestseller lists.

When adding your book to Amazon's sales listings, be sure to list it under as many categories as you reasonably can, up to the limit of categories you're allowed. "Reasonably can" is a phrase that's open to interpretation, but avoid stretching the truth too far. For example, Adelaide Einstein is a comic, hen-lit novel; listings under General Fiction, Women's Fiction and Comic Fiction are obvious, but I also listed it under Motherhood because a great deal of the story centers on the heroine's relationships with her kids. I wouldn't list it under Mystery, Sci Fi, Fantasy, or Romance, however. You must balance your desire for more category listings against the risk of alienating readers who could end up buying your book under false pretenses—and may never forgive you for it.

When publishing for the Kindle, adding your book to categories is all part of the publication process. If you've published your trade paperbacks through an outlet such as CreateSpace, iUniverse, Lulu, etc., the publisher will generally ask you to specify listing categories before they submit the title for sale on Amazon.

The Award Winner Press Release

This one is fairly self-explanatory, but it's worth mentioning that the award ought to be directly related to your writing. In other words, if your book wins the "Tri-County Women In Love" award for excellence in Romance books, go right ahead and whip out a press release. Likewise, if you win a "Community Mentor" award for your volunteer work teaching creative writing to disadvantaged kids, because the award is directly related to your involvement in writing this is also worthy of a press release. However, if you win the "Cub Scout Den Leader of the Year" award, unless your books are about Scouting, there's no obvious relationship between the award and your writing, and no justification for a press release.

The 'Something Interesting' Press Release

You can have a 'something interesting' press release anytime you want: just do something interesting! This is the sort of thing which, in the mainstream media, is commonly known as a "publicity stunt," but it doesn't have to be anything as obvious (or expensive) as a staged Martian invasion or pie-eating contest. Many of the promotional activities covered in this Guide, such as speaking engagements, book signings and interviews are interesting enough to warrant press release coverage. Volunteerism related to literacy, involvement in community activities related to the subject matter of your book, and participation in library or book fair events are just a few of the many other opportunities.

Anatomy Of A Press Release

Acceptable press release format is standardized, and fixed in terms of layout. A sample press release is shown here to illustrate. At the top left, the source of the press release is listed. Beneath that is the press release headline, followed by the author name and date. Next comes an optional sub-headline, in italics. Beneath that is the main body of the press release. While this isn't shown in the sample, the release may also include a final paragraph with a brief description of the company or person about whose product or activity the press release is written.

Contact details are listed at the bottom, so that anyone who would like to contact you for more information can easily do so. Traditionally, the legend "<END>" or three pound signs ("###") are inserted at the bottom to indicate the end of the transmission, a holdover from the days of teletype machines, but this is becoming less common.

You can find many, many more examples online by doing an internet search for "press release", or clicking the "news" link at any major corporation's website.

Source, Byline And Contact

By default, the source, byline name (the name listed for "By:") and contact for the press release will be you. While having a source, author and contact name other than your own is desirable, since it won't be so obvious you're tooting your own horn, do not make up a name just for this purpose. Remember that the press release is supposed to be a reliable source of information, and therefore the source, author and contact person must be real, accessible entities.

If you write your books under a pen name this is a no-brainer because your press releases about Joe Pen Name can be written by you under your real name. If not, an easy way to get a legitimate source, byline and contact other than your own name is to have someone else publish your press release. Consider swapping press release duties with a writer friend; not only will each of you get a legitimate source/byline/contact name different from your own, you may find it's easier to write about someone else than it would be to write about yourself.

If you can't do press release swaps, another option is to go with a different source and/or byline name while still keeping your own name as the contact person. When a press release is published by a distribution company, that company's name is the source of the press release. Free and low-cost online press release distribution services are covered in more detail in the Distributing Your Press Releases section of this chapter.

As for byline, if your website or blog has a name other than your author name, you can use the name of the website/blog as the byline on two conditions: first, you must post the press release at the byline website/blog when it's published, and second, you still must provide your real name and details in the "Contact" section. In my case, my author website name is the same as my author name, which is the same as my legal name, which doesn't help me. However, my blog name is IndieAuthor, so I could list IndieAuthor as the byline if I desired.

Don't overthink the source/byline/contact stuff, though. If the content of your press release is newsworthy and interesting, so long as the source/byline/contact information is legitimate, it won't matter much that you wrote it yourself. Your goal is to drive traffic to your website, blog or event with the ultimate purpose of selling books, not to convince the general public that you've got a ton of money to spend on publicity. Listing your own name for source/byline/contact won't kill the credibility of your press releases, but sales hype or dishonesty will.

Content Of A Press Release

While the press release is a promotional tool, it should not read like sales copy. You're writing an announcement, conveying factual information that your intended audience would want to know regardless of whether or not it helps you sell books. If you follow the guidelines already given for the appropriate timing of press releases, you should have no trouble avoiding the dreaded, baldfaced sales pitch in press release clothing because you won't be writing a press release unless you've got something newsworthy to write about. Still, you need to avoid the hard sell. Consider the following two examples.

GALE ADAMS THRILLS IN NEW THRILLER

Don't start reading *Mercy Me*, author Gale Adams' terrific new book, until you're ready to stay up all night with the lights on! In this fact-based thriller, a serial killer is on the loose and private investigator Caitlin McElroy has reason to believe a modern-day Dr. Frankenstein is at work in her sleepy New England town of Cordley. As tensions and suspicions divide the once close-knit community, McElroy finds facts and evidence piling up against the one person no one else would ever suspect…

AUTHOR GALE ADAMS REVISITS "CORDLEY FRANKENSTEIN" CASE

Thirty-seven years ago a serial killer terrorized the small New England town of Cordley, abducting a dozen citizens in as many weeks. The killer's basement charnel house, where he dismembered and re-assembled the bodies of his victims, was eventually discovered, but no charges were ever brought in the bizarre case. Based on newly-discovered evidence and painstaking research, author Gale Adams advances a shocking and plausible theory in her new book, *Mercy Me*…

The first example reads like jacket copy, whereas the second could pass for a news item. The book sales pitch couldn't be any more obvious in the first example, but in the second the book-promotion aspect of the release seems almost incidental, with the primary focus given over to re-examination of an unsolved murder case.

When you write a press release, try to get into the third-person mindset of a reporter. Identify the most newsworthy aspect of your press release and focus on that. Bring in additional facts and quotations only in support of the main focus. If you don't have quotes from outside sources, "interview" yourself.

Instead of writing, "As a former resident of Cordley, Adams had long been troubled by the Frankenstein case and was even acquainted with one of the victims," consider, 'Asked why she chose to write about this particular case, Adams replied, "I lived in Cordley at the time the murders took place, and I was even acquainted with one of the victims. The affected families never got any closure or justice, and I wanted to do something about it.'" Quotes are a good way to keep an active voice in the narrative while revealing more about yourself.

Distributing Your Press Releases

The easiest way to distribute your press releases is through a service. An internet search on "press release" will turn up many such services, and two that distribute online, at no charge, are www.prlog.org and www.openpr.com . You can go to either site and enter your press release information online, review it in a print-preview mode, and then release it to all the major online media outlets (i.e., Google News, Yahoo!, etc.). At the prlog site, you can even sign up for your own, free 'press room', where you can keep track of all your press releases from a single location.

Even if you use an online distribution service, you should still prepare your press release in advance. This allows you to spend as much time as you like writing and revising the release before publishing it, and also gives you an original version for archive purposes. When you're ready to submit, all you need do is copy and paste from your saved file.

The alternative to a distribution service is good old-fashioned elbow grease: look up the fax numbers of all the media outlets you'd like to hit and fax your press release to each of them. The term "media outlets" includes newspapers, magazines, radio stations, TV shows and websites. You can find their fax numbers by looking them up online and clicking the "contact" link on each website. You can also fax your press releases to The Associated Press, which is the granddaddy of all news outlets. Go to http://www.ap.org and click the "Contact AP" link. You'll be taken to a page where you can look up contact information for the bureau office closest to you.

11.5.5 EDITORIAL REVIEWS

☺ - ☺☺☺☺	$-$$$	✗✗	✎ ✎

Most industry experts agree books are sold on word of mouth, so reviews are very important. Don't be discouraged by the fact that mainstream media outlets are rarely willing to review indie books, because polls have shown reviews from professional book critics don't carry much weight with the average reader. Reviews that matter to readers are reviews from other readers: people who read for the joy of it, and post reviews as a public service, not because they're getting paid to do so.

The scale provided above is for soliciting a single editorial review. The time factor can vary widely, as the first part of the task is locating likely reviewers and writing to them to solicit a review. Locating and contacting 1-4 candidates may take just an hour or less, so if time is tight you can limit your efforts to that one hour per day until you feel you've got enough reviews.

The expense factor varies also, depending on your cost to buy a copy of your book and mail it to the reviewer, plus the number of review copies sent. The only skills involved are basic letter- and email-writing, and you only need as much confidence as it takes to write and send your solicitation letters and emails.

Why Should You Solicit?

Editorial reviews have many uses beyond the press kit. You can pull quotes from them to use as book cover blurbs and press release fodder. Positive Amazon reviews help to raise your book's profile, and therefore sales, on Amazon. Reviews can be reprinted on your blog or website. Lastly, and most importantly, editorial reviews appearing in publications or on popular websites are among the best advertisements you can get, and all they cost you is some time and the price of one copy of your book.

Whom Should You Solicit?

If your book is listed for sale on Amazon, try some Amazon Top Reviewers. Go to the Amazon Top Reviewers information page to access the reviewers' profiles (http://www.amazon.com/review/top-reviewers.html). Each profile will usually say something about the reviewer's taste in books and his or her review policy. You want to find reviewers who like your kind of book, have indicated they're open to accepting submissions for review, and have their email address listed in their profile. Where a given reviewer hasn't specifically said they will not accept submissions for review, if they've listed an email address you can take that as a sign of receptiveness: contact them.

Another good source for editorial reviews is the LibraryThing online community (http://www.librarything.com). This is a site where people list and rate their own books, and participate in discussion groups about books. Go to LibraryThing, click the "Groups" tab, and browse the discussions till you find fans of your type of book. You can click the member name on any discussion group post to view the poster's member profile, and if an email address is listed you can proceed with a solicitation email.

Blogs are also a great source for potential reviewers. Lots of book fanatics blog, and there are many who specialize in book reviews. Do a Google blog search for "books," "book reviews," "reading" or the like and browse till you find some likely candidates who've listed their email address on their profile. To do a Google blog search, go to http://www.google.com and click the "more" link. In the drop-down list, select "blogs". Now run your Google search as usual, and Google will limit its result set to blogs.

While most large newspapers and magazines have a policy against reviewing self-published books, your local papers and community magazines are likely to be more receptive. Such publications are particularly interested in news and events related to the communities they serve, so a book from a local author is right up their alley. Get a copy of the publication you're considering, first to make sure they publish book reviews, and secondly to see if the publication's likely audience is a group that would be at all likely to buy your book. For example, a publication that's aimed at seniors or families with small children may not be the best outlet for a review of your steamy, vampire-erotic thriller. If the publication seems like a match, call their office or visit their website to get a phone number or email address for the reviewer you'd like to contact.

Finally, sign up for a free account at http://www.bookconnector.com. Once signed up, you can search BookConnector's extensive database to locate editorial reviewers who have expressed an interest in your specific type of book. You can also find listings for bookstores, libraries and other venues receptive to hosting live readings and book signing events.

How Should You Solicit?

When soliciting for reviews, keep your phone calls or emails short, polite and on-point. Email is preferable to phone calls, as there's no risk of catching the reviewer at a bad time and you can take as long as you like in wordsmithing your solicitation. Greet the reviewer by name, spelled correctly. If you can't tell the reviewer's gender from the name, you can fudge it by omitting any gender-specific titles (Mr., Mrs., Ms.) in your greeting. In the body of your email, explain how you found the reviewer, why you think your book will appeal to the reviewer, include a link to a free excerpt if you've made one available online, then close by asking if you may send free review copy, and if so, where you should send it. Here's an example:

Dear Lesley Drummond:
I've found your book reviews in the Daily Bugle to be well-written and insightful. Because you seem to especially enjoy true-crime thrillers, I hope you might consider reviewing my new novel, Mercy Me. The novel centers on the real life, unsolved 'Cordley Frankenstein' case, in which 12 Cordley Township, New Hampshire residents

were murdered over a period of 3 months in 1970. Based on extensive research and interviews with many of those involved in the case, I've developed a plausible, if shocking, new theory about the killer's identity. That theory forms the basis of Mercy Me. If you'd like to take a look at it, I've posted an excerpt from the novel online at http://www.galeadams.com/MMexcerpt.pdf. May I send you a review copy of the novel, and if so, where should I send it?

Thanks For Your Consideration,
Gale Adams

Notice that the solicitation does not merely parrot jacket copy, or sales hype of any kind. Rather, it states why you're contacting the reviewer and only provides details relevant to that specific reviewer's area of interest. If you were soliciting Dollmaker's Monthly for a review of your Young Adult novel about a doll that comes to life, you wouldn't need to provide a whole plot synopsis—the mention that it's about a doll that comes to life would be enough to pique their interest.

Because you will be sending out many, many solicitations, it's a good idea to save a boilerplate version of your solicitation, or a few different boilerplate versions. When you need to solicit, paste the most appropriate boilerplate into a new email and customize it for the individual reviewer.

11.5.6 ARTICLES

Articles you've written are additional press kit candidates, as they can show your range as a writer or your ability as a researcher. Aside from press kit considerations, writing and distributing articles is a great way to build up readership and drive more traffic to your website, blog, and ultimately, your books. Writing articles for print media is a Traditional Tactic, while online articles are New Media.

Many writers blog, but a blog entry is not the same thing as an article. An article in this context contains informative, useful content, whereas blog entries can consist of amusing observations, editorial essays and anecdotes.

Article Content

What can you write about? If you've done research for your writing, you've probably amassed all kinds of interesting factoids that may be of interest to the general public. In the course of education and experience, you may have developed particularly keen editing skills, or an uncanny ear for dialog. Maybe you don't consider yourself a subject area expert in writing prose, but you're the person everyone calls when they need help with the advanced formatting features of their word processing program, or when they can't figure out how to set up an Amazon author profile. Maybe your fellow writers shower you with praise for your insightful and thoughtful manuscript reviews and notes.

Or perhaps you feel you have no expertise whatsoever to speak of, but you frequently attend writers' seminars and events, and can report on your experiences there. If you've got anything of interest to share, you've got another promotional tool in your belt.

Article Distribution

You can post your written articles in .pdf or .html format on your website or blog, though a blog isn't necessarily the best way to go if your articles may be lengthy or could include illustrations. Pasting all that text directly into the pages of your website isn't such a good idea either, because it clutters up your site and your articles will be a lot harder on the eyes than if they were presented in typical, black print on a white background format. It's preferable to provide a link to each article, which can then be accessed as a standalone document.

Another option is one of the many public websites that solicit for submissions on an ongoing basis. Some of them even pay for the articles they print. While sites like www.payperpost.com and www.associatedcontent.com claim you can actually make a living writing articles for their sites, in reality it's not too likely. Another site, www.squidoo.com, doesn't promise you can make a living writing for them but they do offer the option of donating your earnings to the charity of your choice. Even so, forget about the money because it's not going to amount to all that much. Your reason for doing this should be twofold: first, to help out your fellow authors with information they can use, and second, to increase your visibility in the crowded world of authorship.

Check out the sites I've mentioned here, and also do an internet search for "articles" to find more sites to consider. It's a good idea to settle on a single content site for your articles, partly in order to increase your earnings potential (however small it may be) and partly to raise your profile as an article author. If you write six articles for the same content site, you've got a body of work there. If you publish two articles on three different sites however, you may come off looking like a dabbler.

11.5.7 APPEARANCES

① - ①①①	$$$$$	No Skills!	✎ ✎ ✎ ✎

A live appearance can be something as humble as giving a career day talk at the local high school, something as prestigious as being a speaker at a writers' retreat, or any number of things in between. A speaking engagement merits a press release, and every audience member is a potential purchaser of your books, so unless you're painfully shy don't pass up any writing-related live appearance opportunities.

In fact, drumming up such opportunities yourself is an excellent way to promote your books. Whatever you've written about, chances are there's a group or club out there interested in, or dedicated to, that very thing.

What To Speak About

You can talk about your experiences as a writer or the content of your books, or you can develop a talk based on an article you've written. Whatever you choose to speak about, tailor your talk to the group. For example, a writers' group may want to hear about your technique or experiences in publishing, whereas a book club (readers) will likely be more interested in the content of your book.

Where To Speak

You can quickly obtain a long list of bookstores and clubs interested in hosting author talks by signing up for a free account at www.BookConnector.com. Once your account is set up, you can do a search of the site's extensive database, specifying details about your geographic location and types of venues desired to narrow the results.

Contact your local public and university libraries, and also consider soliciting clubs and groups with a specific connection to your work. For example, if your historical fiction novel deals with the Civil War, you might approach Civil War re-enacters. If wilderness survival or wildlife conservation plays a major part in your book, you can reach out to the local chapter of the Sierra Club. Apply some creative thinking, and you're sure to come up with many options of your own.

If you're good at public speaking, don't hesitate to make those calls and volunteer to speak. Libraries and clubs are always looking for ways to keep things interesting for their members and visitors, and guest speakers are a popular solution.

11.5.8 LIVE READINGS

☺ - ☺☺☺	$$$$	No Skills!	⚡ ⚡ ⚡ ⚡

Libraries, independent bookstores and community fairs are all good venues for live readings from your books, as are book club meetings. Just as you would for appearances, you'll need to make calls and send emails to solicit for readings. You can also make some calls to local coffeehouses and bars to locate open mic nights, when anyone is allowed to go up onstage to read or speak. It may be possible for you to make serial appearances, gradually working through your book from beginning to end.

It's easy enough to look up libraries, bookstores, coffee houses and bars, but you may have to do an internet search or check with your local community center to find out where and when book clubs and writers' groups meet in your area, and when community fairs will be held. Try searching on [your town name] + "book club".

Doing the reading only costs your time, but it's a good idea to have copies of your book(s) available for sales and signings on the spot, as well as some cash to make change if you'd prefer not to accept checks, and this is where the expense comes in.

11.5.9 BOOK SIGNINGS

☺ - ☺☺☺	$$$$	No Skills!	⚡ ⚡ ⚡ ⚡

Book signings can be held at a bookstore, library, community fair, or anywhere else people congregate—so long as you get any necessary permissions or permits ahead of time. You can rent a booth at a community fair and work the "local author" angle. You can work out a deal with your church to set up a table at their rummage sale in exchange for a share of your profits. One writer I know has an arrangement with public libraries in her area, which invite her to do readings and book signings in exchange for 10% of her sales at the events.

It may surprise you to know that even the big chain bookstores may welcome you to do a signing event, but they will require you to provide all the books you intend to sell and will still want their cut of each sale (typically 40% of the retail price). Just call the store manager to make your inquiries. Note that the manager may want to meet you or even read your book before agreeing to host your event.

11.5.10 THE MEDIA TIE-IN

☺ - ☺☺☺	Free! - $$$$$	No Skills! - ✖✖✖	✄ - ✄✄✄✄

A media tie-in is connecting yourself or your work to something already being widely reported in the media. The connection is not literal, nor does it even necessarily reference the larger story you're connecting with directly. Rather, the tie-in is more about timing promotional materials and activities strategically, to capitalize on buzz and publicity already out there in the marketplace. Don't think of tie-ins as single, self-contained events. Tying in to larger media stories should be an ongoing process, something you do as a regular part of your promotional efforts.

The variance in cost and skills is due to the variety of methods you can use to establish your media tie-in, and depends on how much of the effort will be DIY versus paying for outside services. Confidence requirements vary based on the strength of the connection between yourself or your book and the story you're tying to. For example, if your book is a fictionalized account of events leading up to the Bay of Pigs conflict, it's easy to tie in to the anniversary of that event, as well as any news being reported about Castro's government. However, when the subject matter of your book is related to events in the news, though not truly about those events, some salesmanship is needed.

What To Tie In

Keep an eye out for media coverage of people, places and things in your book. By "people," I don't mean specific characters—unless those characters are real-life historical figures. I'm talking more about their professions, major interests, ethnic identities, socio-economic position, and so forth.

Novels that feature adult children caring for their elderly parents can be tied in to media stories about caring for the elderly, or the increasing size of the elderly population. A book of essays about various jobs you've been fired from can tie in to media stories about layoffs and employment data.

Also be on the lookout for news stories about the publishing industry or the arts that affect you, as an author, personally. If the small press you've published with is bought out by a larger publisher, you can write an insider-view article about how the merger will affect you and your books. When Amazon released its Kindle eBook reader, there was an opportunity for authors to weigh in with their thoughts on how this new technology might affect them and their future work. In such a piece you may not have a reason to mention your book in the body of the article at all, but you can still include a link to your website or list your book's title in the author summary typically given at the end of articles (i.e., Matt Pulley, a writer based in Spokane, WA is the author of four novels. His latest, The Craven Ones, was published in January of this year. For more information about Matt and his work, visit www.mattpulley.com).

Do not attempt a media tie-in unless the connection you're establishing between yourself/your work and the reported subject is clear and legitimate, because that connection cannot be stated directly: it must be inferred by your audience. In a book tie-in, your goal is to draw the attention of people who are already interested in the topics, places or types of people you've written about, then inform them about a book that will provide more coverage of those topics, places or types of people. In an author tie-in, you want to comment about current events of interest from a position of special knowledge or expertise, adding your informed opinion to the body of information available about an event or topic.

How To Tie In

Most tie-ins take the form of articles or press releases, but authors can tie in to community events by making live appearances as well. For example, the author of a book that prominently features knitting can tie in to a local arts and crafts fair by setting up a booth to sell and sign her books at the fair. She can also donate some copies of her books as raffle giveaways for the fair in exchange for a mention in the fair's printed program. Another possibility is volunteering to give knitting lessons to beginners, or to give demonstrations of advanced techniques, either from her booth or from a performance stage, if applicable.

My own community hosts an annual folk music festival each spring. Authors whose books involve folk music, or cultures strongly associated with folk music (i.e., Appalachian culture is strongly associated with bluegrass, devotional and banjo music), could tie in to this festival. As with any live appearances, a supply of books should be on hand to sell and sign.

Events related to literacy, books or libraries are no-brainer tie-ins for any author. In addition to live appearances, consider writing an article for your local paper (or community newsletter). For library-centered events, you can write about what that library means (or has meant) to you, both as an author and a community resident. Literacy events invite you to wax philosophic about the state of literacy in today's changing world from an author's perspective. Book fairs are also obvious tie-ins, regardless of the subject matter of your book, as are anniversary celebrations for local, independent bookstores you frequent.

On a more personal note, be on the lookout for media coverage of places or topics that concern your development as a writer. When the little neighborhood shop where you used to sit and scribble in your journal for hours on end celebrates an anniversary or goes out of business, it's an occasion worthy of remembrance—and an article or essay from you. Similarly, if a teacher who mentored or strongly influenced your writing is about to retire or receive some kind of service award, volunteer to speak at the event, to share how his tutelage helped make you the writer you are today. Teachers rarely get the thanks or credit they deserve, so your words will be greatly appreciated.

If you aren't comfortable with public speaking, or you can't afford the time or money to travel to the fete, make some inquiries to see if any type of event program or memory book is being compiled. If so, you can offer to send a brief letter or essay for inclusion, along with your author details. You can also just write a letter to the editor of your local paper to sing your teacher's praises.

11.5.11 HANDOUTS

◷ - ◷◷	Free! - $$$$$	⚒⚒ - ⚒⚒⚒	ϟ - ϟϟϟ

Handouts are printed cards or bookmarks you can keep on hand at all times to hand out to anyone who inquires about your writing. The confidence required to actually hand the cards out varies, depending on whether you're whipping them out in a face-to-face social encounter, or simply stacking them on the table in a shop or at a book signing. Handouts you make yourself cost very little, but take considerable time to design and print. Office supply stores with a print shop on the premises can usually print promotional cards in various sizes, colors and the like, but you will have to provide "camera-ready" art in an electronic file and will also have to order a minimum quantity of your chosen card.

You can print your own bookmarks on card stock at home, and you may find your word processing, photo editor, or desktop publishing program provides a bookmark template. You can find many template choices online by searching on "bookmark template". If you own the rights to your book's cover art, use that cover art on the bookmarks. If not, try to approximate the look of the cover with similar clipart, colors, and the same font. Be sure to include your website address and/or where-to-buy information.

Handout cards can be printed on business card stock or postcard stock, both of which are available at any office supply store. If you buy Avery brand paper stock, you can look up project templates at www.avery.com based on your paper stock's product number. Some of the available templates will be free, others will be downloadable for a fee. Most generic, or 'store-brand' paper stock will also be labeled with the Avery equivalent, so you can still find a template that will work on the Avery website. Also try the website of your printer manufacturer (i.e., HP, Canon, etc.) for projects and templates.

Business cards will be easier to carry around in your purse or wallet, but the postcard may be a better handout for live appearances since it can feature your book's cover (or an approximation) on one side and jacket cover copy on the back. If you have the appropriate paper craft tools and skills, you can even make a bookmark part of your postcard design and perforate or score the card ahead of time to make the bookmark easy to remove.

11.5.12 MERCHANDISE

☺ - ☺☺☺☺☺	$ - $$$$$	✸ - ✸✸✸	No Confidence!

Merchandise such as t-shirts, tote bags, magnets, pencils, mugs, mousepads and the like, printed with art and/or text, are excellent promotional tools. Many of these items can be made at home using your own computer and printer, while others must be ordered from an outside vendor. The time, money and skills involved all depend on how much you plan to do yourself, and how much you plan to pay someone else to do.

Most office supply stores carry DIY promotional magnets, which allow you to print a business-card sized promotional piece and stick it onto the front of a pre-glued refrigerator magnet. You can also buy sticker sheets to use in your printer, as well as iron-on sheets you can use to make your own mousepads, tote bags and t-shirts. The per-item cost of these DIY items is higher than if you ordered them in bulk from an outside vendor, but the advantage is that you don't have to buy a minimum quantity of items up front.

An option halfway between total home-based DIY and total outside vendor is the on-demand or small-run vendor. Two such companies are www.cafepress.com and www.youdesignit.com . Both companies operate online exclusively, and allow you to upload your own designs to go on various items. Cafepress even goes so far as to let you open your own CafePress online shop if you'd like to sell your promotional items to the general public. An example of this is my IndieAuthor shop (www.cafepress.com/IndieAuthorShop).

Your "design" can be as simple as a copy of your book cover art (or an approximation), a quote from the book, or even just your website address. Whatever you put on your promotional items, you'll want to be sure to provide where-to-buy information, such as "Available Now At Amazon.com," or your website address. If your website has sales links, use the website address for your where-to-buy information since that will drive traffic to your website as well as to your book sales pages.

Promotional items can be costly, so if you're on a budget you'll want to choose your items carefully, and distribute them even more carefully. Consider how much advertising bang you'll be getting for your buck when deciding what to buy, and to whom you should give your promotional items. Ordering your items from an on-demand vendor like Cafepress makes it easier to control costs, and also saves you the trouble of having to store boxes full of mugs, t-shirts, etc.

T-shirts and tote bags are big-ticket options, but people love getting free t-shirts and tote bags, and whoever wears your shirt or carries your bag in public is a walking advertisement for your book. Give your t-shirts to people who are likely to wear them, especially people who are frequently surrounded by readers. Bookstore sales clerks and library volunteers are good candidates, so long as they're allowed to wear t-shirts to work. A quick glance around at the staff will reveal the likely dress code. College students are another good bet for t-shirts. Tote bags are very much appreciated, and always used, by teachers. Don't rule out grammar school teachers, because they'll carry their stuff in your bag all over the place, not just to their classrooms.

Coffee mugs and magnets can work if you give them to people whose job involves meeting with other people throughout the day. Lawyers, customer service reps, real estate agents, accountants, insurance agents and sales people are just a few examples.

The next time you're asked to contribute something to be raffled off for fundraising, offer some of your promotional items or copies of your books. Promotional giveaways are real crowd-pleasers at live readings and public speaking appearances too.

11.5.13 WORD OF MOUTH

⏱ - ⏱⏱⏱⏱	Free!	No Skills!	✏✏ - ✏✏✏

At the low end of the time and confidence scale, "word of mouth" just means mentioning your book to anyone who asks about your career or hobbies. Another step up the scale means that you mention your book and also give the inquirer one of your handouts, and the next step after that is trying to discuss the book whenever the opportunity arises.

People at the highest end of the scale are those who don't wait for opportunities to arise, they actively seek out and approach others to talk about their books. They also attempt to enlist everyone they know to assist with getting the word out. Your own comfort level will determine where you fall on the time and confidence scales.

11.5.14 PAID ADVERTISING

⏱	$$$$$	No Skills!	No Confidence!

Authors with a few hundred dollars to spend can pay for a small ad on a website, or in a local newspaper or magazine. Those with a couple thousand available can go for a larger ad, or a newspaper or magazine with slightly larger circulation. If you've got more money than that to spend, your best option may be to hire a professional publicist. A publicist can handle as much or as little of your promotional efforts as you like, but if you intend to continue doing certain promotional tasks yourself you should coordinate your efforts with the publicist to ensure there's no duplication of effort, and to maintain consistency across your promotional materials.

11.6 NEW MEDIA TACTICS

In terms of promotional opportunities, the internet offers an embarrassment of riches—and an awful lot of the riches are free! In the era of Web 2.0 (large quantities of internet content being created by internet users instead of paid professionals), authors who aren't using the internet to promote their work are at a distinct disadvantage to their more tech-savvy peers.

While basic computer and internet skills will be enough to get you by with most of the options discussed in this section, you'll need moderate to advanced skills to take full advantage of all the web has to offer. If you're completely intimidated by the idea of setting up a website, even a free one built with fill-in-the-blanks templates, skip ahead to the Author Blog section.

11.6.1 AUTHOR WEBSITE

☺ - ☺☺☺☺☺	Free! - $$$$$	✗✗ - ✗✗✗✗	No Confidence!

An author website serves as a centralized clearinghouse for all official information about you and your books. Your website can provide your readers (and potential readers) with information about you, your work, where to buy your books, and what's being said about you and your work in reviews and the press. You can also use an author website to host excerpts from your published work so readers can try before they buy. And of course, your website is the ideal location to publicize your books, signings, appearances and so on. The amount of time, money and skills required to get an author website up and running are highly variable, depending on the type of site.

Generally speaking, your site should include a "Home" page, an "About" page (author biography), a "News" or "Press" page (links to your press releases and any articles in which you're mentioned or quoted), a page about your books (with thumbnail images of the covers, jacket copy and a where-to-buy link for each), a "Links" or "Favorites" page (links to sites of interest to readers and writers), and an email link for site visitors to contact you. Optionally, you may have a "Blog" page or link to an outside blog. If your site will include excerpts from your novels, you can provide links to the excerpts in the page about your books or have a separate, designated page just for links to excerpts as I've done on my site. The choice depends on how much content is already present on the page about your books. More site design guidelines are provided in the "...Or The Hard Way" section below.

We Can Do This The Easy Way...

There are many, many places online to set up a website for free, using simple, fill-in-the-blank templates. Googlepages (www.pages.google.com), Homestead (www.homestead.com) and Tripod (www.tripod.com) are just three options for this type of site, but there are plenty more. Free websites from providers such as these usually have ads from the provider displayed on their pages, though the providers typically offer an ad-free option if the website owner is willing to pay a small, monthly maintenance fee. The providers also generally offer website upgrades, such as more server space, a wider variety of website templates and the ability to host video or music, on a fee basis.

If you can possibly afford it, I strongly recommend you go with the no-ads option. Ads clutter up your pages and make it painfully obvious you went the cheap-and-easy route with your site. Furthermore, you don't usually have any control over what appears in the ads on free, ad-supported sites and may be surprised to find listings for products or services you don't like, or even for other authors' books!

Aside from the ads, there are three downsides to this type of website. The first is that your design options are limited to the available templates. The second is that your website address may be long and hard to remember, since the provider's company name is in the address. "www.GaleAdams.googlepages.com" may not seem all that unwieldy, but it's not as clean, simple and professional-sounding as www.GaleAdams.com.

The third, and perhaps most important, downside is that the number of hits (visits) your site can receive in a given period (per day, per week or per month) is limited, and when that limit has been reached no one can visit your site until the start of the next hit-counting period. Providers aren't stingy with their hit count allowances, and most of the time you'll be far from any risk of going over your limit. But if you're lucky enough to get some major media attention, such as a mention in a syndicated column, you may burn through your hit count allowance in a matter of minutes; it is the world wide web, after all. Anyone who gets an error message instead of your site probably won't come back.

It's also worth mentioning that totally free sites don't typically offer much in the way of technical support. You'll probably have access to a Frequently Asked Questions (FAQ) guide, a community forum where site owners share their problems, ideas and solutions with one another, and an email form you can use to send questions to the technical support department. It's typical to get automated, boilerplate responses to such emails, directing you back to the FAQ and community forum. Fortunately, because free, template-based sites are so simple, you'll rarely have the need for technical support. If you're not yet published, you might consider setting up a free, template-based site as sort of a starter site. You can always upgrade to a full-featured, paid site later.

Another option is to join an online community that hosts websites for its members. Some such communities are free (again, ad-supported) and others charge a modest membership fee. One such community that's geared specifically to writers is AuthorsDen (www.authorsden.com). The main advantage to this option is that site features are tailored to the needs of the community. For example, AuthorsDen websites make it easy for members to sell books directly from their website.

If you want to go with a free, template-based site and don't care for any of the options mentioned thus far, try doing an internet search on "free website" to find many, many more choices. If you're willing to pay for your site but still want something template-based, search on "easy website".

...Or The Hard Way

Authors with advanced skills can set up an author website the old fashioned way: register a domain, sign up with a hosting service, build their pages, and upload everything to the web. The main advantage of this approach is control: since you own the site and build the site, you can make it exactly the way you want. It's more expensive and time-consuming than the 'easy way' described above, but well worth the effort if you've got the skills.

A common mistake in web design is thinking that the goal is to make every page element as impressive as possible. In fact, the goal is to make every page element as easy to use or read as possible. In the final analysis, effective web design can be boiled down to a single rule: don't annoy site visitors. Anything that makes your site harder to use is annoying, and an annoying site won't get repeat visits.

Strive for elegance. In terms of software and website design, "elegance" means simplicity, clean design, and consistency. An elegant website is one that's easy to navigate, uncluttered, and predictable. The site serves as a delivery system for content, and shouldn't draw attention to itself any more than a picture frame should distract you from the picture inside it.

Simplicity – Keep your site design basic, relatively static and uncomplicated. Less is definitely more when it comes to websites. While it's true that you need to add new content on a regular basis to keep visitors coming back, that doesn't mean the "bones" of your site should look substantially different each time a visitor comes back.

Don't assault the site visitor with content; when you want to include streaming video on a page, display a thumbnail or icon on the page rather than just having the full-sized video load and begin playing immediately when the page loads. Sites with many videos will often contain a dedicated video page with clickable thumbnails of all available videos gathered in one place. Music and videos that load automatically when the page loads slow down the browser, and if the visitor wants to click on a link to a different page on your site, she may have to wait until the music or video is finished buffering first. I can tell you from personal experience, this is annoying.

The question of whether or not to put ads on an author website is a matter of opinion, and my opinion is that with few exceptions, you should not put advertising on your site. Aside from the clutter factor, recall that free, template-based sites are usually ad-supported. Placing ads on your site makes it look like a free, template-based site, undermining all the expense and effort you've sunk into building a custom site. Another consideration is the fact that your author site is, in and of itself, an advertisement for you and your work, and should already contain 'ads' for your books in the form of where-to-buy links. Placing ads on your site is like putting commercial breaks in an infomercial.

The 'few exceptions' are when advertising is being used to help cover the expense of giveaways, and even then, it's best if the ads are unobtrusive. For example, the only page on my site with ads is the 'Indie Author Guides' page, where I offer free, downloadable excerpts from this book to site visitors. A small AdSense strip appears at the bottom of the page. AdSense allows the site owner to select the ads shown, as well as the size and format of the ads.

Don't stuff every square inch of your pages with content; balancing positive and negative space enhances readability. Avoid the style-over-substance trap: animated graphics, flashing banners, garish colors and unnecessary widgets are out. Follow the rule of three for fonts and colors: use no more than three different colors and fonts, and only use fonts from the same family (i.e., Arial, Arial Narrow, Arial Rounded). If you intend to offer a blog, photos, video, an online shopping cart for books or merchandise, etc., don't embed these items directly into your home page. Either have a dedicated page for each different type of content, or use other sites (i.e., Blogger for blogging, Picasa for photos, YouTube for video, etc.) for those purposes and just link to them from your author site.

Clean Design – It's all about attention to detail. Don't take shortcuts, and always review every page online after you've made changes because some mistakes will only show up on a real web server. Never go "quick and dirty" when it comes to your author site, do everything the right way. Use tables, not the spacebar, when you want to create columns in your pages. Take the time to embed links within text, don't just type out the URLs, thereby forcing visitors to copy and paste the address.

Always set the target for linked content outside of your site to "_blank" so that when those links are clicked, the sites will open in a new window instead of letting the browser navigate away from your site. The user may want to return to your site after looking at the linked material, and providing a "_blank" target makes that a lot easier for them.

Take the time to crop, clean up and resize any photos or graphics before loading them to your site. This helps avoid the dreaded "jaggies", your pictures will load faster, and once loaded, they won't completely fill up the browser window.

Consistency – Every page of your site should have the same layout and basic functionality. The link menu is in the same location on every page, it always contains the same links no matter what page you're on, and clicking on the links will always take you to the same locations no matter which page you click them from. Use the same naming and capitalization conventions on every page: the link to your "About" page shouldn't be "About" on some pages, "About Me" on others, and "about the author" on the rest. Use the same font, same icon set, same bullets and same colors on all your pages.

...Or The Slightly-Less-Hard Way

Starting with templates can save time and increase the "wow factor" on your site, but these will not be fill-in-the-blanks templates. For example, my author website (www.aprillhamilton.com) features some very nice graphic art elements that serve as my banner, page frame and navigation menu.

All of these items are part of a template package I bought from HitGuru (www.hitguru.com) for about US$8, but I still had to work with HTML to add my own text, pictures and links to my pages. The template package included a few different sample, blank web pages I could customize for use on my site, as well as separate copies of each graphic element (i.e., bullets, banner, frame pieces) provided as individual .jpg files. I could've spent a lot of time working in a graphic art program and writing the HTML to create my own site design, but since I'm not a graphic artist I doubt my finished product would've looked as nice as my bought template. An added bonus of purchased templates is that you can extend their colors, fonts and graphics across all your promotional materials, from business cards to one-sheets, creating the same effect as that achieved by hiring an artist to design a "look" for you.

If you're considering templates, do an internet search for "website templates" or "web templates," but beware of templates offered for free. In my experience, free templates either have advertising embedded in them or have such limiting terms of use that they're more trouble than they're worth. Also, you definitely can't use elements from a free template in your other promotional materials.

Another time- and effort-saver is using a web page authoring tool with a graphical user interface, such as Dream Weaver or Front Page. These tools look and behave a lot like a glorified word processor, allowing the user to type and insert graphics directly on the page, but instead of outputting documents they output web pages. Don't think that using such a tool will get you off the HTML hook, however. As you insert your graphics and type and format your text, the tool is writing the HTML for you, behind the scenes. It sounds great, but the tools often misinterpret what you're trying to do, making it necessary for you to go in and clean up the HTML manually.

It's not difficult to learn HTML. A very basic HTML primer is provided in this book, and there are lots of free tutorials available online if you'd like to learn more. Just search for "learn HTML" or "HTML tutorial". However, don't use your author website as an experimental sandbox as you go through your learning curve. Whatever you post to the web is instantly visible to the whole world, and you don't want anything defective out there representing you and your work.

If you intend to do this the hard way, you undoubtedly already have the knowledge and skills to do so and there's not much point in me giving a how-to here. However, be sure to read Creating Your Brand chapter before you start down the road toward building your own website.

...Or The Expensive Way

The author who wants a truly professional-looking site but doesn't have the time or skills to make one can always hire a web developer to do it. The best way to find a reliable web developer is through a personal referral. Look at others' websites, not just authors but people in various professions, and bookmark sites with the look and features you want in your own site.

Sites designed and maintained by outside persons or companies usually have contact information for the site designer listed at the bottom of every page, but contact the person or company who hired that outside service first, to inquire about their satisfaction with the outside service. You can also ask what the service cost, both in terms of initial setup and ongoing maintenance expense.

Narrow the field of candidates to just two or three, and then conduct email or phone interviews with them. Topics of primary concern include technical support (i.e., hours and days available, telephone vs. email-only support), throughput capacity (how many site visits and file downloads are you allowed each month before incurring additional charges, and what will visitors to your site see if you've exceeded your throughput allowances), and the process for making site changes and updates (whom do you contact, how do you contact him/her, can you see changes in a preview mode before they go "live" on your site, and how long does it take for changes/updates to go "live"?). You'll also want to find out how frequently, and in what form, site statistics will be reported to you: how many visitors, what links they followed to get to your site, what keyword searches led people to your site, how long site visitors stayed, etc. etc.

Apart from expense, there are a few other downsides to this approach. First, there will always be delays between the time you notice a mistake on your site or want to update it and the time changes take effect online. Second, the site designer's interpretation of what you want won't always be accurate, and this introduces further delays while you wait (and possibly, pay) for corrections. Finally, once you've tied your wagon to a certain site design service, you're stuck with that service for the duration of your contract.

11.6.2 AUTHOR BLOG

☺ - ☺☺	Free! - $$$	✗✗	∥ ∥ ∥

The term "blog" is an abbreviation for "weblog," or online journal. A blog is a natural supplement to an author website, and if necessary, can even substitute for full-scale site. There are lots of blog services out there, many of which are free. Some options to look at are www.blogger.com (free), www.typepad.com (fee-based), www.wordpress.com (free) and www.googlepages.com (free). To find more, just do an internet search on "blog". Googlepages is mentioned both here and in the Author Website section because it offers fill-in-the-blanks templates for both traditional websites and blogs.

How To Blog

Blogs all work in basically the same way: you type an entry (a "post") into an online form that's much like an email form, apply the same types of formatting options to your text as you might in an email (i.e., bold, italic, font, etc.), click a button to preview your post, go back to make changes if necessary, preview again, then click another button to publish your post. The blog service will automatically date- and time-stamp your posts. Text formatting options will generally be much more limited than what you get in a word processor, but they will generally work the same way they do in a word processor: highlight the text you want to format, then click a button to apply formatting changes.

Most blog services will also have a button for inserting hyperlinks in your posts, and some even allow full use of HTML to insert pictures, video, widgets, etc. The blog service will also provide a profile page, on which you can provide as much or as little personal information as you like, and most allow you to choose whether or not blog visitors will be allowed to post comments and feedback on your blog. In most cases, there's an option allowing the blog author to review and approve any comments and feedback before they become visible on the blog. You can blog under any name you wish, but since the purpose of your blog is to promote your work, it makes sense to blog under your author, or 'brand' name.

Most blogs will automatically generate a link to every post you create and keep a running list of those links displayed on your main blog page. It's typical for blog authors to be able to categorize the list by topic or date by adjusting their blog settings. Increasingly, blog services allow users to employ HTML and site widgets. Blogger, for example, has an "Add Page Element" feature in the "Layout" section of the user dashboard.

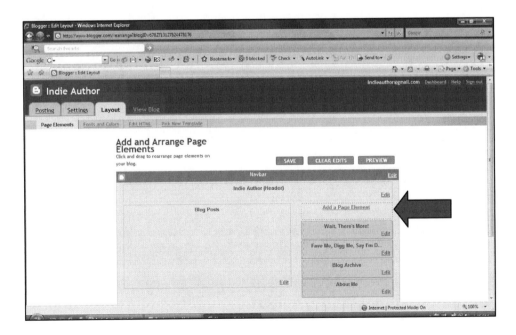

When the user clicks the "Add A Page Element" link, a new window opens and displays all the available site tools and widgets that can be added.

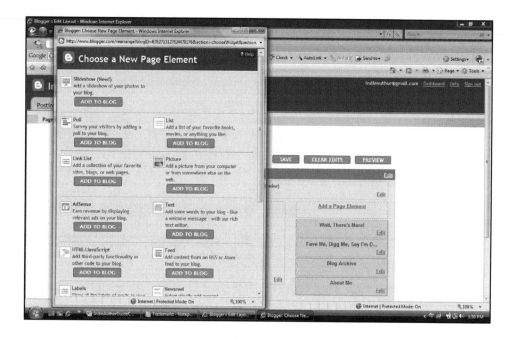

The "HTML/Javascript" feature presents a text box into which the user can type (or paste) HTML and internet scripts to add special features to his blog. Like Blogger, most blog services provide widgets like those shown above (i.e., photo slide show, visitor poll, link list, etc.). Users can add the widgets and services to their blogs with just a button click, or by selecting the item from a list.

What To Blog

I indicate that above-average written communication skills are needed for blogging because your blog entries must be compelling enough to keep people coming back. Since anyone can write a blog, there are lots of boring and pointless blogs out there. Your blog posts will be most effective if you wait until you've got something worth writing about, but not every post must be a wellspring of pithiness.

Most writers are interested in learning more about other writers' technique, or even just commiserating over common challenges. You can blog about your process, your stumbling blocks, your frustrations and triumphs in writing. When you attend a writers' seminar or class, blog about it. Blog about great new writer resources or websites you've discovered, promotional activities and your degree of success with them, books you've read and your opinions about them, and of course, about your works in progress. You can blog about contests, writers' groups, the publication process...just about anything writing-related, so long as it's interesting, informative, surprising or provocative.

Blogging about your experiences querying or dealing with agents and editors is another popular option, but if you do this be careful not to write anything that could be construed as slander or libel; it's safest not to name names at all unless you're showering someone with praise and admiration.

About the only people who can get away with mere pontificating in an author blog are nonfiction authors. Plenty of people would love to read David Sedaris' description of a typical day in his life, because it would undoubtedly be just as funny and insightful as his published articles and essays. As for the rest of us...the general public probably won't be all that interested in reading that your cat threw up on the quilt again this morning and you finally figured out how to send pictures with your new cell phone. Remember that people visit your blog because you're a writer, because they're seeking a writer's viewpoint on things. Try to keep your posts relevant and on-point.

Blog Integrity

While blog services allow the author of a post to go back and edit or delete the post anytime they want to, you should only use this feature sparingly, and only to correct mistakes on the order of typographical errors. From the time your post goes "live", people all over the world may be linking to it or telling friends about it via email. These people will be very annoyed if the post they were excited about has changed since they linked to it or told other people about it, especially if the particular thing that piqued their interest in your post is no longer there. Consider the following scenario.

You blog about a writing seminar you'd like to attend. Other writers who are interested in the seminar bookmark your post and email their friends about it. Some writers even put the link to your post on their websites. You decide not to attend the seminar after hearing bad reviews from members of your writers' group. You don't want to have any part in promoting a bad seminar, but you also don't want to badmouth anyone online, so you decide to simply delete the post. All the links to it on websites where it was added are now broken, which reflects badly on the owners of those sites. People who received the link in an email find the link is broken, which reflects badly on the person who sent them the link. All the bookmarks to it are now broken, which annoys the people who bookmarked it. In the end, all of this confusion and annoyance reflects badly on you, and it's a safe bet none of those people will visit your blog again.

It would've been better to leave the original post intact and enter a new blog entry about your decision not to attend the seminar. You can avoid seeming to badmouth the seminar by choosing your words carefully, and limiting your remarks to statements of fact (i.e., "My writing partner attended last year and he said it was disappointing...").

I recently read an article that said bloggers should never delete a post, nor even edit a post without making the edits known, even if the blogger learns she has written something that's factually inaccurate. It was suggested that in such a case, the blog author should handle the situation the same way a magazine would: by leaving the original post intact and printing a formal retraction or correction notice. Given that people who have bookmarked, or linked to, the original post may not see your notice, a suggested alternative was to edit the original post by formatting the incorrect text as "strikethrough" (like this:

strikethrough), then entering your desired changes. This makes it clear to the reader that something has changed without breaking any links or bookmarks, and avoids any hint that you may be trying to hide your mistake.

One good way to avoid blog mistakes and revisions is to compose your blog posts offline in a text editor or word processor first. Take all the time you want to write, revise, spell check and polish your post offline, then copy, paste and post with confidence.

11.6.3 AMAZONCONNECT BLOG

Authors with at least one book for sale at Amazon can blog on Amazon's site using AmazonConnect. You can learn more about this service at www.amazonconnect.com. Any Amazon customer can set up an AmazonConnect page, but only authors with books listed for sale on Amazon get to blog on the page.

The page displays an author blog, bibliography, profile and other items per the author's display choices. AmazonConnect is a powerful marketing tool, as it puts you in almost direct contact with your readers and potential readers. Even if you blog elsewhere, don't pass up this terrific promotional opportunity if you're eligible. I maintain both an AmazonConnect blog and a Blogger blog, addressing my Blogger posts to writers and my AmazonConnect posts to readers.

Blogging on AmazonConnect works the same as anywhere else, but you're not allowed to enter HTML or widgets in your blog posts. Buttons are available to format your text with color, boldface or italics, and to insert hyperlinks, images of products available on Amazon, images or video, but that's all. Compared to other blogging services AmazonConnect may seem a bit limited, but it has two huge advantages: you have the option of displaying your AmazonConnect blog posts directly on your books' Amazon product pages, and a link to your blog will be included in the 'Amazon Daily' portal page of any Amazon customer who has bought one of your books.

Note that you can only add blog posts to "verified" books in your bibliography, and only going forward from the day each book is verified. When you 'claim' a book as yours by adding it to the bibliography section of your AmazonConnect page, you must specify a verifier: someone who can vouch for the fact that you really are the author of the book. Amazon contacts the verifier for approval, then adds the verified title to your bibliography upon receipt of approval.

All your AmazonConnect blog posts will appear on your AmazonConnect page, but each time you post a new blog entry you can specify whether or not you would like the post to also appear on any or all of your books' Amazon product pages. You can tailor a post to a specific book, then display the post only on your AmazonConnect page and the product page for that specific book. You can have some posts show only on your AmazonConnect page, and you can have others show in multiple locations.

One of the best uses of this feature is to provide potential customers with a link to a free, online excerpt from each of your books, since not all self-published and Kindle books are eligible for the 'Search Inside the Book' feature on Amazon. Note that you don't have to have an author website to do this. See the next section of this chapter for more details.

In terms of other blog content, you must follow the AmazonConnect Terms of Use. They're fairly standard and self-explanatory, but do take the time to look them over when you first set up an AmazonConnect account. In addition to the Terms of Use, apply the same common sense when posting to your AmazonConnect blog as if you were posting to any other blog: always consider the impression your post will make. You may want to keep your AmazonConnect blog entries shorter than entries you'd make in a dedicated blog, because they will appear on your books' product pages between the product description and the reviews area. You don't want to discourage anyone who's read your book from scrolling down far enough to enter a review. Note that your AmazonConnect blog entries cannot ever be deleted. They can be edited, or 'emptied out' into a blank space, but a dated entry will always remain wherever you've created a blog post in the past.

Aside from the blog and bibliography sections, your AmazonConnect page also includes a profile. A simple form is provided for you to enter as little or as much personal information as you like (i.e., location, hobbies, etc.), and you can upload a photo as well. By default, your public wishlist(s), recent purchases and other Amazon activity (i.e., reviews you've written) will appear on your AmazonConnect page as well, but you can edit your profile to hide anything you'd prefer to keep private. Personally, I think it's a good idea to hide everything but your profile information and blog posts, because other types of content may detract from the professional impression you hope to make. People tend to think of authors as creatures somehow distinct from other humans that don't do anything but write and make public appearances. Allowing them to see that you not only bought the Clorox Toilet Wand but gave it a detailed and glowing 5-star review tends to break the illusion.

Here's the URL of my AmazonConnect page, to give you some idea of how it works: http://www.amazon.com/gp/pdp/profile/A2USJVB92E9Q90. After reviewing the page, scroll down to the bibliography and click on the links to my books' product pages to see how my blog posts are integrated into the pages.

11.6.4 MAKE A FREE EXCERPT AVAILABLE

🕐 - 🕐🕐	Free!	✗✗	No Confidence!

It's not too difficult to overcome any trepidation readers may have about buying a book from an author they've never heard of if you let them read some of the book first. You will have to create an excerpt and 'park' it somewhere on the web, but it's definitely worth the effort. Anyone who reads through to the end of your excerpt is probably hooked enough to buy the book, especially if you've provided a very lengthy excerpt. Also, anyone who buys your book on the strength of an excerpt is likely to enjoy the whole thing, so posting an excerpt helps ensure all you customers will be satisfied customers, thereby reducing the probability of negative customer reviews.

Create Your Excerpt

Open your manuscript. Create an excerpt by copying the title page and first 25-50pp (according to your preference) from the manuscript and pasting all of that content into a new, blank file. Add a page at the end with a blurb to the effect of, "Thank you for reading this excerpt. If you would like to continue reading [book title], you may purchase it from [where to buy information]."

Omit the table of contents and copyright page, but add a one-liner copyright legend to your title page, if applicable. Save the file in its usual format, though under a different name than the complete manuscript. Use a pdf maker program to save a pdf version of the excerpt file.

Besides Adobe Acrobat, there are many shareware and freeware options. Do an

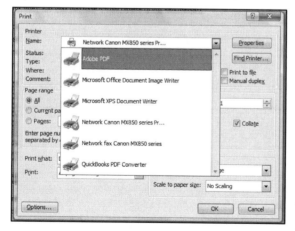

internet search on "pdf maker" to find them. They all work essentially the same way, appearing as a printer option in the Print menu of your programs. In the screen shot at left, Adobe PDF is the top option in the list of printers. To create a pdf version of your file, select the pdf printer from the list and specify a location for the pdf file on your hard drive when prompted.

Post Your Excerpt Online

If you have an author website, you can 'park' your excerpt there. If not, there are other options geared specifically toward writers.

Two that are free of charge are 1 Chapter Free (http://www.1chapterfree.com) and Scribd (http://www.scribd.com). You have to sign up for an account to post your excerpts at either site, but it's free and easy to do.

If you intend to offer your book in eBook format(s)—and why wouldn't you, since it's free and opens up a whole new market for your work—you can publish to various eBook formats and offer a free, lengthy online excerpt at Smashwords (http://www.smashwords.com), which is also free to join. See the Publishing To Other EBook Formats chapter for more information.

Link To Your Excerpt

Once your excerpt is posted, view it online to make sure it was posted in its entirety and appears normal. If there are problems, you can re-upload the excerpt. When you're satisfied with the excerpt, make a note of its URL. Now you can provide the link to your excerpt on your blog, your AmazonConnect blog, your author website, in the description of your book in your publisher's online store, and anywhere else it's appropriate to do so.

11.6.5 ONLINE COMMUNITIES

⊙ - ⊙⊙	Free!	✗✗	↗ ↗

Online communities are web-based clubs and discussion groups. This is where your non-writing interests can come into play as part of your marketing efforts. Such groups are great places to promote your work, but I do not recommend joining any online community purely for the sake of promotion. To do so would be an abuse of the group, and more likely to generate ill will than sales anyway.

Rather, I suggest making fuller use of the unobtrusive marketing opportunities inherent in any communities to which you already belong.

First, edit your user profile to include links to your author website and/or blog. Revise your biography to make brief mention of your books, if desired, but don't rework your biography into a sales pitch. Also edit your 'signature', adding a link to your author website (or blog if you don't have an author site), or a link to the product sales page of the book you're promoting; now the link will appear in every one of your posts to the discussion group. If a given community doesn't offer the signature feature, get in the habit of signing all your posts with your name and the desired link.

Some community sites provide an 'insert link' button in the window where you compose your posts. In that case, highlight the text you want to make into a link, click the button, and type or paste the desired link into the provided pop-up window. See the HTML Primer in this book for more information about how to create links manually. Be sure to test your link after your post is up, and edit the post as needed if the link doesn't work. If all else fails, you can simply include the full text of the web address in your post. It's less elegant and a lot less convenient for the user, who must copy the link and paste it into their browser, but it's better than not including a link at all.

Now use the presence of your link as motivation to become more involved in online community discussions. Take every opportunity to contribute to those discussions in a meaningful way. If people find your posts interesting or amusing, they're likely to click your link in order to learn more about you and your work. Don't post solely as an excuse to get your link displayed in a discussion, however. Your motives will be obvious and your posts will be ignored. Be willing to give back to the community in exchange for the opportunity to display your links.

Avoid gratuitous mentions of your books, but in cases where there's a legitimate reason for doing so, germane to the discussion, be sure to make your book titles hyperlinks to their respective product sales pages. If you can't use hyperlinks, include the product page web addresses at the bottom of your post, under your signature. Again, be unobtrusive.

11.6.6 COMMENT FORMS

☺ - ☺☺	Free!	✗✗	⚡⚡

To date, the majority of traffic on my author website has come as the result of my entries to online comment forms, either directly or indirectly. My entries in comment forms have drawn the attention of other writers and potential book-buyers, as well as journalists who've gone on to interview me for inclusion in an article. I get site visits from those who saw my original comment, and then many more visits from people who read about me in articles.

Whenever I have time I scan popular media websites, seeking articles related to writing, publishing, or any other topics of particular interest to me. By "popular media websites," I mean the sites of print magazines, TV news networks, newspapers, blogs and e-zines (magazines that exist only online, such as Salon and Slate).

I'll also do a periodic internet search on topics related to indie authorship (i.e., "POD", "self-publish", etc.) to locate relevant articles. Most sites offer online comment forms at the end of their articles, where readers can respond to the article and discuss it with one another. If I feel I can add anything worthwhile, or have a strong opinion about the article, I use the comment form to enter my reply and sign off with my author name and desired link.

As with posts to online communities, I avoid any outright salesmanship in my comments, and even avoid mentioning my books at all when they're not relevant to the article—which is most of the time. Look at the comment form as a micro-writing sample opportunity rather than a promotional opportunity, and you won't often go wrong. Anyone who follows your sign-off link can learn about your books on your site, and anyone who doesn't won't be left with the impression that you're a spammer. Of course, articles about writing and the publishing industry often provide legitimate reasons to talk about a book or author website/blog in a comment form, so put a little extra effort into seeking out those articles.

Unfortunately, spammers have gotten wise to the power of the online comment form too, and it's become a favorite vehicle for posting baldfaced advertisements. To discourage this, some comment forms will automatically reject any post with "http:" or the "@" sign in it. You can get your links past the filters by omitting the "http:" part of your link, substituting the word "dot" in place of the 'dots' in your link (i.e., www dot aprillhamilton dot com), and in the case of an email address, substituting the word "at" for the "@" sign. So long as my comments are truly there to add to the discussion, inclusion of my link is incidental and I'm complying with the site's Terms of Use, I have no compunction about sidestepping the security bots. You'll have to decide what sits best with your own conscience.

If your comments draw the attention of journalists seeking an interview or quotes from you, make sure that in exchange for your participation the journalist will include a link to your site, blog or book in the published article. A comment I posted at Business Week's site got the attention of Michael Brush, a regular columnist for MSN Money. He was writing an article about Barnes and Noble and wanted to get my perspective as an indie author. I was only quoted twice in the article, very briefly in both cases.

Nevertheless, the day the article was published my website traffic went through the roof. Quite a few of those site visitors checked out my press page and online novel excerpts, and book sales followed.

11.6.7 ONLINE PRESS RELEASES

☺ - ☺☺	Free! - $$$$$	✗ ✗	✗ ✗

My second-highest source of author website traffic is press releases. If you go completely DIY and distribute your press releases via a free, online service such as PRLog or OpenPR, this promotional activity won't cost you any money but will take some time. If you pay someone else to write your press releases and/or use a paid distribution service for them, you'll save some time but variable costs are involved.

Refer to the Press Releases section earlier in this chapter for more information about how to create and distribute press releases. If you have an author website, be sure to save .pdf copies of your press releases on your site and link to them from your "Press" or "News" page. If you have a blog instead of an author site, you can add links to where your press releases are being stored on the distribution service's website, but press releases will only be stored by the service for a limited time. Check periodically to ensure the links are still active and remove any that have become broken.

11.6.8 KEYWORDS AND TAGS

Keywords and tags are the terms people enter into online search boxes. The search tool scans all the pages it has cataloged, looking for those terms, then returns a set of links to pages on which the desired terms were found. The terms can be found in the body of a page or in "metadata". Metadata is data added to a page via an online data entry form or written directly into the HTML. As you can imagine, the more and better tags and keywords are associated with your web pages, the more people will find them when doing searches. "Better" in this instance means more commonly-used; for example, "free" and "complimentary" mean the same thing, but "free" is a better keyword to use because it's more likely to be entered into a search box than "complimentary".

Working with keywords and tags to improve your pages' visibility to search tools is called Search Engine Optimization (SEO), and entire books are written on the topic. SEO is judged to be so important by so many marketing people that they even hold international conferences about SEO strategies. The goal of SEO is to design page content such that popular keywords feature prominently and repeatedly, making the page easier for search tools to find and making the page rank as high as possible in the list of search results.

Web pages designed with an eye to SEO are easy to identify, since certain terms (or versions of those terms) show up in the page text repeatedly. You may notice this in articles printed online at newspaper and magazine websites. The editors of such sites are trained in SEO, and part of their job is to revise print articles for SEO before the articles are posted online. SEO experts know the most popular search terms and make every effort to incorporate those terms into the text of pages they write or edit.

Even though there are thousands of popular keywords, compared to the entire English language the list of popular keywords is pretty small. Application of SEO techniques tends to result in a sort of homogenization of the web: SEO does not encourage originality or variety in expression. One of a writer's primary goals is to cultivate an original and appealing "voice", and SEO works in direct opposition to that goal. For this reason, I advise writers against writing blog entries or web page text with SEO in mind. Instead, I encourage making maximum use of metadata tagging.

On Amazon.com

① - ①①	Free!	✗✗	No Confidence!

If you have books for sale on Amazon, tagging your books with keywords is one of the best ways to increase their visibility in Amazon's vast database. Every product page on Amazon includes a "Tags Customers Associate With This Product" area, which is located immediately above the Customer Reviews section of the page. Two methods are provided for adding tags to a product: "your tags" and "tag this product for Amazon search". Use both for maximum effect.

Tagging allows you to effectively add your book to countless categories beyond the standard genre categories (i.e., General Fiction, Sci Fi, etc.), as well as to create your own categories. However, note that with both types of tagging, your name will be associated with the tag in a way that's visible to the general public. Anyone who clicks on an assigned tag on a product page can drill down into more information that will ultimately reveal a list of customers who used the tag, so it's not a good idea to apply boastful, smart-alecky, or otherwise potentially objectionable tags.

The "your tags" feature gives customers a way to mark products with tags that are personally meaningful to them, in order to make those products easy to find on future visits to the site. For example, someone shopping for a Mother's Day gift might tag all the products being considered with the phrase "Mother's Day".

Your tags

Manage Your Tags | Manage Your Tags Suggested for Search | Learn More
amazon breakthrough novel awards (6), comic fiction (4), womens fiction (4), comedy (3), chicago (2), chick lit (2), comic mystery (2), coming of sage (2), dark comedy (2), ebook (2), funny (2), hen lit (2), humor (2), kindle (2), media bias (2), midwest (2), missing persons (2), physics (2), abna 1000 (1), abna semi-finalist (1), april hamilton (1), april l hamilton (1), best of the abna (1), comic (1), dark humor (1), family (1), female protagonist (1), fiction (1), mom lit (1), mystery (1)

› See all 35 tags...

Amazon keeps track of the tags entered by each customer and stores them as part of the customer's profile information. Tags you've entered using the "my tags" box on product pages will appear on your AmazonConnect page as links under the "My Tags" heading, shown above. When you click on one of them, Amazon locates all the items you tagged with that term and returns a list of results.

Note that on product pages, just above the customer reviews section, there is a "Tags Customers Associate With This Product" area with a "Search Products

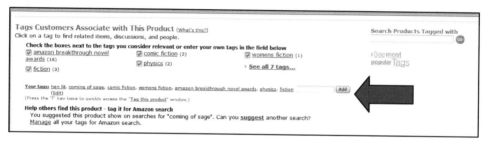

Tagged With" box at the right-hand side. This search incorporates all the tags entered by all customers who have used the "my tags" feature. Going back to the above example, if you search on the tag "Mother's Day" in this box, you'll get a list of products tagged with the phrase "Mother's Day" by all Amazon customers.

Use the "Your Tags" feature (indicated by arrow above) to tag your books with words and phrases you think Amazon customers are likely to search on in the "Search Products Tagged With" box. To create a tag, enter your desired word or phrase in the "Your Tags" box and click the "Add" button. Repeat for all the tags you wish to enter. Amazon displays a list of tags other customers have already applied to your book and books similar to yours; you can use these as a starting point, but don't miss the opportunity to apply more specific tags that only someone who's read your book would think to use.

For example, if Quaker life or culture feature prominently in your story you can tag your book with "Quaker", "Quaker life" and "Quaker culture" so that people looking for stories that feature Quakers will be able to find your book. Consider tags that touch on the time period or geographical location of your story, your protagonist's profession, historical events included in the narrative, and so on.

Also employ tags to overcome limits imposed by your book's genre classification. Your book may be officially classified as Romance, but if it's also historical fiction you can tag it "Historical Romance". Fictionalized accounts of historical events can be tagged with the names of historical figures, battles, settlements and the like included in the book.

Try to think outside the box a little with your tags, but don't be misleading. You may think it's a good idea to tag your Sci Fi book with "espionage" because you think many customers will search for books with that tag, but if espionage isn't

prominent in your plot, readers who buy the book based partly on that tag will be disappointed.

The "Help others find this product – tag it for Amazon search" feature is located just below the "Your Tags" box in the "Tags Customers Associate With This Product" area. Tags added this way are incorporated into general Amazon product searches: searches entered into the "Search Amazon.com" box which appears at the top of every page on Amazon's site. Click the "suggest" link to access the submission form.

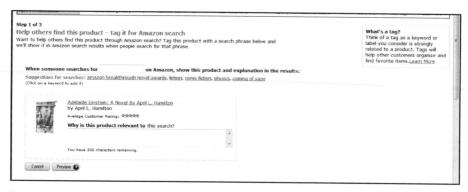

Because unscrupulous people can manipulate the tagging system to make their products appear in the result set for virtually any search, Amazon verifies the validity of any tags entered for Amazon search. Along with your suggested tag, you must also enter a brief reason for why you are suggesting the tag. If the Amazon verifier determines the tag is valid, it will be added to the product in question. If not, it won't. Either way, you will be notified via email.

Tagging your book for Amazon search is a more powerful technique than tagging via the "my tags" feature. The "Search Amazon.com" box is right at the top of every page on Amazon's site and therefore gets more use than the "Search Products Tagged With" box, which is buried far down in each product page. Also, when customers search using the "Search Amazon.com" box, they're able to select a product category from a drop-down list. Doing so returns a smaller, more specific result set. Your book may appear higher up in the list of results than it would in a result set from a "Search Products Tagged With" search, which isn't designed to employ categories.

Note that your book will already be tagged with the author name(s), book title, and the main genre(s) in which it appears in Amazon store listings, so it's not necessary to add these tags yourself.

On The Internet

☺ - ☺☺	Free!	✗✗	No Confidence!

Tags and keywords can also be used to help internet search engines find web content you've authored: your website, your blog, your online press releases and so forth. People who create their own web pages using HTML can incorporate tags in the "metadata" and "keywords" sections of their pages' HTML header code. Those who use fill-in-the-blanks forms to create online content can add tags and keywords in the "tags," "keywords" or "labels" box which is typically provided as part of the form, but such forms usually place a limit on how many words or characters will be accepted.

On Blogger, there's a large box provided for composing blog entries and a second, smaller box directly beneath the large box for adding "labels". You type in the words and phrases you'd like to use as tags, separated by commas, and when you save the blog entry the tags are saved as well. OpenPR and PRLog provide a similar box for entry of keywords/tags on the page you use to enter your press release details. Most fill-in-the-blanks web page templates have the feature, but you may need to search on "tags" or "keywords" in your provider's Help files to find out where it is and how to use it.

Tagging really does make a difference in search results, so take advantage of every tagging opportunity available to you when creating online content.

11.6.9 PODCASTING

☺ - ☺☺☺☺☺	Free! - $$$$$	✗✗✗✗	✗ ✗ ✗

Podcasting is creating an audio, or audio and video, recording that people can play on a web page, in iTunes or on an iPod. You can record a podcast using the media player software that came with your computer, or buy a program designed specifically for that purpose. A specialized program can range from freeware to a very expensive, high-end computer recording studio. Some of the programs are designed for maximum simplicity, but offer few controls and options. High-end programs offer a wide variety of recording, editing and sound mixing options, but are harder to use. Podcasts can be added to your author website, for visitors to download and play in iTunes or on their iPod. If you provide a media player widget, visitors can listen to or watch your podcasts right on your site, no iPod or iTunes needed. You can also list your podcasts in the iTunes store.

A complete primer on podcasting is outside the scope of this Guide, so if you're considering podcasting but don't know much about it, you'll need to find a more thorough discussion of the topic elsewhere. Many articles, tutorials and community discussions about podcasting can be found on Apple's website in the iPod+iTunes support section. You can also do an internet search on "how to podcast" to find more information. Here, the topic of podcasting is limited to content: what to put into a podcast to help promote your books.

In the days before video iPods existed, podcasting started out as a way for performers, DJs and talk show hosts (as well as wannabes in every one of those categories) to create their own radio shows that could then be offered to the public in recorded form instead of being broadcast over the radio.

Many podcasters still follow this basic format today, blending commentary, interviews and music in an audio-only podcast. Others approach audio podcasting as a kind of spoken blog, and record themselves talking about the same things they might otherwise write about in a blog. When video-capable iPods came along, program types common to movies and TV became a part of the podcasting universe: skits, movie trailers, music videos, TV talk shows, documentaries, full-length films, etc. etc. Different formats will be suitable for different authors, but in every case you'll need to include your name, the name of your book, and website address at the beginning and end of the podcast.

Nonfiction authors and fiction authors whose books required a lot of research can make good use of the radio talk show, TV talk show or documentary format with podcasts about the topic(s) covered in their book. How-to programs are popular, as are interviews with subject area experts. Subject area experts are only an internet search away, and are usually flattered by a request to be interviewed for a podcast.

Authors can also read excerpts from their books, providing a kind of audiobook sneak peek, or even stage scenes from their books to create podcast advertisements in the format of a radio spot or movie trailer.

11.6.10 YOUTUBE

☺ - ☺☺☺☺☺	Free! - $$$$$	✗✗✗✗	∥∥∥∥

YouTube is an online repository of film clips submitted by site visitors. There are copies of clips recorded from TV shows or movies, music videos, movie trailers, funny or amazing advertisements, and lots of videos produced by average members of the general public. YouTube visitors can search for the kinds of clips they'd like to see (i.e., karaoke, cats, battle of the bands, etc.), and then rate and review the clips after watching them.

You can promote your books with YouTube in the same ways you would using a video podcast, but the finished video is uploaded to www.youtube.com instead of iTunes or your website. You can link to the video from your blog or website, or embed the video clip in a page on your author site or blog.

Detailed directions for how to shoot, edit and upload your video are beyond the scope of this Guide, but help and tutorials are available in the Help area on YouTube's site.

The main advantage of YouTube over a video podcast is that videos loaded to YouTube are ranked by popularity in real time, on a constant basis, according to viewer ratings. The more popular your video becomes, the higher it climbs in the search results when users search for clips on the site. If viewers like your clip, it will get increasing exposure. Funny, shocking, weird and instructive videos seem to perform best.

11.6.11 ONLINE SOCIAL NETWORKS

◷ - ◷◷	Free!	⚒⚒	ϟϟ

Online social networks are online clubs that provide members with an "About Me" type of fill-in-the-blanks website and tools to easily connect with other members who have similar interests. MySpace and Facebook are two such sites. Most indie bands and filmmakers have a MySpace page, and comedian Dane Cook famously leveraged his MySpace page to attract a huge and loyal following. Facebook began as a social networking site exclusive to Harvard students, but has since expanded to other colleges, then high schools, and finally to the general public.

If you're already a member of an online social network, by all means use it to promote your work by adding links to your blog, author site, press releases and book sales pages. Also use it to publicize appearances, sales accomplishments, positive reviews, etc. However, I don't recommend joining an online social network for book promotion, for a few reasons.

First, there are only so many hours in the day and you should already be maintaining an author website and/or blog. Online social networks can be very time-consuming and even addictive. Having a social network site is like having a whole new author site to maintain.

Second, remember that the whole point of such services is—surprise!—social networking. Members who "friend" you on such networks are expecting to have a cyber-relationship with you, and they don't take kindly to neglect. If your main purpose in joining is promotion, you're certain to annoy other members with your self-serving presence.

Finally, while social networking sites lend themselves very well to music, video, photos and a plethora of widgets, in my opinion they are not the best platform from which to promote books. The target audience of most online social networks skews young, so member pages tend to be stuffed to overflowing with chat boxes, photo slideshows, mini games, animated icons, virtual bulletin boards, video clips, music clips, and flashy templates. Books can seem pretty staid and boring in comparison. Also remember that MySpace is infamous for countless incidents of members' extreme cyber-bullying; it's an enormous, and at times, unruly crowd. Things can go very bad quickly on a social networking site.

11.6.12 LINK TRACKING NETWORKS

☺ - ☺☺☺	Free!	✗✗✗	No Confidence!

Link tracking networks are online services that allow people to submit links to websites and online articles they wish to recommend. Like YouTube, these sites provide a search mechanism and constantly update popularity rankings. The most-submitted links get promoted to the service's front page, where they may be picked up by major media outlets. Link submissions also raise the linked page's rank in internet search results.

Some services also provide a membership option, which allows users to rate other users' submissions and may also allow the user to maintain a personal, centralized list of favorite links on the service's site. Anytime a user adds a link to her personal list, it counts as a vote in favor of the link. Digg, De.licio.us,

Technorati, StumbleUpon and furl are just some of the many services, and it seems new ones are springing up all the time.

In order to make your web content eligible to receive 'votes' in the form of submitted links, you have to add a little widget to your pages and blog entries. You must supply a widget for each different service for which you'd like to be eligible, and this requires a bit of HTML knowledge. Each service provides a block of HTML code for its voting widget, which you can paste into your site pages or blog, but you will have to customize the code to make the widget look and act the way you want. When a visitor clicks the widget, he is taken to the associated service network and is prompted to fill out a brief form describing your page/content. If you become a member of a given service, you will be able to check the popularity of your links on that service whenever you like.

Most marketing types will tell you to join every one of these networks and actively solicit link-submission trades with other online promoters, but they're not as effective as they once were. While it's true that a lucky page can take off in popularity one day, skyrocket to the front page of the link tracking service's site and go on to be picked up by a major news outlet, the marketplace is so flooded with link tracking networks that the odds against any given page rising to the top are getting longer and longer.

With the glut of tracking networks out there it's less and less likely a given major news outlet will happen to pick up a story off the front of a tracking service site to which you subscribe on the day your page happens to be highlighted there. The proliferation of tracking networks also makes it that much less likely your content will get enough votes on any one of them to truly increase its visibility on the web overall. Now that these networks are so commonplace, advertisers have found ways to manipulate them, further reducing their value. Finally, some networks make those page widgets into a double-edged sword: users can vote for, or against your content. If you attract a web troll with an axe to grind, he can make a career out of burying your content.

Personally, I don't feel link tracking networks are worth the time and effort. Still, if you have basic HTML skills, feel free to experiment with them. They may work for you, and if they don't, you can remove the voting widgets from your pages.

11.6.13 LINK TRADING

🕐	Free! - $$	✗✗	✗

Link trading is just what it sounds like: offering to put other writers' links on your site in exchange for their agreement to add your link to their site. This is a quick, easy and cost-free way to increase your exposure while providing the same service for other writers. A link trade instantly grants each author visibility to the other author's online audience.

11.6.14 AMAZON CUSTOMER REVIEWS

🕐 - 🕐🕐🕐🕐	$-$$$	✗✗	✗ ✗

Positive customer reviews of your book on Amazon are one of the best ways to raise your book's visibility on the site, because customers can (and often do) sort search results by Average Customer Review.

This type of sort is a "simple" sort, which means all the items with an average customer review rating of 5 out of 5 stars appear at the top of the list, followed by all the items with 4.75/5 stars, followed by all the items with 4.5/5 stars, and so on down to the bottom of the list, where items with no reviews will appear. Review count is used as a secondary sort within each customer rating level.

For example, imagine your Young Adult, Science Fiction novel only has two customer reviews, but both are 5-star reviews. Let's say that under the heading of Young Adult Science Fiction, there are 2,500 books listed—but only 15 of them have an average review rating of 5/5 stars. When a customer sorts a list of Young Adult Science Fiction titles by Average Customer Review, your book will appear on the first page with all the other books that have an average rating of 5/5 stars. Your book's position within the group of 5/5 star books will be determined by review count: those with more reviews appear higher in the list, those with few reviews appear lower.

The Average Customer Review sort is one place where the little guy (or in this case, indie guy) can actually have an advantage over bestselling mainstream books. First, as review count goes up, average customer review rating tends to go down. This is because no book can please everybody, and many bestsellers eventually fall victim to reader backlash, especially if they've been heavily hyped.

Some authors try to raise their standing in the Average Customer Review sort by creating a bunch of dummy Amazon accounts specifically to enter lots of 5-star reviews for their books, but this is a mistake. Since the dummy accounts won't have significant activity other than entering 5-star customer reviews for your books and those of your friends, their validity will be suspect. Furthermore, anyone who cross-references the dummy accounts' activity can probably figure out you're the one behind them. Any hint of fraud will instantly cancel out the positive impression you hoped to make, and in fact will make the quality of your books highly suspect; after all, if the books were any good why would the author have to go to such lengths to trick people into buying them?

Instead, solicit reviews from friends and family who have Amazon accounts, and also refer to the Editorial Reviews topic in the Traditional Tactics section of this chapter for information about soliciting reviews from Amazon Top Reviewers. Some reviewers will be willing to work with an electronic copy, but be prepared to provide free hard copies. Don't request this favor from family members whose Amazon username includes their last name if that name is the same as yours, since many people will rightly conclude (or at least suspect) the review is from a relative, calling its validity into question. Also, don't solicit reviews with strings attached, such as a demand for a guaranteed 5-star rating. You can request that friends and family members only post a review if they enjoyed the book, but with reviews solicited from others you must be willing to graciously accept the posted review, whether good or bad.

11.6.15 AMAZON LISTMANIA! LISTS

Amazon customers can make lists of their favorite books and products. The lists are displayed, on a rotating basis, on Amazon search results pages where the search results include items from a created list. The image at left shows two Listmania lists that appeared at the left-hand side of a search results page for Nintendo Wii video games.

The Listmania display box offers three options: you can view a complete list by clicking on the list title, you can click the "Create a Listmania! list" link to create a list of your own, or you can use the "Search Listmania" box to search for items other customers have included in their lists. When viewing a complete list, you can also view remarks the list author made about each item in the list.

Having your book added to a Listmania list can significantly increase its visibility on Amazon. Since search results are ranked by "best selling" by default, your book will probably be buried many pages down in most search results.

However, if your book is part of a Listmania list appearing on the first page of search results, it becomes accessible from that first page. Moreover, the fact that a customer put the book on a list stands as a recommendation, making it that much more likely other customers will give it a try.

Before you go off and create a bunch of lists with your book in them, note that the name of the list author is displayed right along with the list. It's considered poor form to create lists with your own books on them, and your promotional intent will be transparent to the list viewer. Call once again on those friends and family members with Amazon accounts, again granting a pass to those whose usernames make their relationship to you apparent.

11.7 FORM A WEB PROMO RING

☺ - ☺☺☺	Free!	✗✗	◣ - ◣◣

Since so many internet promotion techniques involve accumulating reviews, clicks, ratings and the like from others, consider forming a web promo ring with other writers for members' mutual benefit. Members can agree to whatever promotional exchanges they like: adding books to Listmania! lists, writing Amazon reviews, trading links, rating podcasts and YouTube videos, submitting links to link tracking networks, etc. etc.

The keys to success with such a group are open communication and consensus: every member must be able to freely express her comfort level for various promotional activities without fear of criticism, and no member should be pressured to do anything she doesn't want to do. The group should decide at the outset which activities will be undertaken, rejecting any that are objectionable to any member.

It's tempting to allow subsets of members to participate in promotional activities other members don't like, but doing so will splinter the group and give rise to resentments, especially if subset groups seem to be enjoying greater success than other ring members. Start with a base assumption that you are responsible for all your own promotion, and view any shared promo ring activity as a bonus.

11.8 FIGURE OUT WHAT'S WORKING FOR YOU

When you promote your ultimate goal is to sell books, but you're also trying to generally raise awareness about you and your books. You're shooting for some vague familiarity, which may grow into name recognition, which may blossom into sales. But how do you know which of your promotional efforts, if any, are paying off? In a word: statistics.

11.8.1 WEBSITE STATISTICS

① - ①①	Free! - $$$	✖✖✖ - ✖✖✖✖	No Confidence!

Website statistics can tell you who's visiting your website or blog, what sites they came from, how long they stayed, which pages or articles they viewed, how often they came back, and more. The statistics don't name names, of course, but they do distinguish individual site visitors by user "i.p. address", which is the unique identifier assigned to a specific computer or web server. Statistics provide a kind of virtual paper trail from your promotional activities to your website, thereby enabling you to see which activities are bringing the most visitors to your website. An example of statistics for my own website is shown below, as provided by StatCounter (www.statcounter.com).

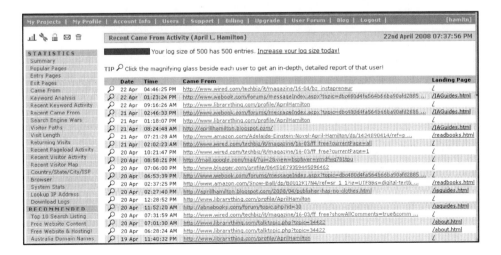

The screen shot shows the "Came From" report, which lists the websites from which my site visitors came. Notice the list of other available reports on the left-hand side of the screen. As you can see, website statistics can tell you almost anything you want to know about your website visitors.

The second "Came From" entry lists a visitor who came from a discussion forum on www.webook.com, and "landed" on the IAGuides.html page on my site. This tells me that someone read a post I made in a forum at www.webook.com, and that person clicked the link I included to the IAGuides.html page on my site. If I click the magnifying glass to the left of this entry, I can drill down into other data about this user and his activity on my site: what region of the world he's from, what browser he used, what other pages he visited, how long he stayed, what page he was on when he decided to exit my site, and more.

Scanning entries in the "Came From" report tells me at a glance which of my online promotional efforts are generating the most traffic for my author website, and that information makes it easy to decide whether or not to continue with a given effort. For example, if I've used a comment form at a certain site and found it didn't generate a single site visit, I won't continue to post there.

The "Came From" report also informs me when someone else provides a link to my site. If there's a "Came From" entry with a web address that's unfamiliar to me, I know someone has posted a link to my site somewhere, and someone else followed that link. I can visit the website shown in the "Came From" listing to see where the link to my site was posted, and in what context (i.e., "Check out this excellent site," versus, "You won't believe what an idiot this writer is..."). If the context is positive, I try to find contact information for the person who posted the link and email to say thanks, as well as to offer a link exchange if she's a writer. If the context is negative, I decide whether to attempt some damage control or just leave well enough alone and hope the post soon sinks into obscurity.

The latter option is usually the better one, by the way, because the more activity takes place on a given thread involving your name in a discussion group, the higher that thread will appear in the results for internet searches on your name. If you get into a tit-for-tat battle with a discussion board troll, you can drive that page up to the #1 slot in no time. As an alternative, if the remarks are truly slanderous you can try contacting the discussion board moderator and respectfully request that the objectionable post be deleted. However, as often as not this will merely spur the offending party on to more mischief. Similarly, if a blogger is talking trash about you it's usually best to ignore it, because a blogger who substitutes insults for insight cannot be reasoned with.

The "Popular Pages" report tells you which pages on your site receive the most traffic. This information is helpful two ways: first, by identifying the most effective pages on your site and second, by identifying the least effective pages. You may learn that all your hours of work to set up and maintain a podcast page were for naught, in which case you may choose to delete that page from your site and stop putting any more time into it. On the other hand, you may decide to look at the most popular pages on your site and try to find ways to make your podcast page more like the popular pages.

The "Popular Pages" report also tells you which pages on your site should be used as the basis for links in your comment form sign offs, profile pages, discussion group signature lines, etc. If you typically sign off with a link to your "About Me" page, but find statistics are telling you that visitors who land on that page promptly click a link to go elsewhere, you may want to start linking directly to a more popular page.

The more frequently you check your site statistics, the more quickly you can adjust your promotional strategies to avoid wasting time, money and effort, or to capitalize on buzz. However, because every statistics service is different, I can't go into great detail about the various reports and options available here. In using different statistics services, I've found the best way to figure out what data is available, and what the data means, is to click on all the various reports and compare them.

There are many website statistics services out there, ranging from freeware to moderately-priced software. Google Analytics and Statcounter are two that are free. Do an internet search on "hit counter" or "site statistics" to find more options. They all work essentially the same way. You sign up for an account (whether paid or free), and the service generates a small block of HTML code you can copy and paste into web pages you want to track for statistics reporting. The block of code is invisible on your pages, it works entirely in the background.

Recall that most blog and template-based website services allow at least limited use of HTML, and since the provided block of code is to be pasted exactly as-is and in its entirety, you don't need to know anything about HTML to accomplish this feat. Open the page or form that allows you to enter HTML on your page, paste the statistics code block into the form, and save your changes. That's all there is to it. If you're adding the code to pages you've authored yourself, follow the service's directions for where to paste the code in your pages.

Many of the services that offer simple, fill-in-the-blanks, template-based websites and blogs include hit counters or limited statistical reports on members' sites, and most hosting services also provide statistics for their customers' sites. Where available, statistics can be accessed from your user 'control panel' or 'dashboard'. These rarely match the level of detail and the amount of information provided by a dedicated statistics service, however.

11.8.2 SALES STATISTICS

$\bigcirc$ - $\bigcirc\bigcirc$	Free!	✖	No Confidence!

Your publisher will provide sales statistics on your books, either in the form of periodic reports or an online reporting service. If your book is being sold on Amazon, you can also watch for upward movement in the sales rank shown for your book on your AmazonConnect bibliography; any sudden, dramatic jump usually points to sales, but you'll need to check an actual sales report to be sure. I use the sales ranks shown in my bibliography as a kind of flag, alerting me to the need to check my sales statistics.

Since it's impossible for you to know who is buying your book and what enticed them to buy it, sales statistics are of limited use. However, a sudden spike in sales following a specific promotional effort on your part probably means that effort was successful. You can also use site and sales statistics to correlate the timing of sales with visits to your blog or author site if you have sales links for your books on a specific page.

11.9 KEEPING THE PROMO TRAIN ON TRACK

Keeping the promo train on track can be boiled down to a two-word strategy: don't stop. Don't stop trying different promotional techniques, don't stop checking your progress, don't stop doing the things that work, don't stop building on your successes, and don't stop looking for opportunities to promote yourself and your work.

Put More Irons In The Fire

Beware of putting all your promotional eggs in one basket. Employ as many different promotional techniques as you reasonably can at all times, but be realistic about how much time, money and effort you have to give. It's better to give 100% to just two promotional activities than to give 10% each to ten different activities.

Setting aside a designated block of time each week to focus completely on promotion can help if you're feeling overwhelmed by the number and scope of promotional strategies available to you. Once-a-week checkups have the added benefit of giving you a set frame of reference for comparing the relative success of different promotional activities, allowing you to see how many website hits or book sales you had per week over time for each different activity. Such insights make it easier to decide where to increase your efforts and where to pull back.

You may have to invest some time, money and effort in acquiring new skills, or improving existing ones, to beef up your promotional arsenal. It's time, money and effort well-spent, as it will pay off for years to come. With all the free tutorials and help available online, anyone with a computer and internet access should have no difficulty scraping together basic knowledge of HTML, graphics and photo editing, or even acquiring some advanced skills if time permits. An HTML Primer is provided in this book, for a start.

Cultivate And Maintain Contacts

This point is pretty self-explanatory. Cultivate positive relationships with writers, readers, reviewers, journalists and people in the publishing industry whenever the opportunity presents itself. You don't have to try to be a best friend to all of these people, you just want to do your best to leave a positive impression.

Maintain lists of contact information for everyone you meet along the book promotion road, categorized by type of contact. You may have a list of other writers with whom you've traded links, a list of publishing industry contacts, a list of people you've solicited for editorial reviews, and a list of writers with whom you exchange drafts for peer review.

Each list is a potential mailing list for future announcements, but don't be too cavalier about sending them. Blanketing your contacts in frequent, unimportant announcements will waste their time and irritate them. Limiting your announcements to events or news that will truly be of interest to the recipients ensures your missives will be read and taken seriously, instead of being automatically redirected to the spam folder.

An announcement about publication of a new book would be appropriate to send to your reviewer list and possibly your publishing industry list. A new website, or website address change, is something to share with your link-trading list. Recent publication of an article pertaining to writing merits an announcement to your writer list, if the article covers a topic that's likely to be of interest. Winning an award, getting a publication contract, optioning one of your books to a movie producer, or earning a bestseller list slot are all things you may want to share with your publishing industry list.

Document Everything, Store Every Document

Again, the title says it all. Save copies of every bit of promotional material you create, as well as every email exchanged with your contacts, and back up your files regularly.

Many of your promotional materials can serve as templates, to be re-used for future projects. Re-using the same basic design and layout for flyers, web pages and so on not only saves you time, but supports the goal of consistency in your marketing campaign.

Save copies of your pithiest and most clever comment form posts and discussion group posts by copying them and pasting them into a Notepad (.txt) or word processing document. The saved text can be developed into blog posts, articles, or talking points for public appearances. It may help to maintain a single "document" for each major topic covered (i.e., writing technique, publishing, contests, reviews and reviewing, etc.), then paste copies of any online posts pertaining to each topic into the appropriate document.

Be Genuine

Perhaps the biggest problem facing any promotional effort in this day and age is the general public's cynicism; while everyone buys things, no one wants to be "sold on" anything. Thanks to infomercials, telemarketing, spam and junk mail, salespeople are almost uniformly viewed as conniving scam artists who will do anything to make a buck. In this environment, it doesn't matter how fantastic or much-needed a new product is, the seller will have a hard time getting consumers to listen to him. Plagiarizing journalists and lying memoirists haven't exactly improved the situation for writers, either.

Honesty, consistency, and time are the only means at your disposal to combat this problem. Potential buyers are looking for any reason to lump you in with the hucksters, so don't give them any. Never be dishonest or even misleading in your promotional materials or any of your communications, and avoid hype. You must absolutely be "the real deal," above-board in all your dealings, respectful and open in all your communications, and willing to give back as much as you take when it comes to opportunities and assistance. While the ultimate goal of your promotional effort is to sell books, think of yourself more as someone with information and stories or abilities to share than as a salesperson.

11.10   WHEN GRACE IS THE BETTER PART OF VALOR

Given that books are a matter of personal taste, you can't really try to "sell" your book to readers. All you can do is make people aware that your book exists, tell them what it's about, and that others have enjoyed it. You can lead a reader to your "Buy My Books" page, but you can't make her click—and you must not resent her if she doesn't.

Resentment is also prohibited if she does buy your book, but doesn't like it. There are plenty of bestselling and well-loved books out there that I don't care for at all, so I know that no matter how many people say my book is great, it's not realistic to expect every reader to agree. Going ballistic on a reviewer who shredded your last effort will leave a negative impression with anyone who witnesses your outburst, and this will not bode well for you as you ramp up the promotional machinery for your next opus.

Attempts to cancel out a negative review with argument will not convince anyone reading your remarks that the reviewer was wrong, and in fact will only convince them that you're one of those petty, self-aggrandizing types with an overblown view of your own talent.

Never forget that as an indie author you're promoting yourself as much as any specific book, and a successful promotion campaign is as much about what you don't do as what you do. Always think before you speak, post or email. Ask yourself, "What is it I'm hoping to accomplish here?" followed by, "Will what I'm about to do help me, hurt me, or make no difference at all in accomplishing my goal?" Unless the unequivocal answer is, "help me," hold back. Of course you're only human, and writers are supposed to be sensitive, so you will make mistakes from time to time. Be willing to apologize, and if the gaffe occurred in public, to apologize publicly.

There will be times when you have been truly wronged, perhaps by an unfair review or a reciprocal agreement in which the other party fails to keep up his end of the bargain, but even in those instances you must be willing to let the matter drop. Your cries of "foul" may be absolutely true, and your charges against the wrongdoer may be completely legitimate, but nobody wants to hear them. Go ahead and warn your writer friends away from these individuals privately, but avoid airing your grievances in public because doing so only makes you look spiteful and shrill.

One caveat: this isn't to say that if you've been ripped off in your writerly or promotional pursuits you must keep mum about it, or that you can't fight back. In that case, you're not a writer conducting an argument in public, you're a consumer who's been cheated. Just make sure that anything you say or write about the matter publicly will not reflect negatively on you in the eyes of your contacts or readers. Remember that anyone can do an internet search on your name at any time, and once something is on the 'net, it never really disappears completely.

12 AN HTML PRIMER

This chapter will give you a good understanding of how HTML works and teach you how to use it to create links, custom-formatted text and embedded graphics. The information provided will also enable you to create your own web pages from scratch, but only very basic pages. If you want to create and maintain your own author website, I recommend using a web page creation program such as Macromedia Dreamweaver or Microsoft Frontpage to get a professional look without having to become an HTML expert. However, even if you use such a tool you will still need basic HTML knowledge and skills.

12.1 HOW WEB PAGES WORK

You've undoubtedly seen all kinds of web pages, and probably know they can only be viewed in a web browser. Still, I bet you didn't know that web pages don't really exist *until* they're viewed in a browser, nor that they *stop* existing when the browser moves on to another page or closes. Universal Resource Locators (URLs), or web addresses, don't actually point to web pages at all. They point to files containing instructions, or "source code", for how to build web pages. The browser "reads" the source code and interprets it, then builds a web page according to the source code's directions in a matter of seconds. It's as if the source code contains a written description of a picture and the browser is a super-fast sketch artist. Technically, when we speak of someone creating a web page, what we really mean is that someone is writing source code the *browser* can use to create a web page.

You can get a better understanding of what's going on by looking at a web page together with its source code. Let's use the home page of my website as an example, since I maintain the source code for it myself: http://www.aprillhamilton.com/index.html. Open this web page in your favorite browser and right-click on any open space in it. A pop-up menu will appear, offering you various options. One of the options will display the source code that was used to create the web page in your computer's text editor.

In Internet Explorer, the option is called "View Source". In Mozilla Firefox version 2.0.0.7, it's called "View Page Source". In older versions of Firefox there's an option called "Page Info", and "View Page Source" is one of the items included in the Page Info dialog box. In the Mac Safari browser, it's an option under the "View" menu.

The screen shot above shows what the page looks like in the browser. The screen shot on the following page shows the source code the browser used to create the page.

This source code was written in Hyper Text Markup Language (HTML). HTML is one of several "languages" used to pass instructions to a web browser. HTML is written as ordinary text, and the text file is saved with a file extension of .htm or .html. These file extensions label the file as HTML source code so a web browser will recognize it. The source code file is uploaded to a web server, making it accessible on the internet.

Anyone who wants to visit my home page does so by either typing its URL into their browser or following a link that contains the URL. Recall that URLs point to source code files; the browser locates the source code file, reads it, interprets it, and creates, or "renders", my home page according to the instructions contained in the source file. The rendered page is discarded by the browser as soon as the site visitor closes his browser or navigates away from the page. The next time that same visitor accesses the page, the process happens all over again and the page is rendered anew and includes any changes I've made to the source code since the previous visit.

The page load buttons on your browser menu or toolbar ('back', 'forward', 'refresh', 'reload') direct the browser to dump its rendered page, access the source code file associated with the button and render a new page based on that source code. The refresh/reload button forces the browser to discard its rendered page, re-read the same source code file and re-render the page—a useful tool when you're waiting for an email or discussion board post to show up.

Browser Cache

Depending on your browser settings, the source code of pages you've visited may be stored, or "cached", on your hard drive up to a user-specified limit of disk space. This speeds up page rendering even further, since the browser can get the source code file from your hard drive instead of having to pull it off the web, but the pages rendered won't include any source code updates made since the source code was cached. Page caching was an important feature back in the days of dial-up internet access, but high-speed internet connections have done away with the need.

Web Page Versus Web Application

ASP, Javascript, VBScript and PHP are examples of programming languages used to create web *applications*. As a rule of thumb, any web page that accepts data input from the user, does something with that input and then returns some kind of response to the user is running a web application. For example, a search engine accepts search conditions from a user, searches for web pages matching those conditions and returns a list of matching pages for the user to review. HTML, on the other hand, is used to create web *pages*, like my website home page. Web pages don't accept data input from users, and don't do any kind of data processing.

Unlike the programming languages used to create web applications, HTML is pretty easy for the average, untrained person to understand. It's all written in plain English, using everyday words and some abbreviations.

12.2 HOW TO CREATE A SOURCE CODE FILE

The best way to learn HTML is to create your own source code file and experiment with it. Look at the following little block of source code.

<HTML>

Hello, World!

</HTML>

Believe it or not, that little block of code is enough to create a web page. The first and third lines contain HTML code, and the page content is contained between them. Most HTML code is enclosed in brackets (<>), and each piece of bracketed code is called a "tag". Here's that block of code again, but this time I've added some comments to clarify what each part of the code is telling the browser to do.

HTML Code	What Does It Mean?
<HTML>	Begin HTML (Hey browser, render a web page!)
Hello, World!	Content (Hey browser, display this on the web page!)
</HTML>	End HTML (Hey browser, stop rendering!)

You can open Notepad right now, type in this same block of text, save the file as Hello.html (being sure the file type dialog is set to "all files", shown below) and presto, you've authored your first source code file.

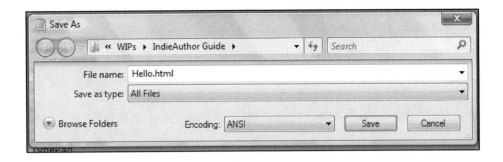

Recall that HTML is written and stored as a text file; you can open the file in Notepad or any other text editor to make changes to it. Just right-click on the file name, select 'Open With' and choose your text editor. In fact, you can open any source file with an .html or .htm extension in any text editor.

Now you know how to make a basic source file and edit it, but you haven't seen the rendered page yet. Close your file, go to the location where you saved it on your hard drive and double-click on the file to open it again. Any file ending with ".htm" or ".html" is recognized by your computer as a web page, and the file will open in your computer's default web browser—even though the file is on your hard drive, not the web.

The Browser Is No Dummy

You'll notice that the browser didn't have to be told what font to use, what color to make the text, or to make the background of the page white. White is the default background color for all web pages, so if you don't specify a different color (I'll show you how later on) the background of your page will be white. There is also a default font setting which may vary from browser to browser, but is generally Times New Roman. That's the font the browser will use unless it's told to use something else. The size of the font and the black color you see on Hello.html are also default values.

Still, it's a pretty sorry looking page. It doesn't have a title at the top, it doesn't have any color or graphics...actually, all it's got is the text, "Hello, World!". That's because the only thing in the content section of the page is the text, "Hello, World!" The source code doesn't tell the browser to render anything else.

12.3 USING HTML TO BOSS THE BROWSER

Every HTML source code file must contain, at the minimum, the two tags used in Hello.html: <HTML> and </HTML>. As described previously, these tags tell the browser to start rendering a web page and to stop rendering the page, respectively.

Tags are typically paired this way, with the first tag of a pair referred to as the "opening" tag and the second as the "closing" tag. The first tag of the pair is like an "on" switch: it turns on an instruction to the browser. The browser will keep doing whatever the first tag of the pair says until it comes to the second tag of the pair, which is like an "off" switch: it turns off the instruction to the browser. "Off" tags always start with a forward slash ("/") and often, that's the only difference between the opening and closing tag. The basic format, or "syntax", for all HTML tags is as follows:

<OPENING TAG> Content to be affected by tag </CLOSING TAG>

The following tables demonstrate tags used to format text, and the resulting changes. We begin with the code saved as Hello.html. Add the changes shown in each step to your own Hello.html, save the file and view the results in your browser.

HTML Code	Resulting Page	Notes
<HTML> <FONT FACE="Arial"> Hello, World! </FONT> </HTML>	Hello, World!	<FONT FACE> tags specify a font. You can specify any standard font in FONT FACE tags. Note that in tags, text entered after an = sign must be enclosed in quotation marks.

The definition of "standard font" varies from browser to browser, but the following fonts are fairly universal: Andale Mono, Arial, Comic Sans MS, Courier

New, Georgia, Impact, Times New Roman, Trebuchet MS, Verdana and Webdings. The next example demonstrates how to apply boldface to your text.

HTML Code	Resulting Page	Notes
<HTML> <FONT FACE="Arial"> <B> Hello, World! </B> </FONT> </HTML>	**Hello, World!**	The <B> tags apply boldface to text.

Note how the <B> tags are "nested" inside the <FONT FACE> tags to apply both the font and boldface. I could've reversed the nesting order, or used either pair of tags by itself, too. Next, you'll see how to change the size of your text.

HTML Code	Resulting Page	Notes
<HTML> <FONT FACE="Arial" SIZE="4"> <B> Hello, World! </B> </FONT> </HTML>	**Hello, World!**	I've enlarged the text by adding the SIZE attribute to my FONT tag. HTML text ranges in size from 1 to 6; 1 is smallest, 6 is largest and 3 is the default. The text you're reading now is set to size 2.

"FONT FACE" and "SIZE" are contained in a single opening tag, and that single opening tag is closed with a single closing tag of </FONT>. Font face, size and color can all be grouped together into a single tag but other text properties, such as alignment, bold and italics, use separate tags of their own.

HTML Code	Resulting Page	Notes
<HTML> <FONT FACE="Arial" SIZE="4" COLOR="Red"> <B> <I> <U> Hello, World! </B> </U> </I> </FONT> </HTML>	***Hello, World!***	I've added three more tags, one for italics, one for underlining and one for font color. Can you guess which is which? About underlining - since in web pages underlined text is assumed to be a link, it's not a good idea to use underlining on plain text.

Look at how the tags are nested, and how I enter the closing tags in the same order as I entered the opening tags. The closing formatting tags can be put in any order, but I find that I'm less likely to leave any out if I repeat the opening tag order in my closing tags. You may prefer to do something different. Again, remember that anything you enter after the = sign in a tag must be enclosed in quotation marks, as shown in the <FONT FACE> tag. And by the way, the <U> tag is for underlining and <I> is for italicizing.

While I've put each tag on a separate line, that isn't necessary. If you wanted to, you could write all of the HTML code on a single line. The resulting web page would look the same, but it would be harder to read and edit your code. Developers have varying preferences for how many tags to use on a single line.

Using Color in Your Web Pages

There are two ways to set text and background colors in HTML: "named" colors and "hexadecimal" colors. Named colors are the eight standard hues on the color wheel: white, black, red, blue, yellow, green, orange and purple. You can set any of these colors just by typing the desired color name in the tag, as I've done in the <FONT> tag on the prior page. Hexadecimal color numbers are used to describe all the other colors you can use on the web - over 250 of them.

If you didn't use a numbering scheme of some kind, how would you distinguish the slightly different shades of green from one another? The use of hexadecimal numbers ensures every one of the available colors has a unique "name", and that those names are known to all browsers. Unfortunately for you, hexadecimal numbers are not easy to remember. You can obtain a key to hexadecimal color names online by doing a web search for "hexadecimal colors", but to keep things simple you can always stick to the eight named colors for text. The eight named colors are a little bright for backgrounds, however (see next section).

Essential Tags – Page Formatting, Links and Email

The following pages begin with new HTML code to demonstrate tags related to page formatting, links and email.

HTML Code	Resulting Page	Notes
<HTML> <HEAD> <TITLE> Hello, World!</TITLE> </HEAD> <BODY> Hello, World! </BODY> </HTML>	Hello, World!	The <HEAD> tags insert a page header. Since we've added a header to our page, we must tell the browser which part of the page is the main body. To do that, we use <BODY> tags.

The header contains information about the page, such as the page title, author name, keywords, or pieces of web application code. Nothing entered in the <HEAD> section will be visible on the page, except for the title, which will appear in the browser title bar. The title will be entered in the next example using <TITLE> tags and is always stored in the <HEAD> section.

HTML Code	Resulting Page	Notes
<HTML> <HEAD> <TITLE> Hello, World!</TITLE> </HEAD> <BODY BGCOLOR="Purple"> Hello, World! </BODY> </HTML>	Hello, World!	The page has been entitled "Hello, World!", and that title will appear in the browser title bar when the page is loaded. The BGCOLOR attribute in the BODY tag sets the background color of your page.

See what I was talking about when I said named colors aren't good to use for backgrounds? If you think that purple is loud in this table, imagine it as the background for an entire page! Instead of a color, you can set the background of the page to a graphic file, or "image", as I'll explain later.

HTML Code	Resulting Page	Notes
<HTML> <HEAD> <TITLE> Hello, World!</TITLE> </HEAD> <BODY> <A HREF="http://www.aprillhamilton.com/Hello.html"> Hello, World! </A> </BODY> </HTML>	Hello, World!	See below

The <A HREF=> and </A> tags make the text between them into a hyperlink, underline the text, and change its color into the default hyperlink color for the browser (usually blue). Note the format, or "syntax" used:

<A HREF="[link address]">
[Text To Display As A Link]
</A>

The "target" of a hyperlink is the location to which the user will be taken when he clicks on the link. The target of a hyperlink will usually be displayed in the footer of the browser window when the user mouses over the link. In the example shown, I've moused over the link for "Press" and the

target is displayed in the footer.

There are four types of hyperlinks: "named anchors", "MAILTO:", off-site, and on-site. An on-site link takes the user to another page on the same website. An off-site link takes the user to a page on some other website. A MAILTO link opens a 'compose mail' form in the user's default email program and pre-fills the recipient email address. A named anchor isn't actually a link, but the target of a link that takes the user to a different location on the same web page.

Named anchors are commonly used on web pages that are very lengthy, to save the site visitor the trouble of scrolling up and down when trying to locate a specific section. In the

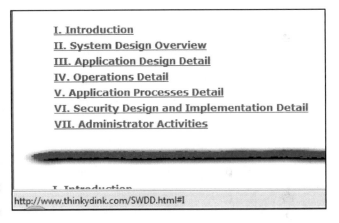

example shown, named anchors have been used to create a hyperlinked table of contents for a lengthy page.

Since named anchors are targets, they must always be paired with hyperlinks. In this case, the hyperlink for "I. Introduction" is paired with a named anchor called "#I", which serves as the target for the link. This is the syntax for the hyperlink:

<A HREF="#I">

The pound sign (#) tells the browser that the text immediately following is a named anchor, not a regular hyperlink. When the user clicks that link, the browser will scan the page to find the named anchor, "I". Once the anchor is located, the browser will scroll down the page until the anchor is at the top of the page, sort of like taking a shortcut. In the screen shot below, the target of the link is indicated by an arrow.

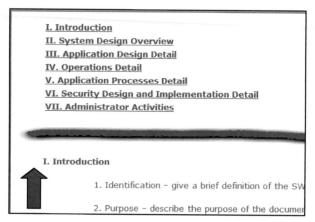

This is the syntax for creating the named anchor, and it was entered in the HTML code immediately *ahead* of the text, "I. Introduction" (under the divider line):

<A NAME="I"></A>

This tag created a named anchor called "I" on the page. In named anchor tags, text is not typically entered between the opening and closing tag where the "text to be affected" usually goes. This is because it's typical for anchors to be invisible to site visitors, so the "text to be affected" is - nothing.

The MAILTO link allows site visitors to send email to a specified email address. In the table on the following page, I've added some more text, and made that text into an email link. When the user clicks on the email link text, the browser will launch its internal mail program and pre-address a mail message to the address specified by the link.

Email link syntax is basically the same as that used for normal hyperlinks, but the linked address is a little different. Where the hyperlink address is normally a web URL, the email link address is an email address with a prefix of "MAILTO:"

HTML Code	Resulting Page	Notes
\<HTML\> \<HEAD\> \<TITLE\> Hello, World!\</TITLE\> \</HEAD\> \<BODY\> \<A HREF="http://www.aprillhamilton.com/Hello.html"\> Hello, World! \</A\> \<BR\> \<A HREF="MAILTO:info@aprillhamilton.com"\> Email me. \</A\> \</BODY\> \</HTML\>\</BODY\> \</HTML\>	<u>Hello, World!</u> <u>Email me.</u>	See below

Notice the \<BR\> tag, just above the email link. This is the line break tag, and each one you use inserts one line break in your page. If I left the \<BR\> tag out, both my original hyperlink and my new email link would've appeared on the same line, one right after the other. As you can see, the \<BR\> tag is one of those few tags that is used alone, not as half of a pair. No 'closing tag' is required for the \<BR\> tag.

\<BR\> tags are useful for controlling line spacing. Text on web pages is single-spaced by default, but with \<BR\> tags you can 'fake' wider spacing. Also, most web page creation tools, including online forms used to create blog posts and fill-in-the-blanks website templates, automatically format any text you enter as paragraphs, using the \<P\> and \</P\> tags, and apply a minimum, default spacing between paragraphs. This wouldn't be a problem, were it not for the fact that you can't easily customize the default spacing.

When using such tools, every time you hit the 'enter' key to begin typing on a new line, you're indicating the start of a new paragraph—whether you want to or not—and inserting empty space between the previous line and the next one—whether you want to or not. This can be a major pain when you're trying to format text that shouldn't be handled as paragraphs (i.e., poems, bulleted lists, mailing addresses, etc.).

To eliminate the problem, you must edit the HTML source. Blogger allows this, and some of the template-based websites do too. Any web page creation software will provide access to the source code of your pages as well. In the source code, delete any <P> and </P> tags enclosing the text you *don't* want to be formatted as paragraphs, then simply insert a <BR> tag wherever you want a line break. Problem solved!

ANSI Codes

American National Standard Institute (ANSI) codes are used to tell the browser to render special characters and symbols that don't appear on a keyboard, such as © and ±. Typing an ANSI code into your HTML is like using the "insert symbol" function in your word processor.

ANSI codes can be entered using a 'name' or 'number', and are typed into the HTML page like ordinary text. However, when the HTML page is rendered, the browser substitutes the desired symbol for the ANSI name or number. For example, the ANSI name for the © symbol is "©". Let's say you want to display the following copyright message on one of your pages:

Page Content © 2008, Joe Author

The HTML code would look like this:

```
<FONT FACE="Tahoma" COLOR="blue" SIZE="2">
```

Page Content © 2008, Joe Author

```
</FONT>
```

ANSI name codes always begin with an ampersand (&) and ANSI number codes always begin with an ampersand and pound sign (&#), and both types always end with a semicolon. The ampersand alerts the browser that the following characters are an ANSI code, not ordinary text, and the semicolon marks the end of the ANSI code. A summary table of the ANSI codes you're most likely to need is presented at the end of this chapter, but there are hundreds more. To find them, do an internet search on web + "special characters".

The Non-Breaking Space

The ANSI code you're likely to use most is the non-breaking space ( ). In a web page, inserting a non-breaking space is like hitting the space bar in a regular document: it inserts a space *without* creating a line break, unlike the 'enter' key. Of course you can hit the space bar when typing text into an HTML page, but by default, HTML only recognizes a single space between sentences or characters, regardless of how many times in a row you hit the space bar. There are times when you need more than one space.

For example, in a normal, typewritten document, it's standard to leave two empty spaces between the end of one sentence and the beginning of another. HTML's default spacing only allows one space between sentences, and sometimes that spacing makes sentences appear crowded when you're using certain fonts or formatting options. Other examples are manually inserting spaces between text and images on a page, or 'faking' a bulleted list.

There are special HTML formatting codes for creating bulleted lists (see next section), but just as with paragraphs, HTML inserts empty space between the

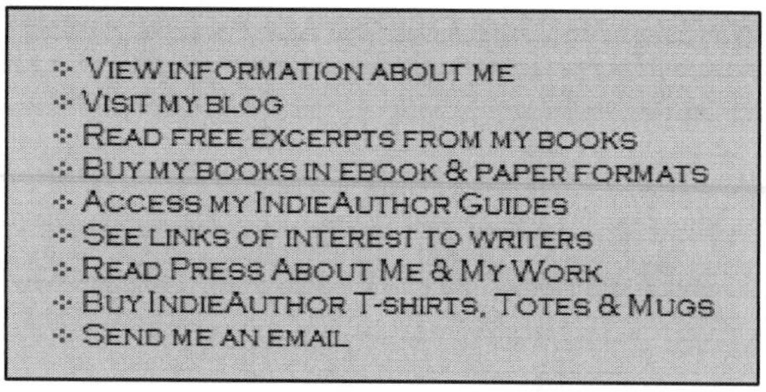

❖ VIEW INFORMATION ABOUT ME
❖ VISIT MY BLOG
❖ READ FREE EXCERPTS FROM MY BOOKS
❖ BUY MY BOOKS IN EBOOK & PAPER FORMATS
❖ ACCESS MY INDIEAUTHOR GUIDES
❖ SEE LINKS OF INTEREST TO WRITERS
❖ READ PRESS ABOUT ME & MY WORK
❖ BUY INDIEAUTHOR T-SHIRTS, TOTES & MUGS
❖ SEND ME AN EMAIL

lines of bulleted lists created with list tags. If you want a single-spaced list, like the one shown at left, you have to 'fake' it by inserting a tiny graphic to serve as your bullet, followed by one or more spaces (using the ANSI code " " as needed), followed by the text of your list item, followed by a <BR> tag. This is how I create all my bulleted lists.

Default Bulleted Lists

The basic HTML syntax for creating a bulleted list is this:

<UL>

<LI> text of item 1 </LI>

<LI> text of item 2 </LI>

<LI> text of item 3 </LI>

</UL>

The resulting list would look like this:

- Text of item 1

- Text of item 2

- Text of item 3

You can enter as many items in a bulleted list as you like, just enclose each list item in <LI> and </LI> tags, and be sure to close the list with the </UL> tag at the bottom. The default bullet is the filled-in dot, as shown, but you can specify an empty circle or a filled-in square in the opening <UL> tag, as follows:

<UL TYPE="circle">

<UL TYPE="square">

There are HTML tags for creating numbered and outline lists too, but they're a bit more complex. Do an internet search on HTML + "lists" to learn more.

Graphics in HTML Pages

Web browsers can only display graphics, photos and art in a limited number of formats. JPG and GIF are universally acceptable, so if you want to keep things simple stick to those two formats. Also, don't use any copyrighted or trademarked images on your pages without the owner's permission. Contrary to popular misinformation, images appearing on web pages are not automatically added to the public domain. The syntax used to insert graphics in web pages is:

<IMG SRC="[filename or URL]" WIDTH="[no. of pixels]" HEIGHT="[no. of pixels]">

Like the <BR> tag, the <IMG SRC> tag appears singly, without a 'closing' tag. Place your cursor where you want the graphic, then use the syntax above to set a pointer to the image and, if desired, specify the exact width and height of the image as you'd like it to appear on your page. If the dimensions of the image to which you're pointing are acceptable as-is, just omit the WIDTH and HEIGHT attributes from your tag altogether.

The image will not be stored as part of your source code file, the <IMG SRC> tag merely sets up a pointer to the image. Therefore, any image referenced in an <IMG SRC> tag must be accessible to that tag at all times, meaning that it must be stored somewhere on the web. People who build and maintain their own websites will usually have a folder on their sites to store all the images referenced by <IMG SRC> tags on their pages, so their pointers will use the 'filename' option. If the referenced image is stored anywhere other than the website of your page, the pointer must be set to a URL address for the image.

If you don't know the URL address of the image, go to the web page with the image, right-click the image and select "properties" from the pop-up menu. Among other details, the image's file format (i.e., JPG or GIF), dimensions in pixels and URL will be shown. Looking at the 'properties' of images can also help you figure out what to enter for HEIGHT and WIDTH in your <IMG SRC> tags, since after viewing 'properties' for a number of images, you'll have a good idea of the average height and width in pixels for small, medium and large images.

To use an image as a page background, modify the opening <BODY> tag:

<BODY BACKGROUND="[filename or URL]">

You don't need to specify height or width because the browser will automatically fill up the entire page with your specified background, laying out copies side-by-side if the image isn't large enough to fill the page as-is. If you use a background image this way, be sure that the image is very light, like a watermark on paper, and that it's not so busy it will distract the viewer from your page content. Also be sure that the chosen image is one that will "tile", or repeat across and down your page, easily. Abstract, repeating designs usually work best.

Text Headers

A text header is a line or section of boldface text that is slightly larger than, and set apart from, the main body text. Text headers are most often used for page or section titles, such as the title "Text Headers" which appears just above this paragraph.

Text headers can be set to a value of 1 through 6, with 1 being the smallest size/emphasis and 6 being the largest size/emphasis. You can set text headers by applying font size and boldface tags also, but many website developers consider it a good practice to use text header tags instead. To set a text header, use this syntax:

<H[1 – 6]>text to be made into a header</H>

Add a text header to your Hello.html and experiment with changing the value to see how the appearance of the header changes.

12.4 BEST PRACTICES

Here's a review of the "best practices", or good habits, mentioned in this chapter and the Author Website section of the Promotion chapter, plus a couple more.

Don't use underlining to format web page text - to the person viewing the page, the text will look like a hyperlink.

Don't use "named colors" as page backgrounds - they're too bright.

Type your HTML tags in uppercase to distinguish them from other page content.

Don't go crazy with graphics, fonts, sounds and animations - too much of a good thing will make your pages busy, harder to read and slower to load, and many web surfers won't have browsers that support all the bells and whistles.

If you set a graphic as your page background, make sure it isn't too dark, bright or busy - the text and images you put on top of it may be hard to read or just hard to look at if the background is fighting for top billing.

Don't use copyrighted or trademarked graphics or images in your web pages without the owner's permission.

Make sure any images reference by your <IMG SRC> tags will be on the web and available for display in your page at all times.

Always make a backup of a page before you begin editing it.

Always preview a page before posting it to the web by opening the copy saved on your hard drive in a browser window.

12.5 SUMMARY TABLES

A summary table of commonly-used ASNI codes is presented below.

NAME CODE	NUMBER CODE	DISPLAYS	DESCRIPTION
&dagger;	N.A.	†	dagger
&Dagger;	N.A.	‡	double dagger
&lsaquo;	N.A.	‹	less than
&rsaquo;	N.A.	›	greater than
&ndash;	&#150;	–	en dash
&mdash;	&#151;	—	em dash
			non-breaking space
&cent;	&#162;	¢	cent sign
&pound;	&#163;	£	pound sterling
&copy;	&#169;	©	copyright
&reg;	&#174;	®	registered trademark
&deg;	&#176;	°	degrees
&plusmn;	&#177;	±	plus / minus
&sup2;	&#178;	²	superscript two
&sup3;	&#179;	³	superscript three
&para;	&#182;	¶	paragraph sign
&middot;	&#183;	•	middle dot
&sup1;	&#185;	¹	superscript one
&frac14;	&#188;	¼	one-fourth
&frac12;	&#189;	½	one-half
&frac34;	&#190;	¾	three-fourths
&divide;	&#247	÷	division

The next page contains a summary table of all the HTML tags discussed in this chapter, as well as a few that weren't discussed, but whose use is self-explanatory.

Experiment with these tags in your Hello.html file until you're comfortable with them. Also try viewing the source code of various HTML pages online to see how others are using them, as well as to learn more tags. When you see something you like on an HTML page, view source to see how it was done.

HTML TAG	PURPOSE
<HTML> </HTML>	declare HTML page
<HEAD> </HEAD>	declare page header section
<TITLE> </TITLE>	set a page title
<BODY> </BODY>	declare page body section
<BODY BGCOLOR="[name or hex]"> </BODY>	set page background color
<BODY BACKGROUND="[filename/URL]"> </BODY>	set page background image
<H[1 – 6]> </H>	insert page header
<B> </B>	make text bold
<I> </I>	make text italicized
<U> </U>	make text underlined
<CENTER> </CENTER>	make text center-aligned
<LEFT> </LEFT>	make text left-aligned
<RIGHT> </RIGHT>	make text right-aligned
<FONT SIZE="[1 – 6]"> </FONT>	make text size 1 - 6
<FONT FACE="[font name]"> </FONT>	set text font
<FONT COLOR="[name or hex]"> </FONT>	set text color
  (no closing tag)	insert single-spaced line break
<P> </P>	format text as paragraph
<A NAME="[anchorname]"> </A>	insert named anchor
<A HREF="#[anchorname]"> </A>	link to a named anchor
<A HREF="[URL]"> </A>	hyperlink
<A HREF="MAILTO:[email address]"> </A>	email link
<IMG SRC="[filename or URL]"> (no closing tag)	insert pointer to an image – remember optional HEIGHT and WIDTH attributes

About the Author

April L. Hamilton lives in Southern California with her husband, two children, and entirely too many pets. She is primarily an author of comic fiction. Her novels, *Adelaide Einstein* and *Snow Ball*, are available in trade paperback edition on Amazon and in the CreateSpace e-store, in Kindle edition in the Amazon Kindle Store, and in various other eBook formats on Smashwords. When she's not writing, kid-wrangling, working to expand the indie author movement, promoting her work or pursuing her grandiose and hopeless dream of a neat and orderly household, she can generally be found reading, reclaiming the domestic arts (aka "crafting") or taking in a movie.

http://www.aprillhamilton.com

About the Book

This book was designed and laid out by the author in Microsoft Word 2003, using the Tahoma font in various point sizes. Graphics were edited by the author using Microsoft Digital Image Pro 10. The cover was designed by the author using the CreateSpace book cover design template and Microsoft Digital Image Pro 10. The finished manuscript was published through CreateSpace (http://www.createspace.com).

Note that the author is not being compensated by any of the companies or services mentioned herein in exchange for such mention.

Visit the IndieAuthor Shop

http://www.cafepress.com/indieauthorshop

Made in the USA